True to Both My Selves

A Family Memoir of Germany and England in Two World Wars

Katrin FitzHerbert

virago

VIRAGO

First published in Great Britain in 1997
by Virago Press
This edition published
by Virago Press in 1998
Reprinted 1998, 1999, 2001, 2008, 2010

A CIP catalogue record for this book
is available from the British Library.

ISBN 978-1-86049-587-8

Typeset by Solidus (Bristol) Limited

Virago Press
An imprint of
Little, Brown Book Group
100 Victoria Embankment
London EC4Y 0DY

An Hachette UK Company
www.hachette.co.uk

www.virago.co.uk

Katrin FitzHerbert was born in Germany in 1936. She was educated at fourteen schools in Germany and England and read PPE at St Anne's College, Oxford. She has been a journalist, an anthropologist, and trained and worked as a psychiatric social worker. She is the founder and director of the National Pyramid Trust, a charity promoting self-esteem and resilience in primary-school children. She is married, has two daughters, and lives in London and Totnes.

More praise for *True to Both My Selves*

'a fascinating insight into a generally neglected aspect of recent history, the plight of the Germans in two world wars. It is also a moving personal account of how the daughter of an active Nazi came to terms with her father's past'   *Spectator*

'a remarkable and courageous book'   *Sunday Times*

'an extraordinary account of loyalties divided between family and nationality'   *Daily Mail*

'the family history is fascinating and is marvellously well told ... absorbing memoir ... full of sharp and keen observation'
TES

'FitzHerbert ... never slides away from her saving honesty'
Observer

'remarkable, truthful and absorbing'   *Country Life*

'An intensely moving account, told with an honesty and integrity that inspires respect and understanding'   Lord Callaghan

To the memory of
Elsie Hope (1890–1961)

and

Captain Harry FitzHerbert,
the father-in-law I never met, killed in action at Gildenhaus,
Germany, 2 April 1945

'It can be the lot of few to be so missed by those they leave
behind'

A History of the Irish Guards in the Second World War
by Desmond FitzGerald

Contents

CONTENTS

Acknowledgements

The project to put my family history on the record started in 1990 with a tour of churches in the two former Germanies and in Pomerania (now Poland), where my ancestors were once pastors. My first written effort bore minimal resemblance to the text that follows. It was Gwenda David who recognised its potential and but for her vision and encouragement the project would long ago have sunk without trace.

Nor would it have got far without my grandmother's written memoirs or without the co-operation of the other principal characters: my brother, my mother and my step-father. Other participants in the story who have contributed interviews and information are Tom and Paule Armstrong, the next generation of the Sharpe family of Kettering; Erika von Bühler and Joachim Gewiess, neighbours from Mahlsdorf; my cousin Klaus Geld-macher; Ilse Krüger-Lorenzen; Jutta and Bernhard Diederichsen; Roy Chapman; Dr Lieselotte Kleine; Reg Hyne; Tommy Rounce-field; Dot and Ronald Sharpe and finally my intrepid second cousin Bruno Heyne and his wife Stine, who investigated my father's alleged connection with the massacre at Gardelegen.

The staff of the following libraries and archives generously gave time and advice: The Imperial War Museum, the Public Records Office, the Ministry of Defence, the Foreign and

Commonwealth Office, the Wiener Library, the Goethe Institute, the German History Institute, the Yad Vashem Archive, the Simon Wiesenthal Documentation Centre, the Bundesarchiev, Aachen and the Gardelegen town archive, whose archivist, Herr Heiko Bierstedt, deserves a special mention.

The following read early drafts and many of their criticisms and suggestions have been incorporated into the book: Dr Lucy Brown, Alison Browne, Naomi Burns, Roy and Steph Chapman, Anne Charlton, Anne and Ron Farquar, Giles and Alexandra FitzHerbert, Kitty FitzHerbert, Lois Fletcher, Dr Anthony Glees, Reg and Heather Hyne, Rebecca Kerby, Sophie Lewis, Sheelah Martin, Mike Shaw, Eric Mosbacher, Andy Norris, Avoulla Norris, Charlotte and Chris Salveson, Imogen Taylor, Wolfgang and Frauke Thiele and Richard and Rosalind Tolson.

My mother has beautifully translated the text into German.

I would like to express my warmest thanks for all these contributions.

My deepest gratitude for his radical and constructive suggestions, historical insight and domestic tolerance I owe to my husband, Luke FitzHerbert.

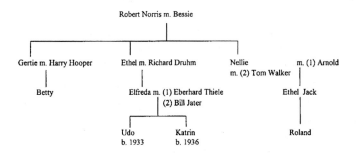

Robert Norris m. Bessie

- Gertie m. Harry Hooper
  - Betty
- Ethel m. Richard Druhm
  - Elfreda m. (1) Eberhard Thiele
            (2) Bill Jater
    - Udo
      b. 1933
    - Katrin
      b. 1936
- Nellie
  m. (2) Tom Walker
- m. (1) Arnold
  - Ethel   Jack
    - Roland

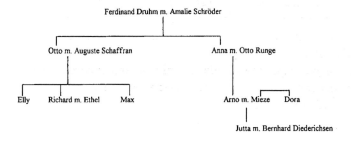

Ferdinand Druhm m. Amalie Schröder

- Otto m. Auguste Schaffran
  - Elly
  - Richard m. Ethel
  - Max
- Anna m. Otto Runge
  - Arno m. Mieze   Dora
    - Jutta m. Bernhard Diederichsen

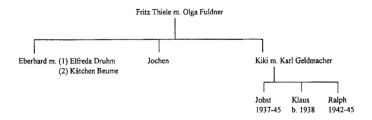

Fritz Thiele m. Olga Fuldner

- Eberhard m. (1) Elfreda Druhm
            (2) Kätchen Beume
- Jochen
- Kiki m. Karl Geldmacher
  - Jobst
    1937-45
  - Klaus
    b. 1938
  - Ralph
    1942-45

The Cast

In England, 1880–1919 and 1946–97

Richard Druhm (also Droome), my grandfather (Opa), 1878–1952
Ethel Druhm (née Norris), my grandmother (Oma), 1880–1966
Elfreda Druhm (Freda in England, Elfi in Germany), my mother,
    born 1910
Gertie and Harry Hooper, my great-aunt and uncle
Nellie Walker, another great-aunt
Cousin Ethel, Nellie's daughter
George Rossell, Oma's employer in the First World War
Elsie Hope (Aunty Hopey), Oma's loyal friend in the First World
    War and after
Kathleen Holness (née Connell), Oma's apprentice
The Sharpe family, Aunty Hopey's Kettering cousins
Mrs Hyne and Reg, my foster-family, 1947–50
Bill Jater, my stepfather

In Germany, 1919–46

Eberhard Thiele, my father, 1907–79
Udo Thiele, my brother, born 1933

The Cast

Katrin Thiele, myself, born 1936
Max Druhm, my great-uncle, 1883–1955
Arno Runge, my grandfather's cousin (Onkel Arno), 1895–1973
Jutta Diederichsen (née Runge), born 1922
Kätchen Beume, my mother's best friend, later married to my
    father
Ilse Krüge-Lorenzen, my mother's partner on her radio
    programme

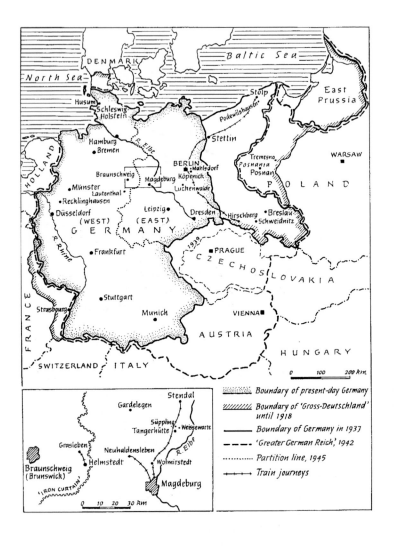

Boundary of present-day Germany

Boundary of 'Gross-Deutschland' until 1918

Boundary of Germany in 1937

'Greater German Reich', 1942

Partition line, 1945

Train journeys

Prologue

THE PEDIGREE

Until that day in the spring of 1951 when my mother handed me a sheaf of parchment papers tied up in pink legal ribbon and labelled 'Pedigree', I had always assumed that only dogs and racehorses had such things.

'You might need this later if you ever have to prove who you really are,' my mother told me and I could see her point. How else would I ever convince anyone of the truth of the very thing I had for more than four years tried desperately to conceal? Namely, that I, Kay Norris, a passably ordinary fourteen-year-old West Country schoolgirl in regulation gymslip and matching flannel knickers, was in reality Katrin Olga Ethel Thiele, born in Berlin in 1936 and not sighted on these shores until 1946, aged ten. The pedigree, consisting of affidavited copies of my birth certificate, parents' marriage certificate and a Home Office document proving my mother's – and, tacked on to it, my – British nationality, explained, sort of, the metamorphosis from my German to my English self.

Katrin Olga Ethel Thiele – what names! Take 'Ethel' for a start. That one was infinitely more embarrassing to live with as a teenager in 1950s Devon than it had ever been in Germany, even at the height of the war. There Ethel, pronounced 'Essel', carried a certain chic as a foreign curiosity; here it was just comic.

Nevertheless I clung to it gratefully; it was English and what did I care about embarrassment when the alternative was the fate I had been taught to dread more than any other – exposure as a German?

Despite the problems they were causing me now, my names couldn't have been chosen for me in a more conventional way, 'Katrin' after the heroine of *Die Katrin wird Soldat*, a best-selling novel – before Hitler banned it – that my mother was reading while she was expecting me and 'Olga' and 'Ethel' after my two grandmothers. If their names made an incongruous pair, so did my grandmothers, or would have done had they ever met – Olga, the daughter of a German country parson, married to a Prussian official, and Ethel, a London hairdresser married to another hairdresser, who was, however, German. It wasn't just the names that were a problem, it was the facts.

My brother Udo and I had grown up in Germany during the Second World War as normal German children. On the wall of our Berlin sitting-room, as of every other sitting-room, classroom, shop, office or public building I ever saw, hung a portrait of Adolf Hitler. Our father, who had been a Nazi Party official before the war, became an officer in the *Wehrmacht*, fighting first in France then Russia. We shared the same wartime experiences as millions of German children: bombing, evacuation and, for the lucky ones of us, successful flight from the Russian advance.

At the end of the war our mother decided to have nothing more to do with our father and, in the autumn of 1946, applied to have the three of us 'repatriated' to England, the country of her birth which we had, however, grown up to regard as our enemy. The problem about England, for which our mother and *her* mother (our grandmother Ethel) took care to prepare us, was the likelihood of being beaten up or even lynched by anyone who discovered our German origins. As we had grown up in a country where *not* beating up your enemies, if you had the chance, would have been considered unacceptably cissy, the welcome we were taught to expect sounded entirely logical and we co-operated fully with the plans to conceal who we really were. We took English names – 'Norris' had been our grandmother Ethel's maiden name – and from the moment we set foot in England pretended that we had been born and spent the war in London. This can't have been very convincing in my case, as I hardly spoke a word of English and what little I knew about life in England had been gleaned from people who hadn't been there for twenty years. My only other sources, a few *Playbox Comic Annuals* and other children's books dating from before the First World War, were hardly more enlightening.

During my first term at an English school, whenever I was quizzed about my origins, I stalled or lied. I couldn't be sure that my tale of being a Londoner born and bred was believed but I assumed that I had at least managed to conceal the terrible truth, since nobody showed the slightest desire to beat me up. In fact, even when they must have suspected the truth, everyone was extraordinarily kind and nice. It was very puzzling.

Our only direct experience of rejection came from our English relatives. On top of long-standing personal jealousies they had never forgiven my grandmother Ethel for starting all the trouble by marrying a German in the first place, nearly half a century ago. Though they grudgingly sponsored our repatriation, when we appeared on their doorstep in the flesh in our extraordinary homemade clothes, with our German hairstyles, speech and manners they couldn't take it. Within a few days they asked us to leave.

This reception confirmed our mother's worst fears and fuelled her determination to transform us, overnight, from typically German to typically English children. Yet, what she was really preparing us for was 1918, trying to spare us the anguish and humiliation she and her parents had suffered through the anti-German hysteria that swept the country during and after the First World War. They, too, had been rejected by their own relations, lost their business and their home and then been deported to Germany.

For, in having me repatriated and changing my nationality, my mother was bringing to three the generations of females in our family who were to spend part of their lives as Germans and part as British, moving to and fro between the two countries in response to the state of hostilities between them.

Yet what happened to us after the Second World War was very different from what the previous generation had experienced after the First. In 1918 anyone with a German connection was indiscriminately detested and that was that. In 1945 the situation was more complicated, with Germans divided into 'good' and 'bad', victims and monsters. Some of the few English people who knew we had been Nazis did, indeed, reject us but nobody who met us for the first time appeared even to consider the possibility that we had been anything so grotesque. We didn't fit their mental picture of Nazi monsters; anyone who realised we were German took it for granted that we were victims and treated us with special kindness. We couldn't understand it.

Nevertheless, with the family's experiences of 1918 indelibly imprinted in her memory, nothing was going to deter my mother from her plan to eradicate our German traces quickly, totally and irrevocably. She had, however, underestimated her task. On the surface my brother and I adjusted quickly enough and within just a few months nobody meeting us for the first time would have suspected that we hadn't been born in England and lived there all our lives. In my case, however, the transformation was largely cosmetic. I had been brought up as one of Hitler's children and, do what I might to pretend otherwise, nothing was ever going to wipe out that formative experience.

Unlike most of my fellow Nazis, I had been too young at the time to feel any responsibility, shame or guilt for the evils of the regime that were subsequently revealed. While all their instincts were to deny, repress and dissociate themselves from their Nazi past, mine were the opposite. My memories of Nazism were an integral part of my childhood and most of them were happy. I had no desire to eradicate them. I also knew that, for the sake of my sanity, I must keep them alive in order to make sense of them one day, to understand what on earth had been going on. Could all the Nazis I had known – just about everyone I loved – really have been the loathsome brutes subsequently portrayed? Could all the Nazi ideals I had been taught to revere, notions like self-sacrifice and dedication to duty, really have been utterly vile? I couldn't accept that. Yet, if they weren't, how was it possible that the worst evil in the history of mankind had been going on in our society, all around me? Once I came to England there was never anybody in my life with whom I could share the contradictions that plagued me. As, externally, I evolved into a passable specimen of English girlhood, in the furthest recesses of my mind a confused closet Nazi continued to lurk.

Whichever way you looked at it, my identity was a mess. My mother's gathering together in one place of the few bits of hard evidence that could prove who I was at least provided a start for sorting it out, as I knew I would one day have to. No present could have given me greater pleasure than my beautiful new pedigree, and I gave my mother a grateful hug.

Part I

GERMANY

I

OMA'S STORY

My grandmother Ethel was a spirited Londoner, very tiny (five foot with an eighteen-inch waist), very pretty, entertaining and, when necessary, very fierce. She once caused an uproar when, as an eighteen-year-old girl travelling to work on a crowded bus, she knocked flying down the centre aisle a large man who was trying to fondle her thigh. She could draw, sing, write and, when in the mood, even speak spontaneously in comic verse. Her general cockiness, combined with atrocious German, became an unbeatable combination for making out under Hitler, as she later had to do. The most officious Nazi bureaucrat was usually stunned into helpless compliance when shouted at, in execrable German, by my diminutive grandmother and, after Germany's defeat, she showed a similar aptitude for bending Russian soldiers to her will.

Perhaps Ethel inherited her spirit from her mother, Bessie. She had been a great beauty, a waitress who married above her station but whose husband, gentleman or no, turned out to be that archetypal Victorian villain, a 'rotter'. He walked out one day, leaving his wife with no money and four children (two others had already died). Some years later there was a knock at the door. Bessie opened it to find her husband standing there. She slammed the door in his face and that was the end of him.

Oma – as I called my grandmother – could see the funny side of this story and laughed at it herself. It was genuine laughter, too, not bitter. I can't recall her being bitter, complaining or feeling sorry for herself. If the worst happened – as it usually did in her life – she would take the line 'It can't be helped' and either try not to think about it or to find something in it to laugh at. She even managed to do this about the worst week of her life, spent in a Berlin cellar as the Red Army overran and ransacked the city. The Russian soldiers' body-search technique of pressing their revolvers into various parts of one's anatomy with one hand, while searching for valuables secreted about one's person with the other would, in years to come, be played out as a piece of comedy to entertain her family.

As for Robert Norris, her feckless father, she had no fault to find with him. 'He had a beautiful tenor voice', was her principal memory of him. His relations – they were a legal family – cast him out for marrying beneath him but, after he disappeared, his mother occasionally helped out, descending on the family in a brougham with parcels of food and clothes. When Oma had rheumatic fever her grandmother even took her to be looked after in her house. But when the old lady died, the contact petered out; the three sisters and their younger brother grew up in poverty and without a permanent home, moving round a series of lodgings in the Brondesbury area of West London.

If a wife hadn't heard of her husband for seven years she could remarry, so eventually Oma and her sisters acquired a stepfather, Uncle Jack, a cutlery salesman who drank. Oma seemed to have forgotten the poverty and drinking, but remembered the curiosities of their family life, like the picture which, after every move, reappeared faithfully on the wall above her mother's brass bed. It depicted two men about to fight a duel; a woman, arms spread out, had thrown herself across one of them as a shield and the caption read: 'Through my Heart First!'

However straitened their circumstances, Bessie allowed no relaxation in their domestic standards. The table had to be properly laid, there had to be a clean white cloth; table manners had to be perfect. Perhaps these values of hers help explain how Oma and her two sisters emerged from their unelevated West London upbringing without a trace of a cockney accent or West London nasal twang.

My grandmother was born in 1880 and left school at fourteen, proficient in the three Rs and knowing the Psalms by heart. She could still recite them at eighty. The three sisters were apprenticed to trades: Gertie, the eldest, to a dressmaker; Oma, the middle one, to a wig-maker and Nellie to an upholsterer. They were a close trio, but Oma, much the prettiest and cleverest, sometimes came in for jealousy and spite, particularly from Gertie.

She first met Richard Druhm, my grandfather, or Opa, in 1899. He was a quietly spoken Prince Albert lookalike who had come to England from Germany four years before as a seventeen-year-old barber just finishing his apprenticeship and ready for a *Wanderjahr* adventure. In 1895 Germany had military conscription, a hangover from the Franco–Prussian war, and it could well have been no coincidence that Opa, an unmilitaristic figure if ever there was one, timed his departure from Germany to the year he would have been drafted. When, for whatever reason, Opa decided to see something of the world, England would have been an obvious destination for his travels. At the time London alone had a German community of 50,000, most of them shopkeepers, skilled artisans and domestic servants. There were a German gymnasium, a hospital, a concert hall, numerous German churches and restaurants, newspapers and clubs, including a German Athenaeum, cultural and sports associations and even charities. The gymnasium, or *Turnhalle*, is still standing, a listed building in the wastelands behind St Pancras Station. In his *Life and Labour of the People of London*, published in 1902, Charles Booth singled out German barbers and hairdressers for special mention, remarking that they were 'exceedingly clannish'. They even had two clubs of their own, the Harmony in Fitzroy Square, 'of imposing character' and the less elevated Concordia in

Houndsditch. I don't know if Opa participated in this organised immigrant scene but he liked England so much that he stayed on and, by the time he met Oma, had dropped all plans for returning to live in Germany.

Opa had fallen for Oma from afar, watching her pass his shop on her daily walk to work, and had used all his ingenuity to get an introduction. When she first met him, Oma too was quite impressed with his good looks and sharp dress. 'As soon as black and white check trousers were "in", he had a pair, and the same with brown shoes and a red tie,' she recalled, in a fragment of memoirs her grandchildren made her write down before she died. When they started going out together, Opa persuaded her to give up wig-making in favour of proper ladies' hairdressing, a career into which he had by this time moved himself and which, he said, held more opportunities.

After a while, Oma wouldn't see him any more. She was influenced by the wave of anti-German feeling building up in England and didn't want to get more deeply involved. She was only nineteen. 'He was terribly upset; never had another girl. Took up cycle-racing instead.'

When they met again two or three years later, both were well established in their new profession, working for Bond Street salons as hairdressers to the aristocracy. They visited their customers in their homes, Opa in a frock coat and top hat, the only trades person allowed to use the front door 'because he had come to the ladies'. They had to grapple with hazards like tiaras that wouldn't stay in place ('A tiara crooked would have been awful!') and debutantes' hair that refused to hold up the ostrich feathers ('They had to be fixed so that it showed there were *three*. Oh, it was a difficult job'). They slaved over coiffures for Edward VII's coronation, twice (the first date was cancelled when the King had to have his appendix out) and, hairstyles being so elaborate that one spent many hours ensconced with one's clients, regularly came under pressure to act as a mentor, or even go-between in their extra-marital affairs.

Oma earned thirty-five shillings a week, enough to fuel the jealousy of her sister Gertie, whose earnings never rose above twenty-five.

Oma and Opa's early life together in Edwardian London can't have been quite as idyllic as their later reminiscences suggest, but there is no doubt that it was the high point of their lives. Opa had joined a cycle-racing club and established himself as an amateur champion with a fine collection of trophies. He got Oma interested in bicycling too, and had a 'dear little tandem' made for them. They started having adventures exploring the countryside, sometimes in a touring club and sometimes on their own or with Gertie and her husband Harry, who became Opa's good friend. 'We did lovely tours; he was such an innocent, good little man; my mother never objected. We even went to Wales once and another time toured round the Isle of Wight for a week. We were such a modest little pair, never a wrong thought in our head. Not like so many young people of today.'

Oma, meanwhile, had become a keen theatre-goer and got Opa to accompany her to plays, musicals and the musical hall. She saw the musical spectacular *Chu Chin Chow* nine times and knew hundreds of Gilbert and Sullivan and music-hall songs by heart. 'There was no radio in those days to popularise songs; they all came from music halls and theatres and spread from person to person. Of course their popularity lasted much longer than the hit songs of today.'

In 1904 Oma and Opa got engaged. To mark the occasion they had some beautiful photographs taken, showing them immaculately turned out in the last detail of fashion. For Christmas Opa took Oma to Germany to meet his family.

He came from Luckenwalde, a medieval town some fifty kilometres south of Berlin, from a family of respectable burghers and trades people long established in the town. Opa loved books and studying but, as his parents' eldest son, had little choice in a career. As was expected of him, he followed the family trade that went back at least five generations and included several military barber surgeons and field doctors. Opa's father, also a barber and the leading light of his local trade guild, was keeping up the family's tradition of finding cures for the sick; his shop offered not just haircuts and shaves, but a wide range of alternative cures and medicines handed down in the family, including homoeopathy. Not all the Druhms of Luckenwalde were barbers, however. Several had branched out into manufacturing and other business ventures, and Opa had several rich uncles in the town. 'They made an awful fuss of me, no nasty feelings against the English like there was here about the Germans,' Oma recalled of her first encounter with her prospective-in-laws. Opa's younger brother Max, believed to be a confirmed bachelor, became seriously smitten with her too; for Christmas her prospective father-in-law gave her a gold watch.

Opa had been saving steadily, so when they got married six months later, 'we went to a big shop and bought a nice little home.' Then, with the help of a 2,000-mark loan from Opa's father, they bought their own hairdressing business on Haverstock Hill, in Hampstead. According to Oma, its principal hazard as a commercial location was the unseemly sound of heavy breathing from horses pausing for a rest as they pulled their busloads of passengers up the hill.

The family moved into the residence above the shop and took in a tenant, a young man called Martin Shaw, who was the organist at nearby St Mary's, Primrose Hill, and an aspiring composer. He was later to make a name for himself as a prolific songwriter, a collaborator of Vaughan Williams, and as a leading light in the movement for the regeneration of church music.

This was where in 1910 my mother Elfreda – Freda in England and Elfi in Germany – was born, their first baby having died when he was only four months old. When I took my mother back there in 1987 for the first time in more than seventy years, she immediately recognised the roads along which she had been pushed in her pram and even identified the house outside which she was sometimes left while her nanny kept an assignation with a boyfriend. Opa had become a keen photographer and his photographs of this period, with Oma in amazing hats wheeling my mother in a pushchair to Hampstead Heath, or of outings to the zoo or the seaside with parties of friends and relatives, recall a purposeful, confident and cheerful lifestyle. Opa's relatives, including his brother Max, by now an official of the Berlin Post Office, and their young cousin Arno, then in his late teens and being groomed to take over the management of his family's department store in Luckenwalde, often came to stay. They couldn't know that, thirty years later during the Second World War, Arno would repay their hospitality by taking in the next generation of the family as evacuees.

Opa's photographs of Onkel Arno's visits are most entertaining. There is one of him as a plump young man peering down from an open-top London bus, with Oma beside him, and another of him adorning Brighton beach in a spectacularly striped bathing suit. Also featuring in snaps of this time was Miss Kathleen Connell, Oma's apprentice, subsequently her assistant and life-long friend, one of the few people who remained loyal to her through two World Wars, and who, years later, was also to reappear in all our lives. Most of the photographs that have survived were made into postcards and a whole stack of them, sent to Onkel Arno to help keep up his English, have been returned to me. Their texts bear witness to the warm and chatty intercourse between the English and German sides of the family as well as to the high morale in force at 72 Haverstock Hill. 'Hoping you are as happy as I am,' is how Opa concluded a card he sent to Arno in May 1912.

Yet all this time anti-German sentiments were simmering beneath the surface of British society. 'The bitterness against Germans was unbelievable,' Oma recalled. 'Even my family were horrid to me and my own mother turned against me. Once she came to see me and said such horrid things that I told her to clear out and didn't see her again for years.'

Germans in every walk of life became bogeys: German grocers, it was rumoured, were liable to 'lace your food with poison', and barbers to 'slit your throat'. Spy-mania was rampant; a German waiter sketching out a seating plan was arrested on suspicion of making a map of military installations.

By the time war was declared, a hysterical press had whipped up such passion against Germans that open victimisation became not only widespread but universally applauded. Germans were dismissed from jobs they had held for twenty years; German music was banned from the Proms and the British-born children of German immigrants made ineligible for London County Council scholarships. The most inflammatory demagogue of the time was Horatio Bottomley, publishing editor of *John Bull*. In May 1915 he called for 'a vendetta against every German in Britain, whether "naturalised" or not . . . you cannot naturalise an unnatural beast – a human abortion – a hellish freak. But you can exterminate it and now the time has come.' The stream of vitriol on the theme of 'the sneaking, slimy Hun who pollutes our atmosphere', which poured from him in editorials and speeches throughout the war years, gained Bottomley such a following that in the 1918 Election he was voted into Parliament as an Independent.

The sinking of the *Lusitania* in May 1915 released the last restraints on Germanophobia and anti-German riots broke out, the most violent seen in Britain this century. Sylvia Pankhurst describes them in *The Home Front*, her book about everyday life in London during the war. 'The prospect of looting without fear of punishment made its appeal to certain sections of the poor and ignorant. Many a home was wrecked; many a peaceable working family lost its all. Stones were flung, children injured.' She tells how a friend who tried to defend German families from the mob was herself injured and how another, married to a German, 'saw her home utterly dismantled, even the tools, so costly and so essential, by which her husband and son earned their living as cabinet makers. She saw her husband, son and daughter dragged out of the house by the mob. What had become of them? Were they killed or imprisoned? A day of agonised suspense elapsed before they were able to rejoin her.' Officially 237 people were injured in the riots, but Pankhurst believed there were many more as 'women like this poor friend of mine made no report of their suffering'. Families lost their homes and livelihoods; there were suicides. The Home Office formed a Committee for the Relief of Destitute Aliens, so did the Society of Friends and other charitable groups.

It is a curiously neglected episode, despite the claims of Panikos Panayi, the leading authority of the period, in *Germans in Britain during the First World War*, that for three periods of the war, the persecution of 'enemy aliens' was the dominant political issue, used to sustain popular enthusiasm for the war.

Oma and Opa's cheerful life on Haverstock Hill came to an abrupt end. First, Opa, 'an enemy alien of military age', was interned. He had by now lived in England for nearly twenty years and considered it his home. However, he could not have failed to notice the surge of anti-German feeling building up all around him, so an obvious question from today's standpoint is: Why on earth had he not got himself naturalised? It is something I could never understand until I had a look at the nationality laws of the day.

It seems that before the First World War the whole concept of nationality wasn't as clear-cut or significant as it is now; what mattered was domicile. A foreigner who had lived in England for ten years or more was deemed to have relinquished the nationality of his birth and become a stateless person; from that position, acquiring British nationality was little more than a formality. Because the whole thing was so relaxed, not many foreign residents bothered to become naturalised. (During the ten years up to the end of 1913, there had only been 10,000 naturalisations in all, and of around 80,000 German and Austrian-born residents living in Britain, only 7,000 had claimed their naturalisation certificates.)

In 1913, just when it began to look as though the remaining 70–75,000, including Opa, might be well advised to get their papers in order as there might be war, Germany introduced a new nationality act which pulled the rug out from under this long-standing convention. It extended indefinite 'state protection' to everyone born on German soil, regardless of how long they had been domiciled abroad. By preventing German expatriates from becoming stateless any more, the act succeeded in making people like Opa ineligible for British nationality. It even affected Germans who had become naturalised. They now had dual nationality, which so offended British practice that when war broke out some had their certificates revoked and were interned along with everybody else. Not that the anti-German rioters distinguished between enemy aliens with or without naturalisation certificates. They didn't even spare the Bermondsey baker, who had resourcefully filled his shop window with photographs of his two sons in uniform, to show that, like several thousand other sons of German immigrants, they were fighting on the British side.

One night a brick landed in Oma and Opa's shop and slogans appeared on the pavement outside. 'Gangs of ruffians went about smashing up shops kept by Germans,' Oma wrote in her memoir for Udo and me in May 1965 when she was eighty-five. 'One of my customers, a gentleman who was an MP – his wife was my customer – was going down Haverstock Hill when he met a gang coming to smash us up. He talked to them and made them turn back but he advised me not to stop there. We hadn't much custom left, anyway. So I sold up my home, the whole lot in a hurry for £7. That was my first home gone. I took lodgings, two rooms. Well, I had to go to work and was forced to go to my mother's and to ask her to take Freda, a tiny girl of four.'

For the next year my mother lived with her grandmother Bessie, her husband and her older cousin, another Ethel, who had an equally pressing need for a temporary home. Ethel's mother, Oma's youngest sister Nellie, had enterprisingly left her husband, emigrated to Australia and married one of her fellow passengers on the boat out, bigamously, of course. The flat must have been small as my mother remembers having to sleep on the sitting-room sofa. She was enrolled at the local infants' school, the

Beethoven School in Beethoven Street, Brondesbury – it's still there, now a Further Education Centre – while Ethel went off to a secretarial course. Every Saturday afternoon Oma collected her daughter for the weekend and every Monday morning she took her back to Bessie's.

So long as she owned up to her German surname – even with its spelling anglicised into 'Droome' – Oma didn't get any work so she reverted to 'Miss Norris'. One day a workmate spotted her on a bus with my mother, who was calling her 'Mummy'. The workmate went straight to the boss to report that Miss Norris was not what she seemed; she was – God forbid – an unmarried mother. Oma was fired on the spot.

She eventually found an employer who didn't hold her nationality against her, a Swiss called George Rossell, universally known as 'Mr George'. 'I had to tell him my circumstances, because at the end of my first week he asked me for my insurance card which at that time all workers had to have. You see, I had no worker's card as I had been mistress of a business. As my luck would have it, he was Swiss (and very pro-German) and he didn't mind. I went as Miss Norris and no one knew who I was, only Hopey, as Mr George had told her.' Hopey was Miss Elsie Hope, Mr George's senior assistant and confidante and she was to become Oma's lifelong friend. She was ten years younger than Oma, only twenty-five when they met and not married, but for the next three years she was to give Oma and my mother unstinting moral and practical support. She did it again after the Second World War, to our much enlarged family.

In contrast to her new hairdressing colleagues, Oma's family abandoned her. Gertie and Harry, to whom she, and Opa too, had been really close before war broke out, stopped seeing them altogether. They also had a daughter by now, Betty, three years younger than my mother, who remembers meeting her cousin only on a single occasion, just before the family left for Germany. 'We were invited to their house in Harrow for tea and to say goodbye,' my mother recalls. 'Betty had bright red hair all done in ringlets.'

'Those were dreadful years for me,' Oma's Memoir relates, 'always living and working in secret, in fear that the others would find out I was married to a German and had a child. Two or three times customers of ours from Haverstock Hill came in and saw me and I had to contrive to ask them to pretend they didn't know me; the same with commercial travellers who recognised me. Also, I was always in fear that the other assistants would see me out with your mother. Anyway, I remained Miss Norris there for three years and they never found out.' Oma stopped sleeping properly. Her nerves were shattered and they never fully recovered from what she went through in the First World War. How was she to know that worse was to come during the Second?

One of Oma's greatest anxieties was being separated from her little girl for most of the week. One day Mr George had a brainwave. He said to her, 'Why don't you take her to the convent school in the next street? You could take her there every morning and fetch her again in the evening. Those sisters are so sweet, she would be happy there.' So that is what she did. They had a lovely nursery and she was very happy.

My mother still remembers the little convent school:

The nuns knew the whole truth but they still took me in and were kind and understanding. I had school lessons and was taught to say a rosary, otherwise there was no effort to make me Catholic. When school was over I played in the nursery with other children till they were collected. I was always the last and had a free run with all the toys. Then Oma and I took a bus and a tube home. I had to walk quickly from the convent to the bus stop and was told that if anyone met us and stopped to speak I mustn't call her 'Mummy'. This arrangement lent a certain air of conspiracy to our relationship.

What I remember most clearly is the winter times when we emerged from the underground and walked out into the cold dark night. Lighting up the sky would be the criss-cross of searchlights, looking for German Zeppelins. Once I caught sight of one that had caught fire, red-glowing and cigar-shaped, breaking in two and falling to earth.

We would walk hand in hand and, because by then I was tired out, my mother would sing to me the popular hits of the day, mostly music-hall songs. 'If you were the only girl in the world' and 'Daisy, Daisy' were my favourites. Whenever I hear those songs today, they remind me of that time.

Sometimes during the nights there were air-raid warnings and I was carried to a house opposite which had a cellar, where the neighbours congregated. I can't remember any bombs being dropped.

Most Sundays we were invited to dinner by Aunty Hopey's parents at their pub in Brondesbury, the 'Wat Tyler'. Hopey also had a family of cousins – the Sharpes – who lived in Kettering, Northamptonshire, and she took me to spend many holidays there. It was a wonderful experience for a London child, living in the country with a large family of children. We played games I had never heard of, climbed trees and had magic lantern shows in the garden. I learned to ride a pony and these were the happiest weeks of my wartime childhood.

Every Saturday for the next three and a half years Oma took my mother, bloomers stuffed full of cigarettes, oranges and chocolate bars, up to the Islington Workhouse in Cornwallis Street, Holloway, where Opa and 400 other Germans were interned. As an enemy alien with an English family, Opa was kept within visiting distance of his home, along with others who had been in England for many years and, as a result, were thoroughly anglicised.

A row of policemen guarded the iron rates through which the visitors had to pass before approaching the austere building. 'They were supposed to search us, but I don't believe they ever did,' my mother recalls, but she was never to forget the scene when they got past the guard. 'There, behind barbed wire, surrounded by a small crowd of eager-looking men, stood my Daddy peering expectantly at the gate.'

'Didn't you find that weekly ritual, seeing Opa locked up like that, terribly distressing?' I asked my mother when I was putting together our story, but she didn't remember it being so. 'I was with my mother and just accepted the whole thing as normal.' I now consider it as one of Oma's most remarkable achievements that, even as her own life was falling apart, her courage and optimism carried my mother through the war years without evident emotional conflict or psychological damage.

Miss Hope, her fur muff also stuffed full of goodies for Opa, often came with them on their visits, and occasionally so did Mr George. Sometimes the visitors themselves received a present in return for their offerings, things like wooden toys and other craft work that their internee had made to pass the time. The favourite occupation in most of the camps was apparently marquetry. Opa, renowned for both his patience and dexterity, became extremely skilled at this and some of his output from that time is still used by our family today; for example, two beautiful jewellery boxes, one made for Oma and the other, with her initials set into the lid, for Aunty Hopey. Another curiosity that has survived is a mechanical cigarette box, built on the principle of a pop-up toaster; while it could never have been a thing of beauty, at least it still works.

Opa was more fortunate in his internment than his seventeen-year-old cousin Günter Wagler, who happened to be on his first visit to England when the internment order was announced. As a bachelor with no close family ties in England, he was shipped straight off to join 28,000 other internees on the Isle of Man. Two years later he died there of consumption, his parents' only child.

Yet, for Germans living in London, even internment in the Cornwallis Street Workhouse was not without hazard. On 7 July 1917 the Germans made their first daylight air-raid on London, killing 44 people and injuring 125. There was outrage and the fiercest anti-German riots yet seen erupted. For four nights running, angry crowds marched on the internment camp, lusting for revenge. Bloodshed was only avoided through the intervention of the Metropolitan Special Constabulary. According to their chronicler W.T. Reay, writing in *The Specials; How They Served London*, their achievement was the more remarkable since 'there could not have been found among the constables who did their duty so splendidly, confronted the fury of the crowds and protected assorted Germans and their property, a man who did not heartily share the wholesome anger which provoked the riots'.

An extra provocation was the name the Germans had given to their new bombers – 'Gothas'; for the British royal family's name at the time was Saxe-Coburg-Gotha. Public fury at the damage – and the insult – rose to such a pitch that within ten days of the raid the King had changed his name to 'Windsor'.

In 1918 the war ended and Opa and the other German aliens were released. However, instead of being allowed back to their families, they were immediately deported. Demands for the expulsion of all enemy aliens, the 'Expel the Hun' issue, was to become a dominant feature of that year's campaign in the run up to what was to become known for ever afterwards as the 'Hang the Kaiser' Election. So, at the age of forty, having spent all his adult life in England, Opa was shipped back to Germany.

The only way for the British-born wives of German enemy aliens to avoid the same fate was by reclaiming the British nationality they had lost on marriage. A special clause had been included in the 1914 British Nationality and Status of Aliens Act to make this easy for them, provided they shed their German husbands, defined in the Act as subjects 'of a state at war with His Majesty'. Many wives availed themselves of the opportunity and the Imperial War Museum has some heart-rending diaries of deported husbands whose British wives and children would have nothing more to do with them after their enforced return to Germany.

Oma decided not to take that road but to join Opa in Germany. She must have formed quite a good impression of the country on her engagement visit there some fifteen years before and was anyway so disgusted by the anti-German hysteria she had experienced in Britain that she couldn't imagine any of them ever living happily there again. Thus, in February 1919, five months after Opa's departure, she and my mother joined a party of English wives and children being 'repatriated' to Germany, a country most of them had never seen. Oma was thirty-nine and my mother eight and a half, two years younger than I was to be for my extraordinary mirror-image 'repatriation', in the opposite direction, more than a quarter of a century later. I must confess to heaving an enormous sigh of relief when, thirty years later still, my own daughter reached her eleventh birthday without a similar upheaval.

It was freezing weather. 'We left King's Cross at midnight and the only person who came to see us off was Hopey,' Oma recalled. 'She had fitted your mother out with a new fur hat and coat, with a muff and lovely little high-legged boots. She gave her a little eiderdown quilt to keep her warm on the journey.'

The trip to Berlin took a week, travelling under guard, sometimes spending the night in a barn or a school. Their luggage, maximum weight allowance 100 pounds, was searched by police several times to make sure they weren't taking out British currency. My mother remembers the journey well:

We set off from London in a special train and then took a boat to Rotterdam. In Holland our transit was supervised by Dutch Quakers. They did their best for us, gave us a hot meal and arranged beds for us in a school. But from the Dutch/German border on it was a nightmare. We travelled for 300 miles through snow-covered countryside in a vandalised or war-damaged train with no heating and no glass in any window. It kept stopping and dodging about; we were told it was because there were mines on some of the train lines and that was why the journey took so long. At each stop a different lot of police or border guards came on to inspect our papers and our luggage. The guards showed us no consideration and were rude to us. Whenever I think of that journey what I remember best is keeping warm, snuggled into my lovely little eider-down.

There is no record of Oma having anything so comforting to keep up her spirits on the trip. She was not one to dwell on past misfortunes and in years to come I never heard her complain about the experience. I can only imagine how she must have felt on that wretched, freezing train with hostile guards and no glass in any of the windows, taking her little daughter away from the only life she had ever known, to join her husband in indefinite enemy exile.

2

KÖPENICK

The discomforts of their journey were but a foretaste of what they were to find in their new homeland. Before the end of 1919, the year my mother and Oma arrived, a million German children were to die of malnutrition. The situation was so desperate that British and American Quakers came to the rescue with an extensive relief programme. Over the next four years they provided 7,300 food distribution stations for mothers and children all round the country. I discovered this little known fact from *Stille Helfer* – The Silent Helpers – an exhibition to celebrate the vital contribution made by Quakers towards keeping the German population alive, more than once this century, that I visited at Berlin's German History Museum in January 1996.

But food shortages were not the only problem. Germany hadn't taken its military defeat well and for the next few years political instability, civil disorder and street violence were to be as much a feature of everyday life as scarcity and want.

The scenes that greeted Opa returning to Germany in September 1918 must have been much like those described by Paul Cohen-Portheim in his classic account of wartime internment in Britain and its aftermath, *Time Stood Still*. After an interminable journey in a train as wrecked as the ones that were to bring Oma and my mother a few months later, he found the capital's streets 'packed with half-starved looking men, there were innumerable war-invalids and still more beggars. Every few minutes motor-vans rattled past, full of red guards with machine guns, and skulls were painted on these vans. Intermittent street-fighting was going on in different parts of the city and one heard the rattle of machine guns and sometimes the deeper sounds of artillery. Endless queues of grey-looking women lined the pavements in front of all food-stores; agitators were haranguing crowds in the squares. It was my return from war to peace; it seemed more like a return from peace to war.'

By February 1919, when Oma and my mother made their journey, the street-fighting had died down, at least temporarily, but in comparison with the victorious, self-confident country left behind, they must have been appalled at the poverty, dereliction and terrible morale everywhere apparent. As Cohen-Portheim put it: 'No matter how much one had read or heard about the state of things in Germany, now that one saw it one was dumbfounded ... the atmosphere was one of listlessness and dumb despair.' Many of the English wives who had gone out to join their husbands couldn't take it and went straight home.

For the first few months the family squeezed in with Opa's parents in the flat behind their shop in Luckenwalde. The old couple did all they could to make them comfortable and shared everything they had, the problem was there being so little to share. Food consisted almost entirely of black bread and potatoes and even those were rationed; having something to eat with the potatoes, like cabbage, was a treat. Worst of all for Oma was the absence of any tea to drink and, until Aunty Hopey, Mr George and Grandmother Bessie came to the rescue with food parcels, she suffered terribly.

The one consolation was the warmth of the welcome they received wherever they went. Overnight my mother became the centre of attention for a whole clan of new aunts, uncles and cousins and when she started school she was a celebrity. On her first day, twelve little girls brought her home. 'They were all round her and looked upon her as something wonderful,' Oma wrote in her Memoir. 'They had never met another foreigner.' Nor, perhaps, a girl with bobbed hair. My mother took it all in her stride. Aunty Hopey received a postcard of the Brandenburg Gate from Oma with the message, 'We came past here today and Freda shouted, "Hyde Park Corner!"'

The extended family organised a whip-round for Oma and Opa. They wanted to raise enough to set them up with their own business again. Within a few months of their arrival they were indeed installed in a perfectly satisfactory shop on Grünstrasse, Köpenick – a historic and, when times were 'normal', agreeable town on the south-east outskirts of Berlin.

Here, throughout the 1920s and part of the 1930s, Oma and Opa traded as successfully as they might on their fashionable London background, introducing such exotica as 'bobbing', Marcel waving and, later, perms, to the stodgy German fashion scene. Their business thrived and within a year of opening they had paid back the loan. 'There was never any ill-feeling because we were English,' recalled Oma, 'just the opposite.'

Yet, for most of that period, the pleasure they might have taken in their business success was overshadowed by their continuing despair at the state of the country. While hairdressing and other service trades could function more or less normally, most of the basic necessities of life, especially food, remained in desperately short supply and their quality was abysmal. The family continued to rely heavily on food parcels from England. 'In 1922 Aunty Hopey came to visit us for the first time and she was appalled,' my mother remembers. 'She called our meals "carrots and oats time", those were our staples. She lost ten pounds in just a few weeks and made me spend the following summer in England so that she could feed me up.'

I have in my possession two items of correspondence from this time which record how desperate Oma was feeling throughout her first few years in Germany. One is a postcard addressed to

Miss Hope and dated 14 April 1920, when she had been in Germany just over a year. The picture is a pre-war photograph of Grünstrasse, Köpenick, showing the shop to best advantage. The message reads:

> Have you received Miss Connell's letter yet from mother? I would like George to read it. Will you take it with you? It is our one and only hope now but oh, it is difficult.
> E.

My mother explained: 'Miss Kathleen Connell, Oma's apprentice from Haverstock Hill days, had gone to Kenya to be a lady's maid/hairdresser to a titled lady. While out there she married Teddy Holness, an engineer working on a government drainage scheme. When Kath heard how terrible conditions were in Germany she suggested that we try to emigrate to Kenya as well. Oma and Opa were terribly excited and applied right away. Teddy Holness recommended them, but after months of waiting Opa was rejected (a) for being German and (b) for being a hairdresser, not considered an essential occupation for a colony. For a couple of years Oma and Opa were very disappointed but after Kath and Teddy returned to England they didn't think about it any more.'

The second of Oma's letters is dated 2 September 1920 and addressed to Horatio Bottomley, then a columnist on the *Sunday Pictorial*. Oma had written:

> Sir,
> I am an English woman living in Germany. My mother sends me the *Sunday Pictorial* every week and I often read statements which I long to contradict.
> I read this week that butter in Germany is 14 *s*. per lb. – I wish it was. Butter is only to be bought by going round the farmer's back door, or from someone who had bought it that way. It is never cheaper than 30 marks per lb, often 40 marks. The 20 gram weekly butter ration is the same price.
> Then a few weeks ago you stated that Germany had gone

back to white bread, well, I have been in Germany nearly two years and I have never seen white bread except once when a piece was given me by an English soldier. Our bread is dark brown, sour and gritty. So-called white bread is allowed for invalids but that is a fawn colour and little better than the ordinary.

No doubt when you state these things you believe they are true but you should first make quite sure. I will willingly inform you of prices and conditions as I find them.

I am, yours faithfully,

Ethel Druhm

I only have the letter because it was returned, unopened and generously rubber-stamped with the word 'Refused'. It is ironic that, having built his fortune on exposing the misdeeds, real or imagined, of others, Bottomley should himself, soon after Oma's one-sided correspondence with him, be convicted of embezzling the £78,000 he had supposedly raised for the war effort. He spent five years in prison and died in 1933, a pauper.

Meanwhile, at around this time, just as there were signs that living conditions in Germany might at last begin to improve, an even more catastrophic phenomenon was gaining momentum, hyper-inflation. At its height, the price of a loaf of bread reached a hundred million marks. Shoppers carried their money not in purses but baskets or buckets. Oma and Opa had to raise prices daily, if not hourly, and rush out to spend their takings, lest their value was lost, almost between customers. Saving money for a rainy day would have been equivalent to throwing it away. In 1923 finance minister Stresemann miraculously brought inflation under control, but economic recovery was slow and did not last. And 1929 saw an even worse disaster: the depression in which six million Germans became unemployed.

As if these economic horrors were not enough, Oma and Opa were having to grapple with another hazard they had not previously encountered in the hairdressing trade: political instability bordering, at times, on civil war. The Weimar Republic's parliament had over thirty parties and the democratic process wasn't working. From time to time different fanatical factions were declaring *putsches*, there were political assassinations and fighting on the streets. At any time a skirmish might erupt outside the shop, announcing itself with a burst of gunfire. Oma and Opa would quickly lock up, close the shutters and hole themselves up in their residence upstairs. If the shooting was prolonged, they would take refuge behind their tile oven. 'Sometimes at night when we were in bed we would hear gunfire and shouting,' my mother recalled. 'We would wonder who would be in charge when we got up next morning. Remnants of the German Army? The police? Right-wing or left-wing street fighters?' Within a few days, normality of a sort usually returned.

They hadn't realised when they went to live in Köpenick that it was – and, it appears, still is – a hotbed of political militancy, a 'red town'. In 1920, during the right-wing *Kapp Putsch*, for example, Köpenick workers made the headlines when they took on, and drove off, army units sent to march on Berlin in support of the coup. Left-wing militancy continued into the Nazi era: on the very day in 1933 that Hitler took power, a red flag was hoisted on the most prominent landmark in the area, the brewery chimney. That gesture of defiance brought forth violent reprisals and yet more fighting in what was to become known as the *Köpenicker Blutwoche* (Köpenick's Week of Blood), when twenty-three anti-Nazis were murdered. With so much militancy all around them, it is no wonder that Oma and Opa, in their high-street location, kept being interrupted in the middle of their bobbing, perming and Marcel waving.

Yet, during the course of the 1920s, in so far as the national problems of the day didn't intrude on their lives, all three Druhms found a lot to like in Köpenick. Its location on a spit of land where Berlin's two navigable rivers, the Spree and the Dahme, join in a wide pool, gave it genuine attractions. Two handsome bridges, one over each river, and a fine baroque castle with lovely gardens were distinctive landmarks. There was always something to see on the water, whether freight barges, pleasure craft or rowing eights; the backwaters were ideal for bathing and skating, there were steamer trips, waterside cafés and beer-gardens where bands played. On Sundays there were open-air concerts in the parks. Last but not least, the whole of Berlin being surrounded by woods and lakes, Köpenick, at the very edge, had two of the most attractive right on its door step, the Müggelberge and the Müggelsee.

With their well-developed instincts for making the best of any situation, the Druhms took advantage of every amenity. Herr Freyer, a teacher at the boys' Gymnasium who had originally cultivated them with a view to practising his English, became their close friend and, being a keen *Wanderer*, led them on weekend expeditions into the Müggelberge. They acquired a canoe and – judging by the photos of them paddling along in the midst of busy shipping, without life-jackets and Oma and Opa unable to swim – were lucky to survive. Some weekends they bicycled the seventy kilometres to visit the Luckenwalde relatives. Dashingly for a man approaching fifty, Opa took up motor cycling and once or twice a year even went touring on his 500 cc machine as far as Bohemia. They took short holidays, their favourite and the one they never forgot to Switzerland. Being such a close family, they shared many interests, like star-gazing with a little star-finder, following the latest excitements in polar exploration and classical archeology.

My mother loved the Dorotheen Schule, her local girls' high school, and joined in with everything on offer, academic or not. Her favourite subjects were music, art and astronomy, but she also took ballet and once did a season in the juvenile corps de ballet of a Berlin show. She learned to play the piano and was taken by her teacher to concerts and operas in Berlin. She became an excellent swimmer, learned ice-dancing, took up rowing and became president of the school's rowing club: 'I was appointed, not elected. We didn't have anything as democratic as elections.' For all its fetching sailor-dress uniforms, the club appears to have been famous for its parties and dances rather than its prowess at rowing and my mother's role consisted more of speaking at functions and welcoming guests than anything excessively sporty.

Throughout her school years my mother was regularly requested to join other classes round the school to read to them in 'real' English, as opposed to the strange language being taught there for the rest of the time by enthusiastic German *Englischlehrer*.

What with my mother being so happy at school, the steamer and canoe trips, waterside beer-gardens and band-concerts, hiking and picnics in the woods, even Oma began to quite enjoy her new *bürgerlich* lifestyle. Yet, however well they managed to adjust to their surroundings, at home the family retained its English character. They spoke English, cooked English dishes and took it in turns to travel into the metropolis to stock up at its one purveyor of English teas. Apart from relatives, most of their social life was with the other Anglo-German families they had got to know while Opa was interned and they also regularly had visitors from England. Every Friday they fell upon the roll of English newspapers that Bessie, regular as clockwork, sent them: the *Schoolgirls' Own* for my mother and the *Sunday Pictorial* for Oma and Opa. My mother had to read out the football results for Opa to record in his notebook. Most Sunday evenings when they returned from their *Wanderung* expeditions Oma would read to them aloud from the English books – mostly classics – with which Bessie kept them supplied. Their favourites were *David Copperfield* and *Treasure Island*, the latter providing the inspiration for the name they gave to their canoe, the *Yoho*.

Their favourite and most frequent visitor was Aunty Hopey, who quickly charmed her way into the hearts of the extended Druhm family. Photos survive of her as the centre of attention at a huge family picnic in Luckenwalde, presided over by Grossmutter and Grossvater Druhm, as well as of her joining in a riotous bathing party by the Spree; Onkel Max, Opa's confirmed bachelor brother, became her regular holiday escort and, back in England, she received fond postcards signed by all the extended family.

In the summer of 1923 my mother returned to England. 'I had a wonderful holiday! I was 12 and travelled by myself. What a different life I found there! I saw a banana for the first time, and heard a radio!' She visited her grandmother Bessie, her aunts and her cousins Ethel and Betty, 'still with those red ringlets'. She accompanied Aunty Hopey to Kettering to the wedding of the eldest of her former playmates and, while there, it was arranged that one of the younger boys would make a return visit to Köpenick.

Aunty Hopey had by now left Mr George's employ and, with a partner, had opened her own salon in Davies Street, Mayfair. My mother spent most of her holiday with her, being driven around in the dickey seat of her new Belsize Sidley motorcar and staying at the Grey Hut, a delightful weekend cottage Hopey had acquired on the Thames at Wraysbury. It was while staying there that my mother made a new friend, Mr George's daughter Gabrielle, who was a year older than her. The two girls hadn't met before as Gaby had spent the war years with her mother in Switzerland, but now they got on famously. At the end of the holiday the Rossells invited my mother to stay in their Oxford Street flat and it was arranged that Gaby would come to Köpenick the following summer. Before she returned to Germany Mr George gave my mother an unusual goodbye present, the very latest hot perm. It caused a sensation when she turned up at school and had to make a tour of all the classes to report on her visit to England.

Oma was finding it very hard to forgive the treatment she had received in England in the war; it was not until 1928, nearly ten years after leaving, that she conquered her hurt sufficiently to join my mother on a trip. She visited her mother and her sister but, like my mother, spent most of her time at Wraysbury with Aunty Hopey and with Mr George, Miss Connell and the rest of the hairdressing mafia who had stood by her in the war.

This was the year my mother left school and was making her first appearance in England as a full-blown eighteen-year-old flapper. As a British-born adult with her own passport, the question everyone asked was: Why didn't she stay in England? Life was better, there were more opportunities, it was her home. My mother was tempted, but rejected the idea. It would mean leaving her parents and the most powerful effect of their years of shared exile had been to bind the three of them together so closely that none of them could ever be happy away from the others again. So she returned with Oma to Germany.

The time had come for her to choose a career but, although she had so many talents to draw on, this proved extremely difficult. While it is such a strong characteristic in our family to always look on the bright side and only remember the good things, my mother can clearly recapture her disappointment and frustration at that point in her life, nearly seventy years ago. 'My parents didn't push me,' she recalls. 'They were always working and too busy to discuss what I should do. It was left to me. The only person in the family who took an interest was Onkel Arno. I really wanted to become a high-powered secretary, somewhere I could use my languages, but he was strongly opposed to that. He said that so many girls could speak English these days and that there were thousands of secretaries. Very few had my artistic talents and I should concentrate on them. He had great faith in my abilities and persuaded me to go to art school. So that's what I did, for a year, and then I joined the advertising studio of Kaufhaus Des Westens' – otherwise known as KDW and Berlin's biggest department store on the Kurfürstendamm – but I always wished I had stuck to my original idea.'

Despite their English lifestyle and their distaste for Germany's social and economic disorder, there is no doubt that, in the course of the 1920s, the Druhm family had to some extent integrated into German society and even started to identify with it. What was the alternative? They couldn't go back to England and, in so far as they belonged anywhere, Germany was their home.

By the end of the decade, for the first time in their lives, they were even taking an interest in politics. After the hardships and chaos of the 1920s, many Germans, including Oma and Opa, were only too delighted when a radical movement appealing for national unity and economic regeneration appeared on the scene. Its leader, previously unknown to them, was an Austrian called Adolf Hitler, and Oma and Opa became his ardent supporters. The lead was apparently taken by Oma who had become so fed up with German politics that she was ready to greet with unqualified enthusiasm anyone who seemed capable of delivering the two things so spectacularly lacking in her ten-year experience of Germany: political stability and goods in the shops. On top of its other attractions, I can well imagine the music and colourful trappings of the Nazi party appealing to her theatrical tastes.

I doubt whether Oma and Opa would have supported Hitler had they been aware of his plan to go to war as soon as he had re-armed, but this was something he worked hard to conceal. On 10 November 1938, he told a meeting of newspaper editors:

> Circumstances forced me to talk almost exclusively of peace. Only by constantly laying stress on Germany's desire for peace was it possible for me to win freedom for the German people bit by bit and to provide the nation with the arms which were the prerequisite for the next step ... I spoke only of peace for so many years because I had to.

He had certainly fooled Oma and Opa. In the spring of 1939, a few months before Germany's invasion of Poland signalled the start of the Second World War, they cheerfully welcomed Oma's sister Gertie on her first-ever visit to Germany. Given what had happened to Opa and his cousin Günter during the First World War, it is unthinkable that they would have let her come had they been aware of the slightest risk of war.

The regime that Oma and Opa helped into power was to

unleash such evil and destruction on the whole of Europe, on millions of Jews and on Germany itself, that anyone subsequently revealed to have been a Nazi has been demonised as a genocidal monster. This interpretation comes from hindsight, however; the reality at the time was rather different and far more complex.

My family's involvement with Nazism – their first excursion into any kind of politics – was not inspired by hatred of Jews, but by the vision of national revival that Hitler held out to them. 'You have no idea what a terrible mood of disillusion and defeat there was in Germany before Hitler appeared on the scene and how he turned that round to one of optimism and hope,' was my mother's overriding memory of those days.

Hitler had an uncanny instinct for touching the button of the innermost yearnings of the German heart. He promised most groups in society – an unhappy society, with a suicide rate three times that of Britain's at the time – the things they craved: jobs, prosperity, security. Yet the deepest longing of Germans at the time, one that was apparently shared by most of the population, including my mother, was for the restoration of their national pride and recognition in the eyes of the world. Germany was still smarting from defeat in war, the loss of its colonies and eastern provinces, and the humiliating peace terms forced on it at Versailles. The rhetoric from those times, with its unqualified assumption that territorial expansion and the domination of other peoples were rights of which Germans had been unjustly deprived, makes curious reading today; so does the popular argument of the time that national 'honour' – undefined – demanded their restoration.

The vision of a strong, revitalised Germany that Hitler held out to his followers was firmly based in its most sacred cultural traditions; he invoked the ancient heroic myths and sagas and reaffirmed such cherished German values as the work-and-thrift ethic, the commitment to public service and efficiency and the love of hiking round woods and mountains, communicating with nature the while. Nazis were made to feel that they were upholding everything that was best in their heritage and they wore their uniforms and badges with pride. But Hitler was a Pied Piper, appealing to their imagination and their hearts, not their heads. He never explained how he intended to restore the country to international greatness without going to war. My family, like millions of others, took his word for it. They had fallen for his charisma, allowed him to cast a spell over them, and laid themselves open to being disastrously bamboozled.

As soon as Hitler assumed power, domestic conditions improved. The reduction in unemployment and the new welfare programmes had an immediate impact on morale. The Druhms noticed the difference right away. In their high-street location they had often felt uneasy about leaving their shop, afraid they might meet a mob on the streets. 'There were so many angry-looking, alienated young men everywhere – unemployed, of course. Then, almost overnight, those same young men had been given jobs to do, roped into the Hitler Youth and become motivated,' my mother remembered. Was this not the start of the very resurgence that Hitler had promised? Adulation of him became ever more fervent. That the euphoria that swept the country probably owed as much to Hitler's propaganda machine, his control of the press and his ruthless suppression of opposition as to real achievements, would not have been noticed by people as politically naïve as the Druhms.

When I asked my mother how the persecution of Jews fitted into all this, she told me that she and many other Nazis had never liked that part of Hitler's programme. Growing up in the Berlin area in the 1920s, used to going to school, to music and dancing classes with Jewish girls and later working for a Jewish boss, she had not witnessed overt anti-Semitism or discrimination; she was used to seeing Jews being treated like everybody else and saw no reason for that to change.

Historical research into the period suggests that my mother's recollection may only be partial. It seems that, however tolerant the face-to-face treatment of Jews in Berlin in the 1920s – and other writers bear out my mother's experience in this respect – there was a powerful undercurrent of anti-Semitism running deep and strong right across Europe, powerful in France, England, Austria and Poland, as well as Germany, where several openly anti-Semitic parties were represented in the Weimar parliament. It was so much part of the culture, yet usually so restrained in day to day personal relationships that people like my mother might well not have been alert to its significance in the society around them. The fact that it expressed itself in caricatures, jokes and attitudes rather than in violence and overt discrimination made it no less dangerous. It was there, ready for Hitler to exploit with a propaganda campaign that linked it to every sensitive nerve in the German psyche.

My mother clearly remembers the stages in which Hitler whipped up even greater resentment against Jews and also that she could not help being influenced by the power of his rhetoric. He claimed, for example, that Jewish speculators had made a killing out of the hyper-inflation in which millions of Germans, including Opa's rich uncle, were dispossessed of their property. He accused Jews prominent in the avant garde of the arts of deliberately subverting that inviolable icon, German culture, with their modernist aberrations and he mounted a high-profile exhibition of 'degenerate art' to prove the point. To begin with, Hitler kept repeating the idea that the worst exploiters were not German Jews, but those from East European countries whose Slav populations Germans historically despised even more than Jews themselves. It seemed to my mother that only when he could be confident that his attack on East European Jews had hit home did he step up his attack on German Jews, gradually moving towards a definition of the German *Volk* from which they were excluded. The Jewish community in Germany identified so strongly with the country that had been their home for centuries that the early days of Nazism even witnessed the spontaneous appearance of Jewish support groups, particularly of Jewish veterans who had fought with distinction in the First World War.

However inaccurate my mother's recollection of anti-Semitism in the Germany of the 1920s and 30s, I have no reason to doubt her claim that Hitler's appeal to her, and many other ardent supporters like her, would have been just as great even without his vicious rhetoric against Jews. 'We only went along with Hitler's Jewish *Klaps* (obsession) because everything else he was doing for Germany was so marvellous,' was her explanation of what ensued.

Where she and millions of other Germans were disastrously to blame was in allowing themselves to be hypnotised by Hitler into suspending their own judgement and handing him their power. By so doing they colluded with his anti-Semitism and left themselves no way of stopping him from doing in their name things that would not have occurred to them to do on their own.

Several aspects of the history and culture of the time would have disposed the population to voting a nationalist dictator into power. One was, quite simply, exhaustion from two decades of war and political chaos with no less than 300 political assassinations in the four years preceding Hitler's rule. Another was the country's authoritarian and military tradition, brilliantly lampooned in the (true) story of 'The Captain of Köpenick'. This was about a destitute, out-of-work cobbler who, in 1906, found a discarded captain's uniform and put it on to keep warm. As he walked down the street a party of Prussian infantry saluted him; when he noticed that, despite his scruffy appearance, they were ready to obey his every order, he marched them to the *Rathaus*, ordered them to arrest the mayor and walked out with 4,000 marks of the town's treasure.

The education system, too, conspired to stop people asking questions and challenging their leaders. My mother's school in Köpenick, an ordinary state high school, was no doubt typical of the time; this is what she remembers of the syllabus.

The only history systematically taught was the origin of the German state, starting with the *Völkerwanderungen*, the migrations of the Germanic peoples in prehistoric times, and culminating in the flowering of the Prussian state under Frederick the Great and Bismarck's unification of Germany in 1871. The Treaty of Versailles and the Weimar constitution were presented as insults to Germany.

The teaching of literature and cultural history complemented this presentation, with the importance of ancient epics like the *Niebelungen Lied* being especially stressed, and their revival in the operas of Wagner welcomed. Science, astronomy and medicine, music and art were presented from the point of view of famous Germans. Even Copernicus, who lived in Poland, was claimed as a German national.

The history of other European countries was taught piecemeal fashion, as a backdrop to heroic characters like Peter the Great and Napoleon Bonaparte. The French, Russian and other modern revolutions were mentioned, but deplored for their cruelty to the ruling classes and the damage they inflicted on their countries; there was no discussion of the evils that had inspired them or of the aspirations of the revolutionaries. All non-German nationalists, especially Poles, were presented as evil-doers. The British Empire was held up as a model institution and an example for Germany to emulate.

Greek, Roman and the principal European cultures were of interest only from the point of view of their literature and myths, not their political ideas. Thus my mother was introduced to the works of Shakespeare, the Romantic poets and even Oscar Wilde, but allowed to remain ignorant of the Magna Carta and the concept of parliamentary democracy.

As for contemporary German politics, neither the principles nor practice of the Weimar Republic featured; there was no discussion of civil and political rights or of the voting system in force. Thus my mother couldn't tell me whether, under Weimar, women had the vote. (They did, when they were twenty-one.)

The teaching style was didactic. Pupils were not encouraged to participate, question anything or think for themselves. Those who showed a tendency in that direction were deplored for being 'difficult' and 'trouble-makers'.

If my mother, with her high-school education, had so little exposure to ideas that might promote an understanding of politics, her parents would have had even less. Thus, in 1930, Oma wrote an enthusiastic letter to Mr George, extolling Hitler and the wonderful impact that National Socialism was having on Germany. He never wrote back and that was the end of a fifteen-year friendship that had already withstood many tests. His daughter Gaby didn't write to my mother or visit again either. Oma and the rest of the family were hurt and puzzled. They couldn't understand it.

Years later, while putting together my family's history, I discovered that Mr George had been a life-long internationalist and communist sympathiser. This, of course, explained why he had hired Oma to work for him in 1915, when nobody else would take her on. Oma herself was always convinced it was because he was Swiss, and pro-German.

I also met up again with my own generation of the Sharpe family, Aunty Hopey's Kettering cousins, who had given my mother such wonderful holidays when she was a child. From them I discovered that with Aunty Hopey, too, there was a political aspect to her support for my family during the First World War. The entire Hope/Sharpe family, it seems, had a long tradition of radical socialism, finding expression in the name Aunty Hopey's father had given to his pub, the 'Wat Tyler'. George Sharpe, my mother's host in Kettering, had been a conscientious objector who spent the war not in the trenches but in a shoe factory. Every time my mother visited he had to report her arrival to the police. Though, unlike the Rossells, Aunty Hopey wasn't very politically minded, that family history does explain how effortlessly she rejected the anti-German fever that was everywhere rampant, in favour of friendship and support for its victims.

Mr George and Aunty Hopey must have been horrified to

witness the rise of Nazism in Germany, and especially my family's support of it. Though, unlike Mr George, Aunty Hopey did not break off her friendship with them, she never visited Germany again. It is a sign of my family's political naïveté that they had no understanding of what anathema Hitler and everything to do with Nazism must have been to their socialist friends.

Yet, contrary to Mr George's fears, Oma and Opa hadn't suddenly become converted to fascism. I doubt whether concepts like 'communist', 'internationalist', 'left-wing', 'right-wing' or 'fascist dictator' meant very much to them, which was why they couldn't understand Mr George's reaction to Oma's letter. As my mother remembers it, 'Being Nazis wasn't about policies; we weren't interested in theories and didn't really understand the difference between them. We believed in a cause and, above all, a man.' Hitler had mesmerised them and I suspect that they would have continued to support him had he, overnight, turned bolshevik.

The final push to the family's assimilation as Germans came in the summer of 1931 when, a few days after her twenty-first birthday, my mother brought home her first serious young man, Eberhard Thiele. He was twenty-four, an engineering student at Neustrelitz in Mecklenburg, good-looking, clever and with an exuberant, forceful personality. He had completely swept my mother off her feet. Oma and Opa were impressed by him too and thoroughly approved of his commitment to Nazism. Their courtship was not only short but mostly conducted at a distance. They can hardly have known one another when, within three months of meeting, they married. In so doing, my mother was not only changing her marital status, but her nationality. On 11 November 1931 she became, in law, German.

3

MAHLSDORF

I was born in Berlin on 6 June 1936, was three in 1939 when war broke out and seven in 1943 when we left the capital to get away from the bombing. Perhaps because the years that followed were so restless and disrupted, I still look back on that first, settled period of my life with special affection.

My family consisted of my parents, whom I called Mutti and Papa, my three-years-older brother Udo and me, Katrin Thiele. Two streets away lived Oma and Opa. We lived in Mahlsdorf, a suburb on the city's eastern outskirts, in the kind of 1930s housing that still sends town planners into raptures: a 'small-is-beautiful' garden estate on a quiet, tree-lined street called Fauststrasse. There were two little apartment houses – ten flats in all – with balconies, verandas, individual gardens and communal spaces our mothers could overlook while we played. It was the ultimate in modernity of the day and, as urban locations go, couldn't have been better for bringing up children.

I didn't discover, until I went back there in 1992 and found some of my childhood neighbours still living there, that nearly half the residents of these delightful flats, including my family, had been moved in by the Nazi party in an attempt to boost its presence in an area that had been something of a left-wing stronghold before Hitler came to power. My father was by then a

Nazi Party official, working in the administration of the Hitler Youth, and with his young wife and two children must have been regarded as a model specimen of wholesome Nazi fatherhood.

Against the odds – for shared political beliefs don't necessarily make for domestic harmony – our socially engineered community turned out a total success. Except that, or perhaps because, the able bodied men only put in occasional appearances when home on leave from wherever they were fighting, a more stable and peaceful community would be hard to imagine. The dominant group consisted of four young families with children of about our age, eight of us altogether; we grew up as a gang, playing in and out of each other's houses and, when we reached the age of six, going to school together. On the rare occasions our fathers were home at the same time, they socialised and played *skat* together. Our mothers co-operated in housework, shopping and childcare; they even had a social get-together every week and, as it was just about their only relaxation, dressed up for it. I remember my mother donning make-up and jewellery in preparation for an evening in the flat across the hall.

Perhaps everyone co-operated so well because it was wartime. The adults were constantly complaining about this and wallowing in reminiscences of life *im Frieden*, peacetime. I had no pre-war memories, so for me everything about it was normal and I got quite irritated at the endless talk about the sacrifices being made by our heroes in the *Wehrmacht, Marine* and *Luftwaffe*. As I saw it, going off to fight was what men were for. They had to do something, and what else was there for them?

Nor could I get worked up like everybody else about the rationing, queuing and shortages. I was never cold and hungry and didn't realise I was missing anything. I could have done with more sweets and chocolates, but that's true of every child, whatever its ration.

Our sparse food supplies, what Gandhi would call 'enough for men's need, not their greed', meant that anything slightly out of the ordinary gave us the wildest pleasure. My most memorable gastronomic experience of the war came when, after months of seeing nothing but sacks of potatoes and cabbages on display at the greengrocer's, the shop was one day stacked with a pile of mysterious green football-size objects that nobody had seen before. My mother brought one home and, cutting it in half, exposed the smiling inside of a water-melon. We weren't sure what to do with it, but quickly discovered it was utterly delicious. Next day the greengrocer was still struggling with his water-melon mountain, reported to have originated from the capture of a cargo-ship on its way to England from darkest Africa. For several more days Udo and I could think of little but water-melons; we had photographs taken of ourselves holding them, cutting them and eating them. Then they were gone, never to be seen again. It was fifteen years before I had my next water-melon experience, by which time my more discerning palate found the taste disappointingly bland and the whole episode a let-down.

As I had no memory of life without air-raids, that aspect of the war didn't bother me either. It was the most natural thing in the world for me to get up in the middle of the night – daytime raids hadn't started – and join the other families from our building in our reinforced basement air-raid shelter for a *gemütlich* session of listening to the radio or playing cards and Ludo. The sirens and anti-aircraft guns, the bangs, the sounds of shattering glass, the drone of bombers passing overhead and the occasional scream of a dogfight caused me no more alarm than a patch of stormy weather passing overhead.

After an hour or so the all-clear sounded and we would emerge from our cellar. Our whole party – eleven if we were all there – would step out into the courtyard for a breath of air and to look west to see how Berlin had fared this time. Searchlights would still be zooming round the sky in criss-cross patterns and after a bad raid the whole sky would be red. I never missed having my gaze to the west, but my interest was purely aesthetic, like looking at a sunset. I felt no concern or involvement.

What did get me quite excited one night was hearing a

beautiful bird-song quite close by. Our neighbour told me it was a nightingale. After that I always listened for the nightingale's song but I never heard it again.

I obviously lacked the intelligence to appreciate the damage bombs could wreak for I felt only gratitude for the one that came closest to finishing us all off. It was a high-explosive one that dropped into the field just across the road from our flat, less than fifteen metres away. The field was earmarked for more housing like ours but, as building hadn't started, the neighbours had helped themselves to extra strips of vegetable patches and the children to the rest for more adventurous games and building projects than our gardens would permit. The bomb had flattened all our mothers' vegetables and shattered every window on the estate but, more importantly, had also produced a magnificent crater whose potential for play got us very excited when we went out next day to study the damage.

The north German plain where Berlin is located was once under the sea. Wherever you dig down more than six inches you reach a stratum that was once below the Baltic. Our bomb had exposed tons of pure white sand, a beautiful beach right on our doorstep. Below the powdery surface the sand was cool and damp, just right for building; we made an elaborate complex of sandcastles with interconnecting tunnels and orifices through which water, fire and smoke could pour. Finally we dug an underground castle to crawl around in ourselves that, we told each other lugubriously, would kill us instantly if it collapsed with us inside.

In view of its position on the edge of Berlin, our suburb would probably have escaped the attention of enemy bombers, had the terminal of Berlin's overland metro, the S-Bahn, not been located there and, more to the point, had the main railway line connecting Berlin with Eastern Europe not passed directly over its main thoroughfare. Thus, on our way to school one morning after a bomber had scored a direct hit on the station, we were startled to see a whole train hanging down from the railway bridge into the street, looking like a giant caterpillar trying to burrow into the ground. Before that, in the spring of 1941, when all attention was still focused on the Western front, we were mystified to see trainload upon trainload of tanks, guns and soldiers trundling over our railway bridge, bound for the East. Then Mutti woke me one day with the news that our *Wehrmacht* had invaded Russia. She tried to make it sound like good news, but she wasn't very convincing. For as long as I could remember, pinned on our playroom wall had been a brightly coloured map of Europe; Mutti used it to teach us the names of all the countries and their capital cities. I was already aware of what dangerous people Russians were and could see for myself how big their country was compared to ours. Under the circumstances, the attack sounded like a thoroughly bad idea to me and I was only five.

Apart from my lack of intelligence, my permanent optimism and sang froid in the face of bombs is, I think, explained by the fact that I grew up feeling so secure – secure in my family, my neighbourhood and the world around me. I had total confidence in my parents' power to protect me from every danger and in their readiness to sacrifice themselves for my safety. I suspect that I owed this over-weening belief in my own importance to the extra care they lavished on me because of a minor birth defect, club feet. Its German name, *Klumpfuss*, makes it sound even worse. It was a fairly common abnormality that could often be corrected in infancy, but with me that didn't work. My feet seemed to have a will of their own and every time a treatment looked as though it might do the trick, the old problem stubbornly reasserted itself.

I was only a few days old when my feet were first operated on and so don't know how they originally looked – scrunched inwards and without proper heels, I'm told. However, as I couldn't imagine having anything other than my own particular pair, they were normal to me and everybody else was out of step. As they didn't hurt or stop me doing anything I wanted to – except wearing normal shoes – their principal interest was as a passport to endless attention and treats denied to other children.

Night and morning my mother had to massage them and watch me do exercises; a special gymnastic apparatus was put up in our playroom, to the exclusion of everything else, including Udo's train-set. Then, when Papa was away in the *Wehrmacht*, I had to sleep in my mother's bedroom so that she could keep an eye on the night callipers I wore to push my feet outward as I slept. Every night she put them on me, reinforcing the buckles with strong tape tied in labyrinthine knots. Every morning the callipers were found undone, with the tapes hanging free. Nobody could fathom how I managed this Houdini act in my sleep and I was just as mystified. I knew for sure I could never have undone all those difficult knots if I'd been awake.

My biggest treats – and my mother's worst nightmare – were our visits to the Charité Hospital. As far as I was concerned, the purpose of the expedition was for me to play with the magnificent toys in the waiting-room: rocking horses, pedal cars, exotic stuffed animals and – oh bliss! – a Wendy house. I always felt cheated if we didn't have a good long wait before seeing the doctor, but I'm glad to say we usually did.

Our doctors at the Charité were apparently not tuned into counselling and supporting the parents of handicapped children and were only interested in the technicalities of treatment. They told my mother there was just a chance that my feet could be manipulated into a normal shape, if she would do the manipulating. They heaped on to her the responsibility for correcting a chronic condition that, in the end, only yielded to major surgery. After that advice my mother could never again enjoy a moment's peace of mind; any time not spent working on me was a wasted opportunity and if the treatment still didn't work, she would be to blame for not doing enough.

While for me my abnormality had definite compensations, it gave my parents only grief. While most of my early childhood memories are happy, my mother's of me as a child are dominated by her permanent anxiety over me, punctuated by extra horrors like having to leave me in hospital for operations, watching me learn to walk in callipers and the perpetual lost cause of finding shoes that fitted me.

I don't remember ever seeing the inside of a clothes shop. My mother made everything I wore on her little hand sewing machine. She had been to art school and was as expert at sewing and design as at recognising the potential of the least likely remnant or cast-off. I always felt I was the best-dressed child in the neighbourhood – the top half of me, that is. The full effect was invariably ruined by my bizarre footwear. Not long into the war surgical shoes became unobtainable and we were reduced to finding me ordinary ones. However, as my feet weren't the same shape or size, I often ended up wearing odd shoes. When even that remedy failed, Udo's outgrown lace-up boots, padded out here and there with cotton wool, were the last resort that could always be relied on to keep me on the road.

As a dedicated Nazi, my father had no doubt been indoctrinated to regard physical deformity of any sort as tinged with moral slur. How mortifying for him to have an imperfect child. It must even have occurred to him that if my deformity had been much worse I could have been in line for extermination. Yet, however purist his ideology in other matters, he didn't apply it to me and I couldn't have had a more doting father. When I was just a few weeks old I was once brought home from hospital strapped into a corrective plaster cemented to a metal frame. It stopped me kicking and I yelled so loud and long that Papa extracted me from the contraption with a hacksaw and took me back to the hospital next day demanding a more humane treatment.

Papa's overriding interests in life were his family and Nazism and he would gladly have sacrificed his life for either. What attracted him to Nazism was, I am sure, the same longing for Germany's regeneration shared by most of his generation; however, in his case there was something else to inspire his commitment. Both his parents had died within a few weeks of one another when he was only nine years old; things didn't go well for him after that and I can imagine that the memories he retained of that first home reinforced his enthusiasm for the Nazi movement.

Both Papa's parents came from clerical families of many generations' standing. I once attempted a tour of all the churches where my ancestors had been incumbents but abandoned the project, incomplete, when I had identified fifty. The Thiele side of the family was firmly rooted in the Prussian clerical tradition of discipline and efficiency, but the maternal influence was softer and more easy-going. My grandfather Fritz had rejected the family trade in favour of agriculture and estate management and when he married my grandmother Olga in 1905 – the same year Opa married Oma – he had already taken up his post with the Prussian Colonization Commission in the province of Posnania. This had been set up to implement the increasingly expansionist policy Bismarck had adopted in 1886 and it was Fritz's job to purchase large Polish estates and divide them up for sale and resettlement by German farmers. The idea was to bring the benefits of Prussian efficiency and culture to a people traditionally despised by Germans as backward and slovenly.

Fritz travelled round the estates he controlled in a private train with three coaches, one serving as his residential quarters, another as his office and the third as accommodation for the livestock he and his party needed to provision themselves on the trip. On top of his job Fritz had taken on the management of a large farm of his own, which meant that the family lived in considerable isolation, miles from the nearest town. From the age of six, the only way Papa could get to school was by harnessing up a pony-trap and driving himself into town and back.

Like any expatriate family living in a hostile colonial outpost, I imagine that the Thiele household in Posnania would have been ultra-nationalistic, passionately committed to spreading the Prussian way of life and laying the foundations of *Gross-Deutschland* (Greater Germany). The family's photo album of that time recalls a lifestyle resembling in many ways that of a district officer's family in some remote outpost of the British Empire. My father's christening picture shows that Fritz's father, a rural dean from Saxony, had travelled all the way to Popilewo, near Tremesno, to perform the baptism, together with other relatives who came to be godparents. All the other guests recorded in the picture are local German landowners or government officials, with not a Pole in sight. Other pictures portray only an occasional Polish coachman or housemaid.

Then, in 1916, Olga died in a scarlet fever epidemic and, a few weeks later, Fritz of diabetes. Their three children were unofficially adopted into the family of Onkel Otto, one of Olga's brothers. Unlike his brother Jochen and baby sister Kiki who, over the years, both learned to fit in, it appears that Papa, the eldest, was too *schwierig* (difficult) and never settled with his new family. Within just a few months, when he was still only aged nine, his uncle enrolled him as a cadet in the military academy at Naumburg. His holidays were spent being passed round innumerable clerical aunts and uncles, but he never seems to have found a comfortable niche and grew up as a loner. Thus when, in his late teens, he first heard Hitler's idealistic rhetoric in favour of *Gross-Deutschland*, of bringing order and progress to the cultural wildernesses of the East, I can well believe that it struck a powerful chord with Papa's memories of the home he lost and gained the Nazi Party one of its most committed supporters.

Papa saw Nazism as a noble and virtuous cause. Though he had studied long and hard to become an engineer and was, I think, extremely talented, he graduated during the depression and couldn't get a permanent job; for most of the first few years of his married life he was unemployed. That humiliation must have disposed him more than ever to taking up the Nazi cause. In 1934 he abandoned his abortive efforts to break into a career in engineering and became a full-time party official in the administration of the Hitler Youth. He was quickly promoted to the rank of *Oberstammführer*, equivalent to a major. Then, when the war started, he was called up into the *Wehrmacht*, serving first in France and then Russia. He loved the military life and around this time wrote to a cousin, 'I wish every soldier was as happy as I am.'

Whatever he was doing, from party work to repairing a light fuse, Papa was a tireless worker, practical, methodical, quick and not stopping until a task was finished. He had a forceful and charismatic personality, was lively and entertaining and, with his impromptu piano-playing, could be the life and soul of the party. His striking looks as a young man, too, made him very attractive to women. However, he also had his darker side when, as seems to have been the expected behaviour of German family fathers of the time, he would become dictatorial, bang and shout, become moody and withdrawn into himself as though he were another person. At such times he ignored us, so his moods made little impact on us. If Papa had *schlechte Laune* (a bad mood), we made sure to stay out of his way until he came out of it, but I could tell that Mutti always found these episodes a strain. Another side of his character she found distressing was his possessiveness when her relatives and Köpenick friends like Herr Freyer, their *Wanderer* friend, came to see us. He could be so rude to them that they stopped coming unless they could be sure Papa was not around. Impervious to all such undercurrents, I could find no fault with my father and whenever he wasn't at home I missed him terribly. I even spared him from my callous attitude to the other 'heroes' fighting for our country and when one of our friends on the estate lost his father on the Russian front, I couldn't stop worrying all the time lest the same thing happened to Papa. I looked forward to his leaves more than anything.

A curious aspect of Papa's war service was that, in addition to his normal leaves, he periodically turned up out of the blue for an overnight stay or a weekend when he was on the way to somewhere else, like a 'course' or 'briefing'. He was never promoted above the military rank of *Oberleutnant* (first lieutenant), but still seems to have had more of such little surprise trips than our friends' fathers. Many years later, long after he was dead,

I asked my mother about these mysterious jaunts. She told me that she had never really understood very much about what he was doing in the war; he had been rather secretive, and she was too intimidated by him to risk upsetting him by asking questions. I have tried to find out from the official records what was going on and have come to the conclusion that he was probably not an ordinary soldier, but a member of the Nazi Party's cadre within the regular forces. I suspect that his task was political education of the troops, indoctrinating them and keeping up their morale and their commitment to the Nazi cause.

When he turned up like that we were always excited to see him. However short the visit, he would do his best to tackle any jobs around the house and garden, including mending our toys. If there was time, he even descended to his cellar workshop and made us yet another of his magnificent creations, such as a steam engine or dolls' furniture.

Even when he was abroad for months at a stretch, Papa continued to make his presence felt at home. One way was by finding ingenious ways to help us out with supplies from wherever he happened to be. Another was by sending soldiers from his unit to call on us when they were passing through Berlin and needed a bed for the night, preferably near the S-Bahn. They always brought an exciting parcel or letter. Most of them came unannounced, but once a telegram arrived with the message: *Herr Hase und Frau Gans Ankunft Montag* (Mr Hare and Mrs Goose arriving Monday). And so they did, in the luggage of a soldier in transit.

At other times, especially when he was in France, Papa sent us exciting parcels of food, clothes and luxury items that were still on sale there, like coffee, brandy and perfume. He once sent Mutti a roll of cloth destined, he claimed, for American army officers' uniforms. The stuff was olive green and of superb quality; she got a tailor to make it up into a classic suit that became the mainstay of her wardrobe until long after the war.

Another way we felt Papa's presence was through his entertaining letters. We loved having them read out to us and tried to replicate his no doubt sanitised accounts of army life in our games, for example, of an *Entlausungsanstalt* (delousing camp) for soldiers on the Russian front. He sent us a plan of the layout and described in detail the procedures he had to go through. First came the reception area where he had to give up his clothes to be fumigated, then the various stages of being steamed, sprayed and hosed down until he reached the exit and received his clothes back. We found this fascinating, and making our *Männekins* go through the same process became one of our favourite games. *Männekins* was a game Udo and I had invented for our collection of little wooden people, which were sold by the *Winterhilfe* to raise funds for the needy, in the manner of a charity flag day. They made ideal Christmas-tree decorations, but we had given each of the thirty or forty in our collection its own name and character and had invented a language for them that nobody else could understand. Whatever was happening to us or our friends also happened to the *Männekins* who, in their time, were also put through many of the hardships suffered by German soldiers fighting on the Russian front.

Once Papa was sent to Husum in Schleswig-Holstein on a month's training course and arranged for us to stay on a nearby farm. It was our first experience of country life, of touching and smelling real farm animals, including puppies and kittens. It was harvest-time and the farmer let us ride about on his hay-wagon and on the massive carthorses pulling it. I loved every minute and after that anyone who asked me what I was going to be when I was grown up was firmly told, *Eine Bäuerin* (a farmer's wife).

I didn't need Papa to be at home to convince me of his total commitment to our family and to me. Our months of separation did not shake the feeling of confidence and security in my family that, I think, made me so fearless and optimistic throughout the war. What unnerved me far more than bombs at around this time was my discovery that there was such a thing as divorce.

When I was about four I had whooping cough and the doctor

ordered me into the country for a change of air. Frau Winter, one of our neighbours, told us about a hotel near Lautenthal, her home town in the Harz Mountains, and gave us an introduction to an old schoolfriend, Kätchen Beume, who still lived there. It was midwinter and the mountains and forests were covered in snow. I discovered how much more fun – and how dangerous – tobogganing could be when done on actual hills, rather than the only place I had attempted it up to now, the oh-so-flat north German plain.

Frau Beume – Tante Kätchen, as I came to call her – was blonde, very pretty and vivacious. She lived with her parents and her two sons, Dieter and Klaus, in a traditional timbered house, half of which was the town's electricity works, owned and operated by her father. We children got on reasonably well but within no time our mothers had become best friends. A few months later Klaus needed some medical treatment in Berlin and the three of them came to stay in Mahlsdorf for a few weeks, partly with us and partly with the Winters.

That was when I discovered the horrifying truth about Tante Kätchen. She was a divorcee – the first I had ever knowingly encountered. When her marital state was explained to me I was speechless. 'You mean,' I finally managed to bring out, 'she could get married again? To somebody else?' I remember it going through my mind that if there were such things as divorce and remarriage, then my parents could get divorced and Papa could marry Tante Kätchen! The thought put me into a panic and I couldn't shed it. Perhaps I had already sensed, deep in my unconscious, that my mother had some reservations about my father. Perhaps that was at the root of my fear – and my uncanny premonition.

4

Belonging

It is well known that war can do wonders for a nation's mental health; the threat of a common enemy gives a sense of purpose and participation to even the most isolated and depressed. Growing up in wartime Berlin, I clearly recall the atmosphere of unity all around and also the feeling of well-being it gave me.

This spirit of common commitment came not only from being at war, but from all being Nazis; that was how it felt, anyway. I took it for granted that everybody shared this conviction because, with one possible but embarrassing exception, I never experienced anyone behaving in a way that hinted at the tiniest doubt about the validity of the Nazi cause. It has emerged since that Hitler had numerous opponents and there may well have been a lot of them in Mahlsdorf; however, as they didn't voice their opposition at the time, they might as well not have existed. They certainly did nothing to dampen the Nazi fervour that pervaded every corner of our suburb and every aspect of our lives.

The embarrassing exception was my brother. I doubt if his opposition to Nazism was on ideological grounds as I can think of no way he could have come across an alternative political philosophy. What he couldn't stand was the emotional compulsion and hype, the militarism, uniforms and, above all, the pressure for *mitmachen* (togetherness) and joining in. His lack of enthusiasm was incomprehensible to our father. Why wasn't Udo counting the minutes to reach the magic age of ten when boys could, or rather, were obliged to, join the *Hitlerjugend?* Since he considered his own time as a military cadet to have been the most enjoyable and formative experience of his youth, Papa put Udo down as a candidate for entry to the nearest equivalent under Hitler, the *Nazionalpolitische Erziehungsanstalt* – the Institute for National Political Education, NAPOLA for short. Luckily for him, Udo failed the entrance exam, with Papa the more put out because one of the Winter boys from the estate was accepted.

Whenever there was a Nazi event that Papa wanted Udo to attend, even if only as a spectator, he would mysteriously go missing, or become ill. As the pressure built up for him to become a Nazi hero, he developed a nervous cough which he didn't shake off till he was an adult.

I couldn't understand Udo's attitude either as I was exactly the opposite way inclined. I loved all the Nazi paraphernalia and, though still several years too young, longed to john the BDM, *Bund Deutscher Mädchen*, the girls' *Hitlerjugend* equivalent. The minute I was six, the youngest age possible, I joined the *Kindergruppe*. We had a sort of, semi, better-than-nothing uniform: a white blouse, navy skirt with shoulder straps and a beautiful stainless steel swastika badge to pin on to the cross-piece in front. Not long after enrolling I got my first chance to serve my *Führer*.

I went on a hospital visit to some Spanish soldiers wounded while fighting somewhere or other on our side. We met up at the station, compared the bouquets of flowers we'd been told to bring and set off in a crocodile to the other side of Mahlsdorf. On the way we passed a fenced-off area like a giant cage in which a crowd of unspeakable-looking men were standing about. They were dirty and in rags, with hollow eyes and sunken cheeks. As we passed they stretched out their hands for food. Our leader told us to ignore them, they were Russian prisoners of war. At the hospital we found the Spanish patients propped up in bed, neat and comfortable and giving us broad smiles. However, as we knew no Spanish and they no German, there was a limit to how much we could accomplish with our brief to cheer them up, so we just gave them their flowers and sang them a few songs.

That was a minor assignment compared with my next, and last, in the *Kindergruppe*. We had been told to turn up at our school one Sunday afternoon; we weren't told why. When we got there it was already packed with boys in HJ and girls in BDM uniforms. At last the wonderful news was broken to us; the *Führer* was going to fly over Mahlsdorf that afternoon. We had been gathered together to prepare a surprise for him that would make Mahlsdorf memorable to him for ever more.

It was the hottest day of the year. We were led in a crocodile through the outskirts of Mahlsdorf till we came to a large hay-meadow. Here, we were told, we were all going to lie down in the grass in such a way that, as the *Führer* flew overhead, he would be amazed to see a huge swastika, as it were growing up out of the field, in the manner of a vast corn circle.

The concept, though magnificent, presented more technical difficulty than anyone had supposed. It obviously had to be a perfect swastika, with all the limbs exactly the same length, but as the human raw material from which it was to be constructed ranged in age from six to seventeen, getting the measurements exactly right presented a distinct challenge. We were dispatched in groups to key locations and told to lie down, head to toe, in the prickly grass, but the first attempt turned out a mess. As the meadow was much too big for the leaders controlling the various extremities of the swastika to communicate with another by shouting and nobody had a loud-hailer, the scene rapidly disintegrated into confusion. What worried me most was that while the leaders were still arguing and making us run hither and thither several planes had flown by overhead. What if one had been the *Führer*'s and he had seen our pathetically deformed version of his glorious symbol?

At last, after yet more shouting and running back and forth

through the tall grass, we were all presumed to be lying in the right place. The sun beat down mercilessly. Crickets and other insects were hopping about on us, biting and stinging us. We waited and waited. At last a further plane, indistinguishable from the others, flew overhead. We were told that one was the *Führer*'s but I was sceptical. Surely, if it was him, he would have waved his handkerchief or dipped his wings in appreciation of our tribute – and our suffering.

We re-formed into our crocodile for the march back to the school. For what seemed like several hours I had needed a pee and by now I was desperate, bursting, and as we turned the last corner and the school came into view I did burst ... simultaneously into tears and into wetting my pants. The whole crocodile came to a halt to watch me and laugh – or so it seemed.

Had it not ended in shame and humiliation, it would have been my proudest day. I had grown up absorbing the Nazi propaganda that surrounded me on all sides, in the air I breathed, emphasised by the flags, posters and slogans on the streets, songs on the radio, Hitler's portraits in every home, office, shop and classroom, on every postage stamp and by his name on everyone's lips, many times a day, in their daily *Heil Hitler* greetings. Though, familiarly, this tended to be reduced to something like *L'Hitler* or even *Litler*, it had become such an institution that when I once asked my grandmother, '*Wie sagt man Heil Hitler auf Englisch?*' (How does one say *Heil Hitler* in English?) there was only one translation she could give me, 'Good morning'.

During my first school year, the Nazi posters and slogans were particularly important to me as the most accessible practice materials for learning to read. Other than our standard primers, we didn't have any reading books at school; apart from classic grotesques like *Struwwelpeter* and well-known fairy stories, no children's literature was available to us. So, after my mornings at school, I got into the habit of dawdling home along the main street, trying to decipher the texts of long-obsolete advertisements for cigars, perfume and sun-tan oil and political slogans that I passed on my way. Outside the station, I remember, hung a huge banner proclaiming that *Die Räder Rollen Für Den Sieg* (The Wheels Turn for Victory). The post office displayed a brightly coloured poster showing a little blonde girl handing the *Führer* a bunch of flowers. The caption read *Auch Du Gehörst Dem Führer!* (You too Belong to the *Führer*). Another I remember went *Wir Glauben an Den Führer!* (We believe in the *Führer*).

As for what Nazism was all about, I knew that the *Führer* had saved Germany – I wasn't entirely clear what from, something to do with the Germans having had a beastly time after the First World War. Then, suddenly, Hitler had appeared and they had work, food and houses, holidays and *Kraft durch Freude* (Strength through Joy); in other words, altogether better lives and – this was most important – renewed pride in themselves. Hitler wasn't just an ordinary leader either, but a special, super-human person, as had been proved in the First World War when he would definitely have been killed, had a premonition not made him move away from a certain spot that was, seconds later, hit by a grenade, killing everybody else.

As for the reasons we were at war, that had to do with our *Volk* being superior to everybody else's. All the world's greatest inventors, thinkers and artists had been Germans; the *Führer*'s programme of invading other countries was part of his mission – his destiny – to let them share in our greatness. The reason little countries like Austria, Czechoslovakia, Belgium and even France gave in so quickly when we invaded them was that they welcomed the opportunity to become part of the glorious new German Empire. Only a few countries, Britain, America and Russia, were opposed to the Nazi cause, because they lacked the intelligence and insight to recognise what was for their own good. Nevertheless, it was their destiny to be included in our empire as well, as would be shown when we won the war. At school we were shown a map of Germany as she would end up after the war, which would be the shape of an eagle with outspread wings. It almost seemed that the whole purpose of fighting the war was to get the map of Europe ornithologically correct.

I was very aware of the moral aspect of the *Führer*'s mission. He was calling on all of us to be heroes and heroines, serving our Reich according to principles like *Pflicht* (duty), *Treue* (faith) and *Ehre* (honour), all of which featured prominently in his rhetoric.

I also knew, vaguely, that there were in existence a few bad people who weren't Nazis; however, as Nazism had been defined as a moral crusade, its opponents must be, by definition, evil-doers. Their opposition didn't need to be taken seriously because of the type of people they were – communists, Jews, cowards and self-centred people, who lacked the courage and generosity to put the *Volk* and the Fatherland before themselves. Thank goodness we didn't have anybody like that in Mahlsdorf! (I prayed that nobody shared my suspicions about my poor deluded brother.)

On second thoughts, there was a Jew in Mahlsdorf, a boy called Günter. He couldn't have been one of those bad people one heard about; he had been Udo's best friend until Papa found out he was Jewish and wouldn't let them play together any more. The only other time I remember the subject of Jews being mentioned in our family was when Papa brought home a lavishly produced book of cartoons and jokes, illustrating supposed typically Jewish characteristics like greed, dishonesty and smelliness, that he wanted us to read. I was so starved of reading materials that I still remember in detail each of the few books I owned, they were so precious to me that I would normally have pounced on such a lovely present. However, this time I could find nothing to enjoy in Papa's colourful offering, but I got the general message. Jews were despicable and, as a good Nazi, it was my duty to dislike them.

Though the fate of the Jews under Nazism has since emerged as by far the most significant issue of the regime, from the perspective of a child growing up in Germany at the time, it was a minor issue. I rarely heard the subject mentioned and it played no part in the essentials of Nazi ideology I was taught to embrace. When I first saw the concentration camp pictures after the end of the war – a moment I can never forget– I was utterly devastated.

Finally, being a really good, first-class Nazi wasn't only a matter of what you believed, but how you believed it. Fervour, total commitment were admired; doubting, questioning, looking at more than one side of an issue were considered contemptible weakness, bordering on treachery. I can't remember hearing anyone having an impartial discussion, where alternative ideas were explored. People just asserted their beliefs and then, usually, shouted. Anyway, there was no need to question anything, because our *Führer* was infallible ... and questioning could get you into trouble. That bit of political reality, too, I had picked up with my mother's milk. When I was three, my mother once heard me ask Udo, aged six at the time, *Udo, wo kommen die kleinen Kinder her?'* (Where do babies come from?)

'Sch ...' was his reply *'Das darfst Du nicht fragen. Niemand weisst das, nur die Regierung.'* (You mustn't ask that. Nobody knows, only the government.)

I don't remember having this precise conversation, but clearly recall perceiving the world in a way that would have made my brother's answer completely logical and acceptable to me ... a world in which asking questions, thinking for yourself, or doing something different from everyone else just wasn't on the agenda.

All the pressures were in the other direction, to conform to the ideals of taste and behaviour set before us. For children the challenge of every game, every piece of art or craft, was imitation and replication. Though it was also a highly competitive society, the competition lay in seeing whose copy came closest to the original, who conformed most accurately to the ideal.

Creativity, initiative, independent thought or any form of non-conformity were not merely despised, but considered dangerous. They made people uncomfortable. Why would anyone want to be different, if not to make a statement of opposition? The normal first reaction to non-conformity was amusement, calling the perpetrator *verrückt* (mad). That gave him an excuse and a chance to retract. But in people's minds the distances between non-conformity, disloyalty and all-out treason were horribly slender.

I'll never forget an incident during my first school year when a 'deviant' girl in our class of six-year-olds was given the full treatment to make her conform. Her family may have been gypsies; anyway, she stood out in the class because of her poor dress and general scruffiness. One day Fräulein Kesselring, our teacher, called her out to the front and made her stand in a corner, facing the rest of us. Then she told us that looking messy was unacceptable, letting down the *Führer* and Germany. She asked us to look closely at the girl's appearance, and pointed out in turn her unwashed face, messy hair, untidy clothes and dirty shoes. Then she commanded each of us to point a finger at her and to subject her to *auslachen*, laughing her to scorn. The class obliged, falling about and shrieking. The little girl cowered in her corner. For the rest of the school year she looked tidy enough, but kept her eyes down and never spoke to anyone again. When, years later, I read an account of a seaman being publicly flogged and of how his spirits never recovered I thought about that little girl in my class. I hope hers did, but I rather doubt it.

Our whole education system was geared to achieving conformity and no child could have worked harder to succeed in that respect, and still failed on so many fronts, than I. Within minutes of entering my first classroom I already stood out as different, and the same torment was repeated at the beginning of every new term. It was the calling of a special register where pupils declared their religious affiliation. Everybody else either called out *Katholisch* or *Evangelisch* (Protestant). When, near the end of the alphabet, it came to me I had to call out *Gottgläubig* (theist). A titter would go through the class and everyone would turn to stare at me. I had no more idea than they of what it meant and could hardly say it, but my father absolutely insisted on it.

In years to come I found my first religious affiliation increasingly puzzling. Papa had brought me up to despise conventional religion and to pity anyone so simple-minded as to believe in

Christianity. My public declaration as *Gottgläubig* was obviously intended as a statement of those values. Yet, taken literally, *Gottgläubig* means 'God-believing'! So what was going on? I asked my mother, who thought it meant something like 'agnostic' but she couldn't be sure. Papa had never discussed the finer points of Nazi philosophy with her, just expected her to go along with what he told her.

My efforts to track down the religion to which I had once belonged led me, fifty years later, to one of the more esoteric areas of debate pursued in National Socialist circles. It seems that even the most die-hard, anti-clerical Nazis like Papa needed God to support their ideology and commitment. In whose name, else, could they swear allegiance to their *Führer* and their *Vaterland*? Apart from not being Christian, they appeared to hold no strong views about Him. His existence was all that mattered, hence the dictionary definition of *Gottgläubig* as 'followers of modern German cult of theism'.

The other horribly visible aspect of my non-conformity was my hairstyle, also forced on me by the foible of an adult in my family, in this case my grandmother. My first school photograph shows Fräulein Kesselring standing at the top of some steps with her class of fifty unsmiling little girls. With one exception they are blonde or blondish and have their hair scraped off their faces, either into plaits or bows and hairgrips. The exception has bobbed, black hair and is the only one whose hair is deliberately combed down to cover her forehead in a fringe.

My hairdresser grandparents were ready to toe the conventional line in most respects, including politics, but, even though they were now retired, where their professional judgement was at stake they stood by their principles. Oma had made up her mind that neither of the currently permitted hairstyles for little girls was right for me. Having my hair scraped back didn't suit me and plaits were old-fashioned. Oma still took pride in having introduced bobbing to suburban Berlin in the early 1920s and for ever after regarded long hair of any sort as irredeemably dowdy. She decided that I looked nicest – and looking at pictures of myself, she was undoubtedly right – with bobbed hair and a fringe. The problem was, I didn't want to look nice, I just wanted to be the same as everyone else. Every time Oma's special hair-cutting scissors came out to trim my fringe we came as close as we were able to a scene – not very close, really, as, like every other child I knew, I wouldn't have dared to challenge an adult, let alone one as fiery as Oma. My only means for expressing displeasure was crying, which did me no good at all.

Thankfully I managed to avoid distinguishing myself in any other way. Given the education system in force, this would have been quite an achievement. Except for one break, our whole morning at school was dedicated to drill in one or other of the Three Rs. Music, art, drama or even stories didn't feature. I spent my first morning filling in page after page of my new triple-lined writing book with columns of the letter 'i', the next day it was the letter 't', and so on. Everything was done in unison, even reading, once we had learned how. Fräulein Kesselring took us through the alphabet and the principles of arithmetic like a conductor taking an inexperienced orchestra through a new symphony. Everyone joined in as best they could. I doubt that she knew me, or many of the others, by name but it didn't matter, as she had no scope for teaching us individually or for developing a personal relationship. She didn't need any discipline, either. We were all much too scared of authority to be naughty or to talk. At the end of the school year we each got a report with grades from 1, *Sehr Gut* (very good), to 6, *Minderwertig* (worthless). Most people, including me, got 3, *Befriedigend* (satisfactory), for every subject. It must have been Fräulein Kesselring's way of coping with the fact that she didn't know who most of us were; I can imagine her reasoning that if she had no cause to identify us individually, she could be fairly confident that our progress was, indeed, satisfactory. Nevertheless, her system was obviously effective as, by the end of the year, when we were seven, she did appear to have taught all fifty-odd of us to read, write, add and subtract.

The pressures to conform and obey were so strong that most of my feelings of fear at that time were about not conforming enough, or even, perish the thought, disobeying. For example, through a propaganda character called *Der Kohlenklau* (the Coal Thief), whose features leered at us from innumerable posters, even inside private hallways, air-raid shelters and homes, we were indoctrinated not to waste electricity. I remember feeling a tingle of nervousness every time I switched on a light. It was the same with not wasting paper, metal, bones and rags that we had to take to school and put into bins in the playground. I have no idea what I expected to happen if I switched on an unnecessary light or wasted a bone or an old tin can, but do remember very clearly being determined never to find out. Who would be offended, what the punishment would be or who would hand it out were all irrelevant. What mattered was *gehorchen* (obeying).

Our obsession with obeying the rules of an invisible but ever-present authority was, I think, reflected in our everyday language. I can't remember being asked very many 'do you like?', 'do you want?' questions, or very often using words like 'favourite', 'choose', 'decide', 'prefer', or 'want' and 'don't want'. I remember much more being told, or just picking up without being told, what was expected of me. The key words were *dürfen* (be allowed), *verboten* (forbidden), *gehorchen* (to obey) and *muss* (must). When I was talking to myself, the most powerful words were 'I must' and 'I will'.

Yet, like the animals in *Animal Farm*, if we didn't step out of line, our lives were remarkably secure. Everything was decided for us, we didn't have to think, we were under no pressure to be clever. The only qualification for being a member of the in-group was accepting the Nazi package. I did and it was the only time in my life I had no doubt that I belonged.

5

THE ENGLISH CONNECTION

During out-of-school hours there was nearly always some communal game in progress around the estate. What helped keep the peace within our own gang was that we were in a permanent state of war with another gang from a few streets away. With hindsight, I suspect they were the offspring of the local anti-Nazis to whom our families were supposed to be setting an example. As they were older and bigger than us and liked nothing so much as beating up the boys from our gang if they had the chance, we had as little to do with them as possible and only confronted them in earnest a couple of times each winter for an almighty snowball fight. The other gang's leader was a beastly bully called Fritz Johne who sometimes sneaked on to the field where we played and smashed up our camp. We were all afraid of him.

One day as we were playing in the field a shower of stones came flying at us from the direction of some bushes in the corner of the fence. We tried to run away but the stones followed us. As our only way out of the field lay directly into the line of fire, panic was about to set in when the stones suddenly stopped. Before we had worked out what was happening we heard a yelp and, next thing, saw Fritz Johne, bent double and with his face twisted in pain, being propelled out from behind the bush by a little grey-haired woman in a black coat with a fox-fur collar, an elegant hat and leather gloves. She was clutching Fritz, who was somewhat larger than she, by the ears and frog-marching him down the road towards his house, scolding him the while in barely intelligible German. We followed at a distance, noting passers-by goggle as the extraordinary punishment detail marched by. Then we listened in awe as our grandmother – for it was she – let out a final volley of threats before handing Fritz over to his terrified mother.

Oma was English. Although she had come to live in Germany more than twenty years before, she still hadn't mastered proper German. Not that she had any difficulty communicating with anybody, but that was to do with her dramatic personality, not her vocabulary and certainly not her grammar. For as long as I could remember, Oma and Opa had lived in a flat above the baker's shop two streets away from us. Their home was a little outpost of England. Oma and Opa (who was, of course, German but had lived in England) spoke English to one another and had surrounded themselves with exotic items unknown in German homes: things like a hot-water bottle, jigsaw puzzles, a biscuit barrel, a pie-dish, a teapot and a tea-caddy and, battiest of all, a knitted tea-cosy! In a war against us tough Germans, we asked ourselves, what chance was there for people so *verrückt* (crazy) as to put a hat on a teapot?

The flat was our second home, and when we went round there Oma always made us something different to eat, like chips, bread-and-milk (which we called Bremmilk) and, when she could get the ingredients, girdle cakes. She taught us to play Snap, Beggar-My-Neighbour and to sing some English songs, one of which I can still sing right through. It had a nice tune and went like this:

Walking through the fields it happened on my way,
Mrs Cow I had to pass,
Lying in the tender grass,
'Mrs Cow,' said I, 'tell me what use are you.'

Solemnly she looked at me and said, 'Moo Moo.'

'Moo, Moo, Moo,' she answered and she seemed to say,
'Every morning without fail,
Mary brings the milking pail,
To the dairy then she takes my milk away,
Butter, cream and cheese to please you get next day.'

Unfortunately I couldn't understand the text, as my father had laid down the rule that we children were not to be taught English. All we knew were a few words like 'please', 'thank you' and 'hoppit'. Enough to show off with to our friends, anyway.

There were also English books, including some left over from our mother's childhood, which we loved looking at and having translated to us. There was nothing like them in German. One of them was *Josephine and her Dolls* by Dorothy Edwards, an account of the heroine's struggles to get her many dolls and bears dressed for a wedding, only to be thwarted at every turn by an unco-operative, one-eyed stuffed duck called Quacky Jack. Then there were some annuals of the *Playbox* comics, featuring Tiger Tim and the Bruin Boys. We often included their adventures in our own games and once I even traced out and coloured a complete portrait gallery of Jumbo, Georgie Giraffe, Porky Boy, Dickie Donkey and the rest and had my mother frame them to hang over my bed.

Oma never talked about her life in England or why she was living in Germany but, whatever the reason, I could tell that it pained her. I also knew that whatever it was had stopped her ever being able to sleep properly at nights again, which was why she had to have a little 'nap' – another English word I knew – every afternoon, and was sometimes tired and nervy. Another thing I knew was that she had a sister called Nellie who had emigrated to Australia; her name cropped up regularly when visitors inquired into the aetiology of our most intriguing toy, *Kolabär*.

Oma and Opa, I knew, had been hairdressers with their own shop in Köpenick, not far from Mahlsdorf. Then Opa got a bad heart and had to retire, so, shortly before I was born, they came to Mahlsdorf to be near our family. Now Opa worked in an office in Berlin. He still did Oma's hair, though, making of it a work of art that contributed in no small part to her glamorous image.

Starting a new career at his time of life couldn't have been easy for Opa. He was nearly sixty, had a bad heart and couldn't practise the only skill he had ever learned. Where could he possibly find employment? Papa came up with the solution – the Nazi Party.

While working there himself before the war, Papa had looked round for a suitable desk job for Opa and found the perfect thing, in the supplies department of the SA, Hitler's *Sturmabteilung*. There was a snag, though: to qualify, Opa actually had to join the SA. Being a slightly built, studiously inclined and self-effacing man who, born in another time and place, might well have ended up as a schoolteacher or a librarian, it is something of a puzzle that the SA should have admitted him to their ranks, let alone insisted that he become a member. Join he did, however, for I have a photo of him, looking utterly miserable and barely recognisable in an ill-fitting uniform, standing in line for inspection.

Once his job was in the bag, Opa abandoned militancy and became a commuter. Udo and I sometimes went to the station to meet him off the S-Bahn which returned him to Mahlsdorf on the dot of six o'clock every evening.

While Opa was at Nazi headquarters, Oma was usually in Fauststrasse, helping Mutti or accompanying her on shopping or queuing expeditions. In the hours they spent together Mutti and Oma spoke only English to one another. They laughed and giggled a lot, but we could never understand a word; their relationship was private and secret, excluding us. It also excluded Papa, when he was around, which no doubt explains his absurd decree that we were on no account to learn English.

If it hadn't been for Oma's presence, nobody could possibly have guessed at Mutti's English background. She was no different, outwardly, from the other mothers on Fauststrasse. She spoke perfect German, had received her secondary education in Germany and studied at a Berlin art school; her maiden name had been German and she was now married to a Nazi Party official and army officer. Our home and my mother's housekeeping were, unlike Oma and Opa's, typically German; some English novels and piano song sheets were the only clues to her English connection. Yet she had been born and spent the greater part of her childhood in England, had often returned there for holidays and, until she married Papa, remained a British subject with a valid passport.

From the map of Europe on our playroom wall, we had learned to identify the jagged-shaped, pink-coloured island on the left as the British Isles. The thought that our mother, a model of everything admired in our German world, should have been born in London, so far away – and on enemy territory – made me dizzy. It was as hard for me to accept as if she had come from another planet. Other than her and my grandmother, I had never met a foreigner. Oma cut such an extraordinary figure that she, at least, fitted the role of some sort of outsider, but Mutti? It was incomprehensible.

Once when we were talking about it she let drop the idea that perhaps Udo and I, too, would one day visit London, but I cast the thought from my mind. It was too fantastic; I couldn't cope with it.

Having Oma around all the time naturally let the cat out of the bag about Mutti's origins but nobody on Fauststrasse was perturbed about the Englishness of either of them. As the only remotely subversive thing Mutti ever did was to listen secretly to the BBC, she was fully accepted in the community as 'one of us' and, being a dynamic, sociable person with many talents, everyone admired her. Oma, too, was popular; nobody could resist her wit and liveliness and, particularly after the Fritz Johne incident, she could do no wrong on Fauststrasse. She felt so much part of the community that she was not afraid to use her well-known fierceness if someone needed putting in his place.

Her cocky assertiveness, unknown in German women of the day, gave the recipient such a shock that in his confusion he nearly always gave in to her demands. When Papa was away from home it was not Mutti or Opa who would be sent off to sort out shopkeepers, bureaucrats and even Nazi officials, but Oma.

For both of them the key to being accepted was the confidence they inspired by the fact that their loyalties in the war were firmly on the German side. And so they were.

It must have been agonising for them having their two countries at war, like watching your parents beat each other up and having to side with one or the other in a horribly final way, but two things would have helped them work out where their loyalties lay. First, both were pragmatists who judged most issues according to one criterion only: what would be best for our family. If they asked themselves which outcome for the war was likeliest to ensure that we all survived with some measure of security, it's difficult to see how, as otherwise ordinary Mahlsdorf housewives, they could have reached any other conclusion than by a German victory. That would, at least, put an end to the British and American bombers coming over, trying to kill us every other night.

The second thing that must have made it easier for them to come to terms with taking the German side was the manner of their departure from England: being deported from their own country. It was something my spirited Oma found hard to forgive.

One day when I was about five, my mother received a letter which got her quite excited. It was from the *Kurze Welle*, short-wave radio station; a man called Herr Cleinow who was in charge of foreign-language broadcasts being beamed to other countries on that frequency was looking for two perfect English speakers to join his unit. He had heard of Mutti through Papa's party connection and invited her along for an interview.

He wanted her to take part in a weekly English language

programme on women's issues. It was to take the form of a fifteen-minute discussion about domestic and childcare matters, slanted, no doubt, towards publicising the merits of the health and welfare services provided by the Nazi state. Her partner was to be Ilse, wife of Kurt Krüger-Lorenzen, a well-known broadcaster and radio personality of the day. Ilse was half-American and, like Mutti, completely bilingual. In *Jane and Janet's Weekly Chat*, as the programme came to be called, Mutti's new friend became Jane and Mutti herself, Janet.

They had to write the scripts themselves, sometimes on subjects suggested by the producer, sometimes from their own ideas. Mutti acquired a rattly old typewriter and taught herself typing – I can still hear her tapping away at it while I am trying to go to sleep in the next room. As, outside their studio, Jane and Janet were both ordinary housewives and the programme had no researchers, a lot of their inspiration must have come from what was happening to us at home.

Occasionally the programme visited other locations or featured a visitor and once or twice even Udo and I participated. The first time was for a Christmas broadcast when I had to sing three verses of a German song that Oma had translated into English. Another time I played the part of the patient in a programme about immunisations. I had two lines. For the first, when the man playing the doctor pinched me, I had to say, 'Ouch!' Then, when he asked me if it was still hurting, I had to say, 'No, not a bit!' So it would be true to say that the first English words I ever spoke in earnest were broadcast to the world.

6

PODEWILSHAUSEN

In summer of 1943, as soon as my first school year ended, our cosy Mahlsdorf life came to an abrupt end. Thereafter we only visited the flat on Fauststrasse a few times, mostly when on the way to somewhere else. Perhaps because it was to be so many years before we settled down again anywhere else, my years in Mahlsdorf came to assume a special meaning for me as the timeless 'home' of my imagination, to which part of me always longed to return.

This is not to say that the years which followed, spent as an evacuee, refugee and repatriatee, were times of doom and gloom. I was a privileged child and, compared with others, had a 'good war', with excitements that would never have come my way if I had stayed in Mahlsdorf. It is these colourful events of my years on the move that have stayed with me most clearly and lent their cheerful air to my personal memories of life in the third Reich.

We left Mahlsdorf when the bombing was already driving mothers and children from even the relatively safe suburbs, but for my family there was an even more pressing reason for suddenly taking off in all directions. We had all been mass chest X-rayed and Mutti discovered to have TB. Everyone was shocked; she had no symptoms and looked in the best of health. The doctor

who broke the news went on to impress upon her that only a
schlechte Mutter (a bad mother) would continue to expose her
children to the risk of lethal infection; she must isolate herself
from us at once. Mutti was distraught, protesting that nobody else
was capable of looking after her children, particularly me, with
my feet. The doctor revised his ruling. I could stay but Udo must
be got away immediately; the implication was that an imperfect
specimen like me catching the disease wouldn't matter as much
as an A1 child like him.

The news caused enormous anxiety in the family, but it gave
Papa the opportunity he had long craved: to have Udo educated
in a proper military academy. He was still smarting from his
son's rejection by the NAPOLA and now took a few days' leave to
find the next best thing. He chose a boarding school in Bavaria
that was housed in a converted Benedictine monastery, but run
– this was the important bit – according to the strictest Nazi
principles. He dismissed Mutti's objections as sentimental and
assured her that the experience would be the making of her son.
Had his own experience as a cadet in a military academy not been
the high point of his life? Udo himself, just ten, was not
consulted. Papa took him down to Passau himself, supervised his
kitting out in Hitler Youth uniform and delivered him up to the
monastery.

Before returning to the Russian front he also arranged for
Mutti and me to be evacuated from Berlin. We were to go to a
village called Podewilshausen in remotest Pomerania, to the
home of an army friend of Papa's who, in civilian life, was the
schoolmaster there.

Mutti didn't usually question any of Papa's decrees, but this
time she refused to co-operate with his plan for abandoning Udo
to his terrible fate. As soon as Papa was safely out of the way in
Russia she took matters in her own hands and sent me off to
Pomerania by myself.

I was just seven and it was my first solo train journey. I was
both proud and frightened at the thought of travelling on my own.

I still felt on top of the world when Mutti took me to the station, installed me in a corner seat of the Danzig train and asked the guard to keep an eye on me; then, when the train pulled out and her waving handkerchief receded from sight, I couldn't stop crying. What if somebody abducted me, or I got lost and never saw her again?

Soon the hanky disappeared and my spirits recovered; travelling alone was as enjoyable as I'd anticipated. The best moment came when we approached Stettin and the train slowed down to trundle across the viaduct over the river Oder, revealing a panorama of docks, cranes and a whole fleet of warships of the kind I had previously imagined only in interminable games of Battleships with Udo. In Stettin I was met by the schoolmaster's wife, unmistakable in the blue and white spotted dress I had been instructed to look out for (her Sunday best, it turned out). She greeted me with a bunch of flowers nearly as big as myself and led me to a different platform for the provincial train to Stolp.

There, a boy of about fourteen was waiting to meet us beside a battered-looking little pony-trap. He wore strange country clothes, including knickerbockers – his Sunday best as well. He also handed me a posy of flowers in welcome. I was touched by this gesture, but also embarrassed. According to the Nazi standards of propriety imbibed in my Mahlsdorf upbringing, for a boy to so much as look at a flower came dangerously close to *Himbeer Heini*, cissy behaviour and therefore ideologically incorrect. It was the first of many moral dilemmas that were to trouble me in life after Mahlsdorf, where everything had been so simple and straightforward, with never the slightest doubt about what one was supposed to believe.

The boy installed us into the worn leather passenger seat, climbed up to the driving seat and set the pony off on the nine-kilometre drive to Podewilshausen. The road ran through a dense, featureless pine forest, the like of which I had not seen before. We had not proceeded very far when I noticed my thoughts spontaneously turning to the hazards that people like

Little Red Riding Hood and Hansel and Gretel had encountered in just such forests. In fact, as it started to get dark I could think of little else.

'Are there wolves in the forest?' I asked the boy, trying to sound casual.

'Sure,' came the reply, 'and escaped Russian prisoners.'

I pressed myself against the worn leather, hoping to become invisible. For the rest of the journey I peered from side to side, preparing myself for what to do if either a wolf or a starving Russian sprang out at me from the black trees.

It was nearly dark when we were set down in front of the village schoolhouse. I was taken upstairs to a room with grown-up painted wooden furniture, including a washstand and porcelain basin and jug. Still more vases of flowers had been placed around the room. Everything was very different from the streamlined modernity of our Berlin flat, but having, as I thought, narrowly survived the dangers of traversing the world's densest forest I was in no mood to find fault.

Next morning I inspected the village. Like many Pomeranian villages, Podewilshausen had a mixed Polish and German population but there was no question about which culture predominated. Poles were only tolerated as equals – sort of – to the extent that they demonstrated commitment to abandoning their regrettable Polish ways and behaving like Germans. It was highly questionable how well the Poles of Podewilshausen were doing; I soon noticed parts of the village that looked distinctly tatty and unGerman, such as the duck pond with its muddy water and slippery banks permanently covered in poultry droppings and the pitted dirt road where you never saw a car or a tram, only an occasional ramshackle horse or ox-drawn cart and, if you were lucky, an antiquated bicycle. Compared with the order and efficiency of Mahlsdorf, it was all pretty deplorable.

The village had only two substantial buildings, a slightly dilapidated but picturesque white church – Catholic and therefore Polish territory – and the schoolhouse, centrally placed, solidly built and aggressively German. It had a single large classroom in which, while her husband was away at the war, my new Tante Bärbel each morning taught, simultaneously, every child between six and fourteen in the village, including me. The experience was in danger of making me big-headed, as after one year with Fräulein Kesselring I could already read and write better than most of the older pupils in the class, including the fourteen-year-old Polish boys.

The only other downstairs room I remember was a large rambling kitchen. One wall was taken up with a huge stove and ancillary bread-ovens. Every other Tuesday afternoon, Tante Bärbel took over the kitchen for a fascinating bread-making ritual. Distributed round the room in cloth-covered pots and basins would be a dozen lumps of rough brown dough, swelling and rising as if under the influence of a spell. When they reached the right volume, Tante Bärbel gave each one a thorough pummelling, shaped it into a rough oblong and consigned it to the depths of the bread-oven. For several hours after her batch of gleaming rye loaves re-emerged, the house was filled with the tantalising aroma of the most delicious *Landbrot* I have ever tasted.

Tante Bärbel had two children, one of them a girl of my age called Rotraut. If our parents had planned for us to become best friends, they must have been disappointed. The strongest memory of my stay in Podewilshausen is of everyone being immensely kind, but of feeling homesick, isolated and often bored. The local children and I were on different wavelengths. Nobody knew my games, I missed my toys, the children on Fauststrasse and, most of all, Udo. Another unsettling factor was the absence of the Nazi ethos, the conviction that we were living at the dawn of a bright new age, which was such an overpowering ingredient of the air I had breathed for as long as I could remember. Without it, Podewilshausen didn't feel part of the normal world, more like a forgotten outpost of the past. What happened there didn't matter.

The only part of my Nazi upbringing that appeared to have relevance there was the prejudice already instilled into me against

Poles. *Polacken* were racially inferior to us, I had been given to understand; however, the ones living on Greater German soil at least had the opportunity to grow into proper Germans, if they only made the effort. I must have doubted that the ones in Podewilshausen were trying hard enough as, when some of the big German boys from school invited me on an expedition to vandalise the Polish church, I had no compunction about joining in. The church looked so pretty from outside, how disappointing that the inside was dark and spooky, with a dirt floor and damp patches on the walls. There didn't seem to be anything worth taking or breaking, so we just spilled out the holy water and scattered the flowers from the altar over the floor.

At last, when I'd been in Podewilshausen for what seemed like an age, Mutti arrived. She came loaded with gear, including her bicycle and her sewing machine, as if prepared for a long stay. Of greatest interest was the news she brought with her. First, she didn't have TB after all; when she went back for further X-rays it was discovered that the spots on her lungs were old pleurisy scars, not galloping consumption.

Secondly, she and Opa had rescued Udo from his monastery. He was now living with some of our Druhm relatives in Luckenwalde – Opa's cousin Onkel Arno and his family. As soon as Papa departed for Russia, Mutti had boarded the Passau train and visited Udo's school. She wasn't allowed to speak to him alone but he somehow managed to convey to her the more spectacular details of his regime – and how he felt about them. If they weren't doing drill, it was long-distance marches, sometimes in the middle of the night, carrying rucksacks and tents. If the boys didn't get their drill right, as happened to Udo more often than not, they got an *Ohrfeige* (boxed ears). Udo was such a hopeless case at every kind of drill that when the school was invited to nearby Regensburg to participate in a parade where the salute was to be taken by none other than Goebbels, Udo was one of only two boys who weren't allowed to go, lest they disgrace everyone else. All the boys slept together in one huge dormitory and everyone, including now Udo, wet their beds. The head-master said it was something in the water.

When Mutti finally managed to get an interview and asked for Udo's discharge, the headmaster wouldn't hear of it. The boy had been put into his care by his father, and would be returned to nobody else. He even refused to let Udo out for a morning or afternoon with Mutti. That was when she conceived her rescue plan. She sent a wire to Opa, summoning him to join her immediately. Next she established herself in a guest house overlooking the school and familiarised herself with the boys' routine. Catching occasional glimpses of her made Udo more miserable than ever, but Mutti took no notice. By the time Opa appeared she had her strategy ready and the next time the column left the gates on a march, Udo was kidnapped. 'I had to leave my things behind, but I didn't mind. It was like being released from prison,' Udo recalled afterwards. So as not to tempt fate, the three of them quickly left the area, but Udo and Opa stayed in Bavaria. They found themselves another guest house in the foothills of the Alps and took a week's holiday to recuperate, Udo from his ordeal and Opa from the emotional strain of the kidnap. They had a lovely time together hiking and picking blueberries. I suspect that Mutti needed the break most but she decided to hurry back to Berlin and on to Podewilshausen to see how I was faring.

She had just started to settle down with me at the schoolhouse when who should turn up to visit us but Papa, with Udo in tow. How did he manage his little jaunts away from the front, whenever family affairs called? He was in a cheerful mood, taking the news of Udo's bunk from the monastery much better than one might have expected. The two of them had brought their bicycles with them on the train, as a result of which the four of us managed to have a rare 'magic moment' together as a family. It was an all-day bicycle expedition, one of very few excursions of any kind I can remember the four of us making. We set off on three bikes into the open countryside – the opposite direction from the scary pine forest – with me balanced on Papa's crossbar.

I hadn't stepped outside the village boundaries since my arrival two months or so before. By now it was deeply autumnal and the countryside looked enchanting. We followed a stream and passed lakes and villages. When we came to a large deciduous wood, Papa led us on a mushroom hunt. Udo and I had scarcely seen a mushroom growing in the wild, but Papa knew exactly which varieties to look out for and we returned to Podewilshausen weighed down with pounds of *Steinpilze* and *Pfefferlinge* (boletus and chanterelles). We ended the day sitting round the table of the schoolhouse kitchen with Tante Bärbel and her children, scoffing ladle after ladle of wild mushroom soup with chunks of her incomparable rye bread.

A few days after that, we left Podewilshausen, Papa for Russia and Mutti, Udo and I for Berlin. I'm not sure why we left, for nowhere could have been safer from bombing. Clearly, Mutti not having TB had changed our situation; the three of us could stay together and perhaps, Udo having reached high-school age, it was felt that the all-in-one Podewilshausen classroom wouldn't do for him.

Our trip back to Berlin in the autumn of 1943 was to be the first of our many wartime journeys, and the one on which we perfected our technique. The same pony-trap took me and our luggage back to Stolp station, Mutti and Udo riding ahead on their bikes. At the station I was put in charge of our thirteen pieces of luggage, ranging from the sewing machine and bicycles to our school satchels and gas masks. As soon as the train arrived Udo leapt on board to get us seats. Mutti watched where he went, stacked the bikes and other big things into the luggage van and then collected me and the small items to join Udo in one of the crowded compartments.

I was more than ready to go home, back to my friends, my toys and Oma and Opa, but it was not to be. My travels had only just begun.

7

LUCKENWALDE

P apa's orders were for us not to stay in Mahlsdorf a moment longer than was necessary but to repack our things and leave again immediately for somewhere safer. This time we were to go to Luckenwalde, to live as evacuees with Opa's cousin and close friend, our Onkel Arno. Oma and Opa told us how, before the First World War, while still in his teens, Onkel Arno had spent a memorable holiday with them in England. They showed us some priceless photos of a rotund, smiling young man with a thatch of carefully plastered-down hair, taking in the tourist sights.

This background explained the warmth of the welcome his family gave us when, thirty years later, we appeared on their doorstep equipped for an indefinite stay. My mother knew them well but I had no memory of having been to Luckenwalde and only knew Onkel Arno from the ancient photos. By now this thick, neatly brushed hair was silver, but the rest of him looked just as amiable and cherubic as in the pictures.

Onkel Arno managed to combine the good nature which exuded from every inch of his body with the shrewdness and wit required by someone like him to survive unscathed under Nazism. For on the train to Luckenwalde the fearful truth about him was whispered to us. He was – shsh – not a Nazi! The first non-Nazi – apart from Udo – I had knowingly encountered. To make matters worse, he was a church elder, everything that could have caused tension between our two families but, thanks to his well-developed diplomatic skills, it never did. Onkel Arno was always calm and good-humoured, never condemning or defending Nazism or, indeed, any other creed. In his house, in our presence, anyway, politics were never discussed. Outside the home, too, he kept his counsel, doing the minimum required to stay out of trouble and keep his business running.

Onkel Arno and Tante Mieze had a small department store on Breite Strasse, Luckenwalde's central thoroughfare. They were a partnership, Tante Mieze directing the glass and china departments, Onkel Arno the ironmongery and tools. He had inherited the shop and the apartment building above it from his father Otto, whose monogram – the letter R cocooned in the letter O – was still the shop's logo. Mutti had designed it when she was a commercial artist and it was displayed on a shield suspended over the shop door, providing a popular and distinctive landmark for the shoppers of Luckenwalde.

The Runge family consisted of Onkel Arno and Tante Mieze, their twenty-year-old daughter Jutta and Tante Mieze's sister Tante Dora. They lived above the shop in a large flat furnished with the sumptuous heavy furniture and carpets beloved by the German bourgeoisie, here given a modern touch by light curtains, dramatic oil paintings and shelves of books. My favourite room was Jutta's, an ultra-modern bedsitter with built-in light-oak furniture and such novelties as a bed that was, by day, pushed up and concealed in a cupboard and a desk that, at the flick of a switch, magicked into a glamorous dressing-table. Jutta was petite, pretty and vivacious; though not that much older than us, she represented for me all the mysteries of being grown up – having her own room, wearing make-up and, most interesting of all, having suitors.

We quickly settled into the Runges' easy-going household. For us suburbans the ancient market town of Luckenwalde, with its confidently laid out high street and massive medieval tower, was much more congenial than rural Pomerania. The atmosphere wasn't that different from Mahlsdorf, with enough Hitler Youth parades through the town, in fact, right past the shop, to make me feel at home. I always tried to be out on the balcony when they went past and, like the people watching from the street below, had my right arm smartly raised in a Hitler salute at the correct moment. For Udo, and I suspect for Uncle Arno too, the parades were a signal for going underground for the rest of the day. As for Tante Mieze, if she was out in the town when a parade came past, she always made sure to have both her hands too full of shopping and parcels to manage a salute.

In that agreeable environment time passed quickly. There was always plenty for us to do, visiting our various aunts and cousins, helping Onkel Arno in his garden and playing in the shop. For me, however, no pastime held as much interest as being a voyeuse of Jutta's love life. Her two principal admirers were Habib, a Persian studying in Vienna whom she had met on a pre-war holiday in Prague, and Bernhard, a *Wehrmacht* major fighting in Russia. Both seemed to be under the impression that it would assist their suit to present themselves as *kinderlieb* (fond of children), for they were always bringing us sweets and exotic trinkets when they came to visit Jutta. Udo wasn't prepared to play this card, but I was in my element, almost ready to believe that they were calling to see me, not Jutta at all.

I suspect that I owe any academic success I had in later life to Fräulein Vogt, my teacher during the time we lived in Luckenwalde. She did not mould my intellect, nurture in me hitherto unsuspected talents or stimulate in me a love of scholarship. Her legacy was to pass on the ability of *pauken* – swotting, grinding on to the bitter end of any task regardless of its purpose. While it is very likely thanks to her that I was to become an expert at passing examinations, in every other respect unlearning the education I received at her hands has been a lifetime's struggle.

Fräulein Vogt was of indeterminate age, tall and dark, emphasising her already considerable height by a military bearing and a formidably upswept hairstyle. She wore severe suits and a pince-nez. I once caught sight of her riding up Breite Strasse on a bicycle; she looked majestic, like a mounted general leading a parade, yet she was only out doing her shopping.

For every minute of the four hours that thirty-five of us seven- and eight-year-old girls daily spent in her classroom, there was utter silence. Each day we had a session of spelling, grammar, arithmetic and reading, with homework set on everything taught that day. Due to the paper shortage, all written work was done on slates marked up like exercise books, one side with lines, the other with squares. We had to buy them ourselves and looked after them with meticulous care; everyone had a length of string knotted through a hole in the frame, with a damp sponge for wiping out at one end and a cloth for drying and polishing at the other. Our slate pencils, which needed constant sharpening, were carefully protected in our pencil cases. To prevent homework from being accidentally erased through our slates sliding about in our satchels, they were kept in special cardboard envelopes designed for the purpose. The whole system was a model of efficiency and if economies are being sought in education budgets today, I can heartily recommend it.

I remember only two occasions when our daily classroom routine was altered in any way. The first time we were taken into the *Aula* (school hall) to hear a child prodigy in our class – who also happened to be the smallest girl and a Shirley Temple lookalike to boot – perform a Beethoven sonata on the piano. Then, a few days before 20 April 1944, Fräulein Vogt devoted the entire morning to preparing us for celebrating the *Führer*'s fifty-fifth birthday. She began by relating, in uncharacteristic, simper-ing tones, the details of his life, then showed us a pile of photographs and newspaper cuttings of him, mostly depicting him receiving flowers and shaking the hands of little blonde girls with plaits of about our age. Next, she gave us a dictation on the theme of the most important achievements he had wrought for Germany and tested us on all the facts she had presented. When she considered us adequately prepared she gave us each, exceptionally, a piece of lined writing paper and instructed us to write the *Führer* a personal, illustrated birthday letter thanking him for his heroic deeds and sacrifices on our behalf. Finally, she collected them all up and told us she was going to send them off to Berchtesgaden.

Twice during our stay in Luckenwalde, Papa returned from Russia, not on leave exactly, but for some more of his mysterious briefings. What was he up to? Nobody else's father fighting in Russia had all these trips back. Both times he wanted Mutti and me to join him. Mutti asked Fräulein Vogt if I could miss a few weeks of school. She considered the matter carefully and then agreed, but only on condition that I take an exercise book with me and not only write a diary of everything that happened to me while I was away, but that I follow up each day's entry with a grammatical analysis of every sentence I had written.

Our first trip was to Münster, in Westphalia. Our train was scheduled to make a half-hour stop in Hanover, not far from Lautenthal, so Tante Kätchen came to meet us at the station. We hadn't seen her for nearly two years and had a happy reunion. Then, in Münster, as we emerged on to the station forecourt I was delighted to see an immaculate black and gold lacquered carriage harnessed to a pair of greys pulled up at the kerb. I stared in wonder and started peering at all the other passengers coming out of the station, hoping to identify the prince and princess the carriage had come to collect. Then a man approached us and asked Mutti if she was Frau Thiele. When she nodded he lifted our cases on to the box of the carriage, handed us into the red plush seats and covered our knees with a fur rug. Then he mounted the driving seat, eased the brake and steered the carriage out of the forecourt. This was the life! I couldn't believe it was happening to me.

One curious thing I had noticed as I climbed into the carriage was that there were hanging straps attached to the walls, just like in the S-Bahn, to stop people falling about when the train was full. What were they doing here? Then, as the carriage gathered speed, bouncing and lurching, first along Münster's cobbled streets and then along rough country roads, their purpose became only too clear. I clutched my strap for dear life. Where had I got the idea that there was necessarily a connection between travelling in comfort and in style?

We were taken to a remote country estate that had been requisitioned as some kind of officers' billet and shown into an enormous, freezing bedroom with four-poster beds and gilt furniture. To my chagrin we were only to stay there for a couple of nights, before transferring to a local *Gasthof*. Still, on day one of my trip alone I had collected so much copy for Fräulein Vogt's diary that I wondered how I'd ever find the time to write it all down, let alone analyse the grammar.

Our second rendezvous with Papa was in Vienna, travelling from Berlin in a sleeper. The weekend before his course started was, I think, the closest my parents ever came to a binge – obviously not very close, as I was in tow. We stayed in a luxurious hotel and on our first evening went to a charming little opera house to see an operetta called *Die Bäuerin* (The Farmer's Wife) – I have never heard of it since – and sat in a box. Back at the hotel my parents announced that they were going out again, this time to the casino. 'What's a casino?' I asked and Papa did his best to explain. 'What will you do if you lose all your money?' I asked, slightly unnerved by what I had heard. 'No problem,' said Papa, 'I'll sell Mutti.' He was always teasing me but this time I couldn't rely on it and made sure to stay awake until they were both safely back.

After that, we once again transferred to a more modest billet. Mutti and I spent the days sightseeing, but all the statues around the Ring were boxed in concrete to protect them from bombs and most of the museums and other sights closed. We went for walks in the woods and parks but my favourite event was our rendezvous with Jutta's friend Habib, who had invited us to *Kaffee und*

Kuchen in a positively voluptuous hotel foyer. Under polished chandeliers hung from an ornate white and gold ceiling, at tables covered in starched lace cloths, ladies in furs and gentlemen in uniforms lounged in gilt chairs; waiters in tails hurried about serving coffee and *Kuchen* piled high with *Schlagsahne*; in the corner an orchestra played and people were dancing. For me the scene was every bit as gripping as the operetta – and that was even before the arrival of the amazing cakes.

In May 1944, just as we were settling back into our Luckenwalde routine, a letter arrived that sent the Runge household into a spin. Bernhard was being transferred to the Italian front and, while in transit, could take a few days' leave. Would Jutta join him in Nürnberg that very weekend? Feverish discussions ensued on such issues as whether there was a train connection, time for Jutta to have her hair done and whether Bernhard's proposal was, in fact, decent? At last Onkel Arno and Tante Mieze agreed to the rendezvous, but only on condition that Jutta took an *Anstandsdame*, literally, a 'decency lady' to chaperone her. Tante Mietze couldn't leave the shop, Tante Dora couldn't abandon her job; that left Mutti.

There followed frenzied preparations while Jutta was coiffed and items of her wardrobe, without which she claimed she could not survive, were washed and ironed in their wet state, because there was no time to dry them. Mutti made an incongruous chaperone, but one that delighted Jutta and Bernhard. She was so embarrassed at being a gooseberry that she took herself off sightseeing all the time, including an all-day expedition to Regensburg to hear the cathedral's famous choristers, the *Domspatzen* (Cathedral Sparrows). This was all the time Jutta and Bernhard needed to consolidate their relationship. When she returned they had become engaged. They still hadn't spent more than two or three weeks together in all, but decided not to waste any time before getting married.

The wedding was fixed for two months ahead, 20 July. Jutta

invited me to be a bridesmaid, the height of my ambition at the time. Mutti, the family's seamstress, was commissioned to restyle dresses and accessories that hadn't seen the light of day since before the war. She sent Oma an SOS for the net curtains that hung against the glass doors of her wardrobe. Papa had sent the material from France, pale blue muslin embroidered with butter-flies – perfect for bridesmaids' dresses. That left only one sartorial problem unsolved, the usual one – my shoes. By now I was permanently down to Udo's outgrown boots, but Jutta had a brainwave. Wasn't Italy the place for shoes? Bernhard must be able to find me some there. Floor plans and elevations of my feet were dispatched to the Italian front.

Just as everyone was becoming so engrossed in the wedding preparations that they had almost forgotten about the war, two events brought us sharply back to reality. On 6 June 1944 I celebrated my eighth birthday. A few days later a visiting neighbour gave us the news that the Allied forces had landed in France. My heart sank. It couldn't be true, surely not! Please not! According to our news bulletins victory was getting closer by the day; how could that be, if the enemy had a foothold in France? The man went on to explain that the invasion was thoroughly good news for us. By foolishly venturing on to our territory the enemy had laid himself wide open to total annihilation; our superior forces would now be able to thrash the living daylights out of him and bring the war to a quick end. He was so convincing that my fears were allayed.

Shortly after that, something else happened to test even my confidence: a series of air-raids on Luckenwalde more frightening than any we had experienced in Berlin. Onkel Arno's cellar wasn't reinforced like our Berlin air-raid shelter. For the first, a night-time raid, we sheltered in the boiler room. Heavy fumes were oozing from the coke furnace; I felt faint and as I keeled over and sank to the floor, my head struck the edge of the cast-iron furnace. I blacked out. When I came to again a few minutes later I was lying on the ground out in the courtyard and voices were urging me, '*Tief atmen! Tief atmen!*' (Breathe deeply! Breathe deeply!) But I wasn't badly damaged.

This raid was followed by a much worse day-time one. As the bombardment started, totally unexpectedly, shoppers and other passers-by came rushing down the stairs to join us in the cellar, which trembled violently at each impact.

In Mahlsdorf I had regarded air-raids almost as a diversion. Now I became very frightened and lost my cool, becoming, to my shame, a *Feigling*, a snivelling coward and, worse still, hysterical. After that experience Mutti decided that, if we were to be bombed, we might as well be in our own home in Mahlsdorf, especially as Luckenwalde appeared to have become the target of a deliberate blitz. She was also anxious to see how Oma and Opa were faring so, as soon as school broke up, we left Luckenwalde, promising the Runges to return in time for the wedding.

Our brief return to Berlin was a disappointment. We had been homesick for so long but Mahlsdorf had become a different place. Most of the shops were damaged and boarded up and all our friends had left. Oma and Opa looked sad and drawn. The air-raids, now mostly happening in the day-time, were far more frightening than before. Mutti feared that our cellar wasn't safe enough any more and one morning, when the radio warned that a heavy raid was imminent, she sent Udo and me to a purpose-built concrete bunker in another part of Mahlsdorf on our bicycles. We were still some distance away when I got a puncture. Stranded in an unfamiliar part of town, we watched helplessly as wave after wave of American bombers bore down on us from the west. We'd only ever heard them before; now, the spectacle of their menacing formations and the sensation of their individual shadows passing over thoroughly unnerved us. We left our bikes in a garden and ran for all we were worth in the direction of the bunker.

We had been back in Berlin for less than a week when our family's affairs suddenly took a surprising turn. This was how my mother broke the news to Tante Mieze in a letter bearing the postmark of Weissewarte, an obscure village in the province of

Brandenburg, just west of the Elbe.

You must wonder what I'm doing here. A week ago Eberhard was summoned by telegram to the *Reichs-Luftsfahrtministerium* (Air Ministry) in Berlin. I had taken the children out for a day's hiking in the Müggelberge and when we got back, there he was, doing the garden. He had been home since 10 a.m.; had opened the front door with a piece of wire. The next day he reported to the RLM and the day after left for this place, a beautifully situated *Wehr-Ertuchtigungs-Lager* (combat preparation camp), to familiarise himself with the set-up and – you'll laugh – learn gliding. He has been appointed to command his own Hitler Youth Flying Camp, but must first be proficient himself. He is training alongside the boys and feels like a teenager. He is also learning 'management' and other aspects. Despite his very tight schedule, after only two days he was already signalling loudly for us to join him and I came right away, in the first instance, alone.

All around are these enthusiastic young boys, desperate to become pilots. It's a wonderful milieu for Udo, but I think Katrin will like it too. After that scare in Luckenwalde the children were terribly nervous and I am getting them out of Berlin at the first opportunity. In two weeks the gliding course here ends. Eberhard leaves right away to take command of his camp and we are to accompany him from the very start. So as you see, my dear Runges, the Thieles are in luck.

The letter – returned to me by Juttta forty-seven years after it was written – ends with the obstacles the new development had put in the way of our plans to attend the wedding. Whatever they may have been, the women of the family, but not the men, succeeded in overcoming them and on the day the three of us turned up in Luckenwalde in full force.

The celebrations began the night before with a *Polterabend*, the ancient custom of hurling crockery at the bride's house to chase away evil spirits. The well-wishers usually bring their own missiles, but in this case it looked as though Onkel Arno, and possibly even his father, had been saving their broken crocks for the occasion from the day they opened the shop. I discovered that hurling them against the back door to make them shatter could become quite addictive and stayed by my post, exorcising evil spirits, till it got dark.

Next morning was devoted to dress. Bernhard had obeyed his instructions and produced a very nice pair of Italian sandals. They were boys' ones and certainly fitted me when I stood still, but I could see right away that there was going to be a problem about preventing them falling off the minute I started walking.

The other bridesmaids and I were dressed up in our net-curtain dresses and had our hair decorated with garlands; we were given little baskets of flowers to scatter in front of the bridal pair as we led the way down the aisle after the ceremony. Then we were conveyed to the church with Jutta in an open carriage; everyone else travelled in Luckenwalde's only taxi, providing a shuttle service for forty guests. Bernhard looked stunning in his uniform, as much of it as remained visible under all his decorations, including his two iron crosses.

Apart from my Podewilshausen vandalism experience, I had never been in a church and was so overawed that I allowed my attention to wander from my main task, hanging on to my sandals. I had only taken a couple of steps up the aisle when one fell off. I tried to retrieve it, stumbled and dropped my flowers. I doubt if anybody noticed – all eyes were fixed on Jutta and Bernhard.

After the service the bridesmaids accompanied the bridal couple back down Breite Strasse in the carriage, this time to the town's principal hotel. There we ate, drank, and danced till late into the night. Tante Mieze taught me to polka and I watched, fascinated, as Mutti abandoned herself to dancing the foxtrot, tango and charleston with some of Bernhard's fellow officers. I had no idea she so loved dancing. Then the band struck up a tune I hadn't heard before; everyone else knew it, though, and started singing it – in English. Bernhard grasped Mutti's hand and led her and the other guests round the room in an energetic promenade. The first few times I couldn't follow the English words, only the shout of 'Oi!' at the end of the refrain, when everyone flung up their hands. Then I got the hang of it and started joining in – 'Doing the Lambeth Walk, Oi!' Mutti told me afterwards we weren't supposed to sing it as Hitler had banned it.

A few days later a letter in curious German, with a generous scattering of English words, arrived in Luckenwalde. It was from Oma.

Dear Mieze,

I feel I must write to somebody, the wedding was so beautiful and the person who, after Jutta, looked the most beautiful was you, really Mieze, you looked wonderfully beautiful, such a nice dress and such a pretty bit of colour in your face, it's immaterial how it got there, it was nice. I found Jutta's headdress, like a little crown, in very good taste and that heavenly little smile on her face simply charming. She was like a bride in a film. Don't be jealous, Arno, you looked very nice too, but, like at every wedding, the men are not really interesting, only the bridegroom. The church ceremony was not to my taste, though. First, why did the poor bridal couple have to stand for so long? It was a real punishment, couldn't they have put a couple of nice chairs out for them until they had to do their personal bit? To expect a bride to put up with that and then smile as well is too much. And did you like the parson's speech? That's what I'd like to know. I didn't think it very sympathetic. It lacked any nice fitting personal sentiments. Also, the music was too heavy and just like a normal Sunday service. Don't they ever play a proper wedding march in Germany? So you see, Mieze, perhaps I'm an old grumbler, but I want to know if those were only my impressions.

Jutta's wedding was crowned with the great blessing, that our *Führer* lives.

Fond greetings from us all,
Ethel.

For, though for the Runges, the Druhms and the female Thieles 20 July 1944 would always be remembered as the day of Jutta's wedding, its significance for everyone else was over-shadowed by an event happening in East Prussia, more than 400 kilometres away. At just about the moment I was dropping my flowers in the church, von Stauffenberg's bomb to assassinate Hitler in the July Plot exploded in the Wolf's Lair conference room.

8

SILESIA

Whatever deal had been struck to enable Mutti and me to get to the wedding, Udo was the sacrificial lamb. While Papa had taken the humiliating end to Udo's military academy project with remarkable grace, he had anything but abandoned his plan for training Udo up into a full Nazi hero. He was merely awaiting the next opportunity, and the telegram summoning him to the Air Ministry and thence to the Weissewarte *WE Lager* was it.

It has proved something of a challenge for me to establish, fifty years later, the precise role of the *WE Lager*, the Hitler Youth Flying Camp, within the overall scheme of Hitler's fighting machine. From the few mentions I have found of the camps in history books, there is no doubt that they served at least one genuine military purpose – that of indoctrinating impressionable adolescents with the commitment to Nazism that ensured their readiness to fight to the death when called on to do so. However, the gliding mania that permeated the camps had less to do with military strategy than with the powerful position of a specialised 'cult' group within the Nazi Party.

In the First World War Goering had been a celebrated flying ace. For him and other enthusiasts, the most humiliating condition of the Versailles Treaty – and the one that fuelled their passionate Nazism – was the ban on Germany's having an air force. Angry and embittered, they put all their energies into developing to new heights the technology of the next best thing, gliding, and in the process established themselves as one of the party's most influential subcultures. For them, the finest hour of the Second World War was, without a doubt, the glider-borne invasion and capture of Crete.

With the passions for gliding and Nazism reinforcing one another so effectively, it could not be long before this group hit on the idea of using gliding camps as a setting for the political education of the next generation of the military elite. Administered by the Hitler Youth but staffed by military instructors, they offered three-week-long courses aimed at firing up the motivation and commitment of sixteen- and seventeen-year-old volunteers in preparation for their eventual call-up. If Mutti's description in her letter to Tante Mieze and my own memories of the two camps I came to know are anything to go by, they could scarcely have been more successful in achieving their aim. No wonder Papa was confident that he would at last make a breakthrough in the education of his hopeless son.

Dispatching Mutti and me back to Luckenwalde in time for the wedding, he summoned Udo to Weissewarte, instructing him to bring his Hitler Youth uniform and his PE kit. The idea was for Udo to drink in the exuberant Hitler Youth atmosphere and receive intensive training from one of the instructors in the skills required for the prestigious Hitler Youth *Sportsabzeichen* (athletics badge). Surprisingly, Udo found quite a lot to interest him at the camp, the gliding – he was even taken up for a spin – the target practice and the outdoor life generally; he even enjoyed the athletics, easily passed his test and struck up a genuine friendship with his appointed teacher. Only Papa's constant pressure on him ensured that he hated his time there.

At the beginning of August 1944, Papa received his order to take command of his own camp. It was to be near the town of Schweidnitz, in Silesia. Once again he found us an excellent billet, this time a flat in the turret of a miniature *Schloss* in the village of Wilkau, just a few kilometres from the camp. Frau von Schöller, our hostess, was a widow of about Mutti's age. Her husband had been killed in the war, leaving her in charge of the *Schloss* and the agricultural estate that went with it, an ancient mother-in-law, who was a *Gräfin* (countess), and three young children. Tall and blonde, she handled it all with an easy, natural authority.

Her children were a little younger than us, but nice, and we quickly settled into a happy holiday routine with them. In addition to the *Schloss* park and a delightfully playworthy stream that formed one of its boundaries, we had the run of the farm, where the grain store became our favourite playroom. The piles of threshed wheat and rye had the consistency of sand on a beach, with the added advantage of not sticking to you or getting into your eyes or mouth; you could slide about on them and in them, partially bury yourself or curl up in comfort on top. The farm was worked by Polish forced labourers who lived in the outbuildings, well away from everyone else. We couldn't communicate with them or they with us. Taking our cue from the adults around us, we treated them, while not exactly with hostility, with disregard, as though they didn't exist, like non-persons.

The farm had a life of its own in which, during our time there, the *Schloss* household only became involved for two annual rituals. The first was the sugar-beet harvest, when hundreds of sacks of white tubers were brought to the kitchen annexe, loaded into huge vats and boiled down into the most delectable, thick, black treacle. Then, in the run-up to Christmas, came the killing of a pig, when the kitchen was turned into a pork-curing and sausage factory.

Towards the end of the summer holidays, the von Schöllers' governess decided to take her two older charges on an expedition and invited Udo and me to join them. We set off in a pony-trap to Schweidnitz, a seventeenth-century fortified town with every kind of earthwork, battlement, armament, secret passage and ancient gunnery tower to be explored. On the way back we made a detour to a medieval castle that was open to the public. We entered by a drawbridge. Coats of armour and ancient weapons lined the halls and galleries; we were shown a secret passage and some dungeons, where we saw a skeleton still chained to the wall. I had my first conscious encounter with relics from the past that day and have never forgotten the exhilaration I felt.

When school started again, Udo was enroled at the high school in Schweidnitz and I at the local school, which comprised once again a single class for every child in the village, except the von Schöllers, who had their governess. After eight months at the feet of Fräulein Vogt it would have been difficult not to be embarrassingly ahead of everyone else in the class. Our teacher sometimes asked me to coach the other children and to correct their spelling and sums. There was one skill, though, that I was introduced to for the first time in Wilkau, and that was embroidery. The stitches on my sampler may not have reached the minimum acceptable standard for the girls of Wilkau, but I have never forgotten how to do them and they have occasionally come in extremely handy.

Skating was another local skill that we pathetically lacked. As Silesia is much further east than Berlin, winter came early and the lakes and ponds remained frozen for months at a stretch; most afternoons the local children turned out to meet their friends for a convivial spin on the ice or to pull their little brothers and sisters on homemade toboggans to anything, in such a flat area, that passed for a slope. I didn't have any skates or a toboggan and concentrated on building snowmen and igloos, but still managed to enjoy the snowy weather, which was more than could be said for Udo. He had to bicycle to school and could have done without the blizzards that howled down from the Russian steppes, making his progress impossibly slow in one direction, but dangerously fast in the other.

Visiting the *Luftwaffe* camp, part of which had been given over as Papa's *WE Lager*, was our favourite pastime by far. The atmosphere there was always brimming with energy and excitement. Because the country was so flat, the gliders were made airborne by a huge winch reminiscent of a Roman army 'machine' used in the attack on fortifications. Watching the boys being launched into the air as if by catapult was excellent entertainment; when that palled we would wander to the parachute-training area and try out for ourselves the somersault technique for landing being taught there.

One day we saw an extraordinary sight: a flying machine with rotating overhead arms, like a sideways windmill, that was stationary in the sky above us. When it had stayed motionless in the same spot for several minutes, its engines suddenly changed pitch and it slid away into the distance. An airman told us that it was one of the five *Wunderwaffen* (wonder weapons) that Hitler still had in the pipeline. Of the whole seven we had been promised, only the V1s and V2s were yet operational, but the others, he told us, were well on stream. The gliders were going to be a feature of one of the most ingenious designs; they would be attached to a larger – as it were — mother aeroplane, enabling it to deliver bombs on to extremely precise targets. It wasn't clear what would become of the hapless pilot afterwards, but we were assured that the gliders were about to make an indispensable contribution to our victory.

When we had had enough of watching gliders and para-chutists, and the camp's one and only helicopter wasn't airborne, we enjoyed taking in the less spectacular features of camp life, like PE, drill and marching. Each branch of the services had its own marching songs and the young recruits would belt out these and other Nazi songs as they marched around the camp. We knew the words of all the songs and joined in whenever we could.

Soon Mutti, too, became involved in the life of the camp. About a dozen of the Hitler Youth volunteers were ethnic Germans from recently annexed parts of Poland. Though technically German nationals, they couldn't speak the language and Mutti was recruited to teach it to them. She loved doing that and, I suspect, she became their mother figure. To motivate them into speaking German she made them tell her all about their homes and families; every evening she related to us what had happened in class and told us the funny things they had said. We got to know all their names and personalities and followed their progress minutely. Vicariously, they became our friends, our protégés even, for how could one not feel sorry for anyone unable to speak German?

Ever since we had left Berlin nearly eighteen months ago, my feet had, of necessity, been neglected. Mutti still massaged them daily and made me do exercises, but I had long outgrown my callipers and as they grew my feet were gradually reverting to their original bunched-up condition. Mutti couldn't bear to see it and towards the end of the autumn she took me to a paediatrician in Silesia's capital city, Breslau (now the Polish city of Wraclaw). A few weeks later it was to be surrounded by the Red Army in a four-month siege, before it was brutally overrun and seventy per cent of it destroyed. I still have a clear memory of what a noble city it was, with broad streets and stately, steep-roofed buildings. The doctor who examined my feet said I needed to have another operation immediately and booked me into the children's hospital for the first week of the New Year. He also told Mutti that a new treatment for club feet, from which I might be able to benefit one day, was being pioneered in a hospital in the Ruhr area by a specialist called Dr Kleine. Mutti wrote it all down.

If there is one Christmas that will always stand out in my memory it is the Christmas of 1944. After several Christmases when Papa was away, this time we were all together and celebrated in magnificent style. How could we know that it would be our last Christmas together as a family? The world was covered in snow and on Christmas Eve we joined the Hitler Youths for their party in the camp's refectory. The room was dominated by a huge Christmas tree and the polished buttons and buckles of several hundred Hitler Youth uniforms gleamed in the light of its many candles. A powerful cocktail of Nazi euphoria and *Weihnachtsstimmung*, Christmas spirit, charged the atmosphere, as several hundred voices broke into '*O Tannenbaum*'. We were the only children present, sitting at the top table with our parents and the other officers, joining in the feasting, carol singing and falling about laughing at an amateur cabaret. Papa commanded his camp with a tough authority rooted less in personal ambition than commitment to his cause; he usually exercised it with good humour and wit and was, as a result, respected and popular. On this night everyone was allowed to make fun of him and he featured prominently in their sketches. In one scene, I remember, a man was reading out newspaper excerpts, including a small ad which ran: 'Wish to exchange comb for duster. E. Thiele,' a reference to Papa's rapidly developing bald pate.

It was long past our bedtime when we got back to the *Schloss*, but this was Germany, and Christmas Eve had to be celebrated properly. We hadn't been allowed into the sitting-room for several days but now, as soon as he had lit the candles on the tree, Papa led us in. There, dominating the room, was the biggest and most magnificent doll's house I had ever seen. The outside was painted to look like red brick and it had a tiled roof. There were attics, a veranda, a balcony and four main rooms including a nursery with a cradle and a pram and a dining-room with a little grandfather clock, tiny silver candlesticks, goblets and, hanging over the dining table, in Mutti's unmistakably dashing style, a miniature portrait of the *Führer*. Every room had electricity and the bathroom running water and a lavatory that flushed. Closer inspection revealed that many of the raw materials from which these wonders had been fashioned were some kind of military surplus; the perfect little buckets, sets of saucepans and beer mugs, for example, had once been different-sized rifle cartridges. Papa had, of course, made the whole thing himself with the help of some colleagues, and with contributions from Mutti and even Oma and Opa. This incomparable present left me close to ecstasy.

On Christmas Day we were invited to join the von Schöllers' large family party. Their table was laid with heavy silver settings, including individual finger bowls. A magnificently crackling roast goose was brought in on a silver platter. After lunch Frau von Schöller announced that a relative of hers from a neighbouring estate had invited us all for *Kaffee und Kuchen*. She told us to be ready in the porch in half an hour and to be sure to be warmly dressed. When we presented ourselves we found, waiting for us in the drive, two large sleighs harnessed to teams of lively horses, impatient to introduce us to the smoothest, steadiest and most delightful form of transport ever invented.

That evening Papa invited his staff round to our flat. Udo and I had so enjoyed the cabaret from the night before, that we had memorised the sketches word for word and needed little persuasion to give Papa's guests a repeat performance.

We now know that there was less than a month to go before the Russians would overrun Silesia, driving out its population and every trace of German culture. The area around would become part of Poland, and be settled by Polish refugees driven out of their homes further east by Russians. Yet throughout the Christmas festivities the atmosphere in the *Schloss* and on the camp was confident and relaxed. Everyone still believed – or at least behaved as if they did – that we were winning the war; we had an inspired leader, a first-class army, moral strength and destiny on our side. What could stop us?

Without a doubt, I owe the fact that I wasn't trapped in the children's hospital when the Russians besieged Breslau – as I know happened to other children – and separated from my family for ever more to a wasp that stung me on the ankle the previous summer. The sting never healed properly and over Christmas it gathered into an angry boil. Glands all over my body swelled up and a doctor was called. He diagnosed blood-poisoning and ordered complete bed-rest; I wasn't even allowed to start playing with my wonderful doll's house. Mutti put me on the couch in the sitting-room where I could at least gaze at it and plan what to do the minute I was released. It was nauseating to think that as soon as I was better I would have to abandon it to go into hospital. I was still confined to bed when, in the middle of January, we started hearing what sounded like thunder, except that it went on day and night. It was obviously gun fire, getting louder. Papa told us it was artillery practice.

It took several more days before, in the last week of January, when the Russians were only twenty-five kilometres away, we children were finally told the truth. The whole *WE Lager* operation had received orders to retreat; the von Schöllers had already left and we were to do likewise, immediately. Papa had found out that one last westbound civilian train was on its way to a town called Hirschberg, some fifty kilometres away, that afternoon and at virtually no notice he piled us into a military car and rushed us there.

Hirschberg station was swarming with what looked like the entire population of East Europe turned refugees, desperate-looking people weighed down with as much as they could carry. A snow-covered train crawled in, bulging with passengers, the doorways and steps up into the carriages blocked solid and people hanging on to the buffers. Papa dragged us roughly through the crowd to one of the carriages, but not to a door, where other would-be passengers were pushing and shoving, trying to get on. He stepped up to a compartment window and jerked it open from the outside. Before anybody had time to protest he picked up first me, then Udo and then Mutti and flung us through the window, on top of the hapless occupants. The train pulled out, the last passenger train to leave the area before it was overrun by Russians.

Papa returned to the *Lager* to supervise the safe conduct of the boys, the staff and the equipment to the west. Whoever received and unpacked everything at the other end must have been puzzled to find, crated up with the gliders, winches and other military equipment a perfectly splendid doll's house with electricity, running water, a lavatory that flushed and a particularly stylish charcoal miniature of the *Führer*. It hadn't even been played with and I never saw it again.

9

WEISSEWARTE

It was late afternoon when Papa threw us into the train and my strongest memory of that journey is of everything happening in the dark. Sometime in the middle of the night we had to extricate ourselves from our compartment to change trains. I'll never forget that railway junction. It was snowing lightly and the stairs and footbridges connecting the platforms were swarming with refugees. They weren't the kind of people I was used to seeing on trains, smartly dressed for travel and carrying proper luggage. These travellers, the women wrapped in enormous shawls and carrying their possessions rolled up in sheets and blankets, looked frightened and desperate, especially some of the old people. While we waited there another train pulled in from a different direction. It, too, had surplus passengers hanging on to the doors and buffers, who joined the crowded confusion.

Mutti didn't panic. She found out exactly where we had to go for our connection and, when the train arrived, pushed us firmly on. Most of our fellow travellers that night thought only of getting west, west, west, away from the Russians. Our train north to Berlin was less in demand and before the night was over we even got seats on a wooden bench in a third-class compartment. It was a slow train, making as many unscheduled as official stops, and when we got to Berlin it was daylight – I had had my first night without sleep.

We only stayed there for a few hours – Papa had forbidden us to remain there overnight – long enough for an ineradicable memory of rubble and destruction everywhere, our *Heimat* in ruins. Among those who had been bombed out of their home were Oma and Opa. They were now living in our flat on Fauststrasse. Mutti did everything in her power to persuade them to come away with us, but they wouldn't hear of it, so we set off again alone. This time our destination was Tangerhütte, a little town just across the River Elbe, about 100 kilometres west of Berlin. We were bound for the Weissewarte *WE Lager*, the one where Papa had received his glider training the previous summer and Udo his athletics drill. For, having dismantled the Silesian camp and escorted its personnel, equipment and my doll's house to safety in Bavaria, Papa's orders were to take over the command of this same camp. We were to join him there but, as it turned out, we arrived at least a week before him.

The Weissewarte camp was, again, part of a bigger air-force operation where adult conscripts as well as Hitler Youth youngsters received their basic training. It was in an entirely rustic setting, surrounded on three sides by forest.

We were allocated a tiny room in the officers' quarters at one end of a long wooden hut. At the other end, beyond a wooden partition, lived a party of Romanians. Their exact status was difficult to fathom. They weren't prisoners of war, but appeared to be under some kind of restraint and made to do a lot of the menial work round the camp. While nobody could communicate with them directly, they were usually in excellent spirits, singing and joking among themselves almost riotously.

Shortly after we had become their neighbours, they started redecorating their end of the hut. Some of them were busy rubbing down with sandpaper while their leader was attacking old paint-work with a blow-torch, cheered on by the rest. We were in our little room one day having lunch with some of the camp staff who had joined us for company. Mutti sent me to the kitchen for a refill of the soup tureen but, as I stepped into the corridor, a tongue of flame came lashing at me from the wooden partition. The Romanians had set their end of the corridor on fire. I yelled '*Feuer!*' Everyone rushed out, grabbing whatever they could rescue. Passers-by came to help but the heat and smoke were so intense that one youth, who made a heroic rescue dash, had to retreat within seconds, holding just one item of salvage, Mutti's bra.

Two young officers who shared the room opposite ours had gone out for the day leaving their door locked. Nobody could find an axe in time to break it down and when they returned everything they owned had been reduced to ashes. They were not best pleased.

We were moved to another hut, the camp commander's quarters, waiting for Papa to arrive. A few nights later there was a loud knocking on the door. Mutti jumped out of bed to open it and in out of the snow, delighted to see us, came Papa. I had never seen him so elated. He wasn't in uniform, but in scruffy civilian clothes and covered in soot. He told us this camp was so off the beaten track that he hadn't found any normal transport to bring him here, no military or even passenger train, so he had climbed on to a goods train, travelling with the driver on the locomotive. He had helped make the steam and actually taken over the controls, fulfilling his lifelong ambition of being an engine-driver. Hence his elation – and the soot.

From the day he took over the camp we, too, became part of its community. We had our meals in the refectory with everyone else and, as the only children, got a delightful amount of attention. The cook, an oldish man who had worked his way round the world as a ship's cook, became our friend. He gave us lots of titbits, let us scrape out his cake-mixing bowls and taught us rude versions of well-known *Wehrmacht* songs; the gunnery instructor fixed us up in a miniature rifle range with a target and taught us to shoot with air-rifles. Sometimes we turned out for the daily flag-raising and lowering ceremonies, joining in the drill and bringing up the rear when the columns marched off. To me it wasn't playing, but making my contribution. Everyone's attitude to us was so easy-going, even Papa's, that for once Udo didn't need to be forced to participate.

Given that this was February and March 1945, when the Allied forces were already well established on German territory, the camp atmosphere was extraordinarily upbeat and confident. If everyone around us was anticipating the imminent defeat of the *Vaterland*, they weren't showing it.

We now know that all over Germany disillusioned soldiers were looking for opportunities to desert and non-Nazis who had kept their heads down throughout the war were preparing to break cover. Yet in the last days of the war, 20,000 army deserters and civilians who dared make public appeals for surrender were still being shot as traitors. The fighting only went on for as long as it did because Hitler still had enormous support both in the armed forces and in the population at large.

Papa was obviously part of that support, though it is incomprehensible to me now how he could have been so deluded. Not only that, but what on earth did a committed soldier like him think he was doing at that stage of the war, teaching starry-eyed teenagers to fly gliders? Was playing around with model aeroplanes while Germany was being bombed to hell not on a par with fiddling while Rome burnt? He clearly didn't think so and went about his business as enthusiastically as ever.

Mutti no longer had any illusions. She was receiving almost daily letters from Oma and Opa in Berlin, letters that must have torn her apart. That spring Oma celebrated her sixty-fifth birthday and Opa his sixty-seventh. For quite a while now, Mutti had been trying to persuade them to leave Berlin and come to us but they still refused. Oma wouldn't leave Opa; and Opa couldn't leave because all Nazi Party staff, down to the most junior, had been made 'essential' workers, like military conscripts, forbidden to leave their posts. Opa had never disobeyed an order in his life and he wasn't about to start now.

A few of Oma and Opa's letters from Berlin that spring have survived. They cover, in one breath, subjects as diverse as the breakdown of public life in Berlin and Oma's dilemma over what to do with an old coat. They bear testimony to people's need, when their world disintegrates, to carry on as normal.

Oma's first letter is dated 6 February 1945:

It is a funny life here. No telephone, rarely post, no newspapers, no telegrams, no buses or trams and only in a few parts the S-Bahn. Today it goes from here to Schlesischer Bahnhof. Daddy went off this morning to try to get to Charlottenburg, saying if it was too hopeless he would come back, but he hasn't. He is unhappy when he can't get to work, his conscience worries him so, he can't sit still. Fräulein Mache (our neighbour) walks from Schlesischer Bahnhof to Potsdamer Platz every day.

We have raids night and day. Elfi, often they come over Stendal way, I wonder if you hear them and know when we get a raid. Will you tell me? Elfi dear, we are so glad you are not here.

I would so like to talk to you but no telephone. Anhalter Bahnhof is very damaged also the U-Bahn there. Travelling in Berlin is awful. Oh dear, aren't we in a mess? Can we get out of it? I still have hope.

I've unpicked that coat and have come to the sad conclusion that I can't expect a tailor to remake it. It's all bits. I'll have to make a dress of it instead. Daddy has come back. He went this morning via Ostkreuz, Gesundbrunnen, Friedrichstrasse, then Charlottenburg, it took two hours. I forgot to tell you, a lot of the wall in the bathroom fell out on Saturday into the bath.

Love to you all,
Mummy

The next letter is dated 17 February, in Opa's copperplate writing and written from his office:

Mommsenstrasse 48
Charlottenburg
Monday

Dear Elfi, Udo and Katrin,

... I want to tell you how things are looking in Berlin after the big air-raid. I had to go into the area that had suffered the most ... It looks as though there has been an earthquake, no house remains undamaged. You certainly need good nerves to keep up any hope in this situation, nerves like steel. In the Berlin streets big panzer barricades are being put up, some streets are completely closed to traffic.

People have become anxious, everyone asking each other what it means. In my office here it is quite unbearable, they are so chicken-hearted that I'm pleased to get back to Mummy, who is still optimistic.

Yesterday was a lovely day and I worked a bit in the garden. We went to the Fischers for *Kaffee*. Dear Elfi and children, when and where we will see one another again is impossible to say, but it is not out of the question that Mummy will join you one of these days. We keep hearing rumours that the eastern suburbs are going to be evacuated, but nothing definite. Anyway, don't worry about us and write us often to let us know how you are, so we can live together in our thoughts. I am sending you a parcel: torch batteries. So take good care of yourselves.

Till we meet again, *Heil Hitler.*
Opa

Another letter from Oma, dated 28 March, is written on a train. She is on her way to fetch Opa from his office. They plan to visit Opa's brother Max and the old aunt who lives with him. She says they have tried to telephone him often, but can never get a connection and now want to find out for themselves how they are.

I doubt whether we shall get there for this morning's raid has upset the S-Bahn again. You said in your last letter that you always know when we have a raid.

Oh my dear, to look out of these train windows is awful, it doesn't matter when you glance out, it is the same picture, ruin. Look here Elfi, you must give up thinking of Daddy and I, or me alone, coming to you. Daddy can't stay away from his job. Nobody is allowed to leave unless they are a complete invalid or about 100 and I couldn't leave him alone. If you saw what a miserable little scrap he is you would say, no Mummy, of course you must stop with him. But we are going to Schöneiche for Easter.

Do you know, Elfi, I must have got *versteinert* (turned to stone), for the raids have no effect on me any more, no diarrhoea or knocking knees, I sit still in my corner and when it's over I couldn't tell anyone if it was bad or not. Last evening Frau Mache said she counted nineteen bombs and the evening before forty. I'm sure I don't know. Isn't that funny?

Elfi, dear, you can't believe how you have helped me with your last parcel. That soap! Oh! It is a godsend for my poor hands. And fancy all that bread. Now I'll get ahead of myself again and when the new ration cards start I'll have some in hand. No one has any bread now and another ten days to go. And next month we are to get 500 grams a week less. I don't know what the people will do. There is a permanent board standing outside Ungers (the grocer), saying: '*Nicht vorhanden ist*! (not available are) – butter, sugar, jam, syrup, artificial honey, cottage cheese, flour.' No one has got their jam ration this month, everyone is eating dry bread, if they have any. Elfi, what is going to happen, can one have any hope?

My pot of daffodils is really a glory, six great big blooms have come out, double daffs. Oh! such a taste of spring!

All the garden is dug and planted except the beans, the idea of the watering frightens me rather. We had sprouts last Sunday, lovely ones, on last year's plants.

Despite ever smaller food rations, it's clear from Oma's final paragraph, and from her next letter, that everyone had been hoarding for even worse times ahead. Mutti had been keeping Oma and Opa supplied with regular food parcels; now Oma is wanting to return the compliment:

> Your cook must be a fine manager to cook for all that lot and make a success of it. I am sending you a tin of pâté de foie gras, a little luxury as a change from always sausage. Shall I send you some sardines?
>
> I will get your hat to you somehow. Yes, Udo's school does sound funny, sitting on a sofa in a *Gasthaus*. That is what makes him like it.
>
> Your last two letters have only taken about a week to get here, that's better.
>
> Love from us both,
>
> Mummy

Of the final letter only one page survives. A dozen soldiers have been billeted in the Fauststrasse flats; some behave as though they own the place, others are very polite and call Oma *Gnädige Frau* (madam). One asks the residents for permission to play his accordion.

This letter has a strong 'the end is nigh' flavour. Oma has no *Ruhe* (peace of mind) for letter writing but wants Mutti's advice on a problem that troubles her: 'Do tell me what I should do with all this grub? I mean the tins. Nobody is hoarding anything any more. They all say the Russians can be here any day. Fräulein Meta said yesterday, "*Nur ein Idiot wird jetzt etwas aufheben*" (only an idiot would save anything now).' But Oma thinks, 'We may have a much hungrier time to go through. Please talk it over with Eberhard, he always knows what to do.'

Even with reports like these coming from Berlin, radio bulletins announcing record numbers of enemy planes over the Reich and the awesome spectacle of American bomber formations passing overhead on the way to the capital, my parents never so much as hinted to us – or, I am sure, to the Hitler Youths – that the diet of Nazi propaganda on which we had all been fed for years was about to prove deadly poisonous. There was no discussion or planning of what anyone should do if, or rather, when the enemy appeared on our doorstep.

Whatever the evidence to the contrary before me, I took my lead from the adults around me and clung to my belief that the *Führer* was still intentionally luring the enemy to his doom, which the next *Wunderwaffe* was about to seal, definitively, any day now. I slapped down any doubts that dared to enter my consciousness and continued to give my full attention to getting through the practical problems of each day, for example, my walk to school.

Once again we had been enrolled in local schools, Udo a bike-ride away at a little school that had been evacuated to the area from Saxony and was squatting somewhere in Tangerhütte, and I at the Weissewarte village school. It was, by my standards, an immensely long walk across fields and a water meadow. The worst part of it was having to cross a stream lined with a row of stunted willow trees that looked, from a distance, like soldiers taking aim at me with their rifles. They were so realistic that every time I walked into their firing line I prayed anew that they weren't enemy soldiers coming to get me.

But for that twice-daily ordeal, the last few months of the war were, for me, a perfectly ordinary, cheerful time. The camp offered many diversions, I had Udo, my favourite companion, to play with and the only other requirement for my peace of mind – Papa's safety – was satisfied.

The event that touched this particular raw nerve of mine most starkly was also the one that came closest to reminding the camp that there was a war going on. One day, as I approached the end of my trudge home from school, turning the corner which put me in sight of the whole camp, I saw, dead ahead, a vertical aeroplane balancing on the ground on the tip of its nose. After a short wobble it collapsed to one side and disappeared from sight. Was this a new way of landing a plane? I had seen so many odd sights lately that I didn't give much thought to this one till I reached the camp. It was agog with the news that its one and only anti-aircraft gun had shot down an American fighter plane; one of the crew had been killed and the other taken prisoner. I ran in the direction of the excitement and soon came to where a crowd had formed round the plane's debris. I squeezed myself between the spectators to the front, but then wished I hadn't. I had emerged at the exact spot where the dead airman's body was laid out on some straw. He was long and thin, with a pale, narrow face and tufts of short blond hair. I noticed that he wore a wedding ring and wondered if he had a little girl. The thought disturbed me deeply. I had grown up fuelled with enthusiasm for the war and for destroying the enemy. Now that I was looking at one who was well and truly destroyed I could feel no pleasure; I just felt sorry for him and sorrier still for his little girl, if he had one.

10

SÜPPLING

When it happened, the disintegration of the only world I had known was swift, but hardly terrible, at least on the surface. Its impact both on us as a family and individually has taken decades to work itself through and the process may never be complete.

The spring of 1945 stands out in the memory of all Germans alive at the time. Everyone can tell you where they were or, almost as often, where they were trying to get to. Two out of every five in the population were on the move, trying to reach their homes before the collapse happened, or if their homes were in the East, trying to get away before the Russians arrived. Twelve million Germans, the entire population of Silesia and Pomerania, were on the move for a different reason, being driven from their homes into Germany's new, much reduced, post-war frontiers. They had to make way for Polish refugees evicted from their homes still further East by a new wave of Russian settlers. All this had been agreed between the Allied powers at the Yalta and Potsdam Conferences as part of the post-war division of Germany.

My immediate family was in the unusual position of not only being together, but in a remote spot, as safe as anywhere could be from serious fighting. It would be madness for us to contemplate going anywhere else, especially to our home in Berlin; we were worried enough about what was happening there to Oma and Opa. So when Papa received orders to get his family off the camp, he decided to keep us in the area.

One day towards the end of our time there, Papa appeared with a small car. Though painted an unpleasant military grey colour and uncomfortably tinny, it was brand new and, apparently, nothing to do with the camp but our personal property. How on earth had Papa managed to get hold of it at such a time? It was just another of the many mysteries about him that struck me so forcibly when, nearly fifty years later, I tried to put together my family's history. He gave Mutti driving lessons and towards the end of March, when we finally had to leave the camp, packed us and our belongings into it and drove us out of the gates for the last time. A few kilometres along the road he turned into a forest track and proceeded along that for another kilometre or two.

When we finally emerged from the cover of the trees the scene was straight out of *Hansel and Gretel*. In the middle of a clearing stood a picture-book forester's cottage, coarsely built of unstripped pine logs; on the opposite side of the track leading past it was a large pond fringed by trees. Geese and ducks were splashing around in the water and a family of tiny ducklings were scooting about trying to keep out of their way. This was Süppling and I was captivated.

Papa had arranged with the part-time forester/subsistence farmer who owned this idyll that we should rent an attic room from him and this was where he now installed us. A driver from the camp had followed to take Papa back and soon the two of them drove off again down the track towards the *Lager*. The grey car stayed with us in case of an emergency.

I have no idea at what point reason triumphed over faith and even Papa accepted that there was no *Wunderwaffe*, that this was the end and that Hitler had made fools of us all. I assume that he and Mutti had agonising discussions between themselves about their disillusionment; however, if they did, they certainly didn't share their fears or dismay with us.

For our first week or two at Süppling, Papa often visited. Then, once again, we started hearing artillery fire in the distance and from then on he didn't come any more. My parents' assurances to me that everything was still all right may have been misleading, but they certainly kept up my confidence that I was safe from harm, so that the sound of fighting in the distance didn't frighten me. I wondered vaguely about Papa's safety again, but not enough to interfere with my enjoyment of the delights offered by my new surroundings.

The little settlement of Süppling turned out to be a good deal bigger than first impressions might suggest, which was just as well, considering the scenes that were about to be enacted there.

Behind the house was a farmyard surrounded by barns and sheds for a few cows, pigs, a horse and various poultry. In the middle was an enormous dung heap and every so often, in the manner of a conductor ascending a concert platform, a handsome cock would climb to the top for a bout of fortissimo crowing.

Attached to the back of the house was a dairy where the farmer's wife and two daughters were often busy plucking chickens, preparing fodder, skimming cream and making butter. To one side of the house was a hand water pump, to the other a powerfully stinking privy, the little farm's only lavatory facility. As soon as the tank beneath was full, the farmer loaded it on to a cart and spread the contents on his fields, a most effective way of informing the neighbourhood of the exact stage his cultivation cycle had reached.

I had never lived in such a bucolic setting or watched spring bursting out at such close quarters. The budding trees, wild flowers and butterflies, a woodpecker, red squirrels, hares and hedgehogs delighted me. Most fascinating of all was the teeming marine life of the little pond. I spent hours lying at the edge, staring into the water and being mesmerised by the antics of millions of tadpoles, while iridescent dragonflies danced on the surface.

My other favourite pastime was helping the women in the dairy and with the poultry. They let me feed the hens, collect eggs and watch a family of chicks hatching out of their shells; they even taught me to make my own portions of butter, using a jam jar instead of a churn.

My first inkling that the world in which I had such confidence was about to collapse came from the arrival at Süppling of some strange-looking characters. They wore ill-fitting garments with ripped seams and crudely cut holes where there had once been a stripe or insignia. It didn't require much imagination to identify them as mutilated items of uniforms, though not necessarily their own. Looking self-conscious, even sheepish, they would emerge from the forest furtively and stroll up towards the house trying, unsuccessfully, to look natural. They were, of course, deserters.

Süppling must have enjoyed a reputation as the neighbourhood's safe house. We had already learned that, before Hitler came to power, our forester had been a well-known local socialist. He had left his house in the village for the seclusion of the forest as a way of lying low, away from daily contact with the Nazi ethos. Now word seems to have got around that Süppling was not only a safe house for deserters, but that it had a forging factory capable of fixing them up with authentic-looking discharge papers.

This was, indeed, the case but it was so hush-hush that even Udo and I didn't realise for several days that the forgery operative was our mother. With her artistic talent and professional training in graphics she was ideal forger-material, but why was she taking the risk? And where had she got hold of her equipment, including a typewriter, an ink pad and two rubber stamps, one an adjustable date stamp, the other bearing the official spread-eagle symbol of the *Luftwaffe*. Everyone treated these items as her personal property, not the forester's, so she must have brought them with her from the camp. Could Papa have given them to her for just this purpose? Was this part of the deal the forester made with Papa when he agreed to take us in? It was obvious from the first day that he only did so reluctantly.

However it happened, Mutti clearly enjoyed her new job, which at last gave her something creative to do in a place that had little else to interest her. She kept her forging kit in a little box buried in the forest and made nocturnal visits there according to demand.

Most of the deserters were in a hurry to get home and moved off as soon as they had their papers. Others, perhaps from the East and with nowhere definite to go, hung about, making the most of the opportunity to down a few meals and prepare themselves properly for life on the run. Out of this mixed crew the ones I remember most clearly were a couple, well past the first flush of youth, called Henryk and Lilo. Henryk had pulled what must once have been an impressive collection of decorations off his air-force shirt; there was hardly anything left of it without rents or lighter patches. Lilo was lean and tanned, with bleached hair and a natural elegance which survived intact after several weeks spent living in the hay loft. Udo told me he had watched Henryk, unbeknown, throw the rest of his uniform into the pond. There was something whimsical and touching about them. Unlike the others, with their maps, water bottles and survival kits, Henryk and Lilo gave no indication of being desperate to get away. On the contrary, they seemed keen to remain in this delightful spot for as long as possible. We later learned that Henryk had been an air force wing commander and Lilo his secretary. Both had homes to go to, but they preferred to carry on with their affair, for which Süppling offered the perfect setting.

I couldn't help disapproving of all these deserters. It was nothing personal, just regret that people could be so ready to abandon their posts and betray their oaths. They certainly weren't exhibiting *Ehre* (honour) or *Treue* (loyalty), virtues I had been taught to respect above all others. Why weren't they sticking to their duty, like Papa?

Not everyone who turned up at Süppling during those days was a deserter. Once a proper military formation came by, asking for water and somewhere to rest. They didn't stay long, but when they moved off again, forgot one of their Panzer Faust hand grenades, which they left lying in the farmyard, next to the dung heap. The farmer didn't know what to do with it so he threw that into the pond as well. Then a couple of young officers we had known from the *WE Lager* turned up asking for civilian clothes, but they weren't deserters either. They had heard Hitler's last command to soldiers to fight to the death and had taken it to heart; they told us that they were going to be *Werwölfe*, saboteurs behind the lines, risking instant execution if they were caught. Both were cultivated, educated men – one of them had been an architect before the war – and they had only been given their *WE Lager* posting because they were unfit for active service; each had lost an arm in Russia. With that injury and papers from Mutti they could easily have got home, unmolested, but they wouldn't hear of it. They were utter fanatics.

The next bit of evidence that order was fast breaking down came one night in the form of a series of explosions from the railway line that crossed our woodland track a few hundred metres further into the forest. A heavily guarded train carrying military supplies, mostly V1s, was passing quite close by when the soldiers manning its escort of anti-aircraft guns received word that they couldn't complete their journey; the Americans were already in control of their destination further up the line. Their orders were to blow up the train and their ammunition. Before the pyrotechnics started they went round to warn people about the imminent explosions, but also indicated that some of the train's cargo might be worth investigating. There was, apparently, enough of certain food stuffs there to feed an army.

Our forester immediately dispatched the entire company who now made up his household to the embankment to rescue whatever they could get their hands on. News had travelled like lightning and within a very short time half the population of Weissewarte appeared on our forest track with handcarts, wheelbarrows and rucksacks, hurrying in the direction of the train. When we got there it was on fire, ammunition exploding and tracers from the AA guns shooting up into the sky. It must have been terribly dangerous, but in the excitement of looting nobody cared. Unfortunately, the ill-fated train's cargo was packaged in such enormous quantities that it usually needed several people to carry just one item. Our prize turned out to be a whole carton of Mondamin, a brand of blancmange powder, enough to feed a normal household for about a century. For other groups, the booty might be a large sack of dried peas or a whole carton of packets of crisp bread.

The whole incident disturbed me deeply. I couldn't feel comfortable in such an atmosphere of lawlessness and free-for-all. What if we were caught?

The next afternoon, 16 April, we were sitting in the sun on the steps of the porch with the forester's daughters when three armoured vehicles, unlike the kind we were used to seeing, emerged from the forest track. They weren't iron grey but khaki, with white stars on the side. When they came level with us they stopped and armed soldiers in camouflage fatigues and khaki helmets jumped out. We all put up our hands in surrender. The soldiers sauntered casually past us into the house, made a fairly superficial search and emerged with whatever they had found in the way of arms, including Mutti's bedside revolver and the farmer's hunting rifle. Some of them tried to initiate a conversation. When Mutti answered in flawless English they were astounded. The last thing they expected in this outpost of civilisation was a beautiful, sophisticated woman speaking BBC English. They looked at her suspiciously and demanded to see her papers. Mutti produced her out-of-date British passport.

This little convoy of our 'liberators' was to be the first of many. Checking up on the curious ménage in the middle of the forest clearly became the favourite detail of whatever unit was locally in control. Who could tell whether it was the unique setting, the forester's two nubile daughters, or our exotic mother that was the greatest attraction? Though always polite, the patrols occasionally indulged in petty looting, but were always sure to make it sound official. One party demanded everyone's cameras; that was the end of the little box camera that had recorded our entire childhood to date; another party confiscated everyone's watches. Others started coming at the cocktail hour in the hope of some fraternisation – illegal at the time – well out of sight of the military police. We began to be kept awake at night by accordion playing, sing-songs and parties in the forester's parlour, which went on into the small hours. Mutti sometimes joined in and was delighted to receive more than one marriage proposal from over-emotional teenage members of the liberation force.

I quickly became thoroughly well disposed towards the Americans. Even if they hadn't taken the trouble to buy us off – not difficult to do – with their delicious meal packs and Hershey bars, you couldn't dislike them. They were so good-humoured, so gentle, so unthreatening. They wouldn't hurt a fly. Furthermore, we found their whole style of presenting themselves, so different from *homo Germanicus*, utterly fascinating.

The difference between the two species struck me most forcibly the day a whole column of Americans came marching past the house. Having spent eight months watching, at close quarters, recruits being taught to march I had become something of an expert on style. Americans, I now observed, were far taller than German men; their complexions were mostly pale and sallow, not ruddy and weatherbeaten like our soldiers; nor did they stand up so straight that they were almost bending backwards, as German soldiers, having had '*Brust raus! Bauch rein!*' (Chest out! stomach in!) shouted at them often enough tended to do. Most curious of all was their funny walk, rolling their hips and sticking out their bottoms. As for their marching, I found it ridiculously sloppy compared with the disciplined goose-stepping of our soldiers. How was I to know that, sloppy or not, their relaxed style enabled them to cover far greater distances on the same amount of energy?

I was just learning to relax a little at the sight of our conquerors, prepared to believe that there might be life after defeat after all, when they suddenly exercised their power over us in the most terrible way imaginable. One morning a military-police jeep drew up in front of the house. We knew all about them by now and assumed that they had come, like others before, to make sure there was no unseemly fraternisation going on. Two officers raced up the steps, barged into the house and demanded to see Mutti. Without a word of explanation they drove off with her. Whatever I had ever acquired in the way of *Mut* (courage) or other relevant Nazi virtue deserted me. My insides went numb with fear. What could they possibly want with her? I had heard about female spies like Mata Hari being arrested and executed. Were they going to convict Mutti of spying and shoot her? Had they found out about her radio programme, which she had warned us never to mention? About the forging? Was it to do with Papa? And what had happened to him, anyway? The hours until they brought her back were like a lifetime.

When she returned, Mutti told us they had interrogated her about Papa, when she had last seen him and, above all, where he was now. As she had no idea about the latter, she hadn't been able to help them. They obviously didn't believe her, as the following day they came back for her, and again the day after that. On that occasion they kept her overnight, well into the next day and when they brought her back, they took Udo. They asked him the same questions, but, though he couldn't help them either, he felt duty bound to lie to them about anything he did know. They always caught him out and their manner was clinical and hard. He found the whole thing extremely stressful. I was quite prepared to be the next victim and decided that if they took me away too I would quite simply, straightforwardly and without hesitation burst into tears. It wouldn't be difficult; in fact, I doubted that I would have any choice in the matter. So much for my *Mut*.

Apart from these special anxieties affecting my own family, the breakdown of the old order was so gradual and the style of the American invasion so softly, softly that, for me, the significance of what was happening didn't fully sink in. Then, two or three weeks after we had seen our first American, Mutti told me that the *Führer* was dead; she had heard it on the radio. According to the report he had died 'fighting in hand-to-hand combat'. I was devastated. It couldn't be true. Life wasn't possible without the *Führer*! Mutti was, as usual, entirely pragmatic, taking the line, '*Tant pis!* so that's the end of him! Let's just get on without him then,' exactly what I couldn't visualise.

When we later heard that Hitler had committed suicide in his bunker even I could appreciate how ignominious and *feige* (cowardly) the manner of his death had been. It went against all the rules of *Treue* and *Ehre* that were such key ingredients of the ideology he had fed us. It didn't take long for my eyes to be opened to the truth that he had not been a superior being after all, but an ordinary mortal who had betrayed us. Yet, even when Mutti first broke her news and I could at last bring myself to believe it, it was not primarily Hitler's loss that shattered me, much as I had loved him. It was all the other implications of life without him that left me bewildered. For if Hitler was dead, then there wasn't a *Wunderwaffe* and it wasn't our destiny to win the war. In my heart, I still hadn't accepted the American presence as final but, at some level of consciousness, gone on expecting our forces to return to the attack and drive the 'liberators' out.

On the rare occasions in the past that I had tried to imagine what defeat might be like my mind had gone blank. Other than as a joke, nobody ever talked or, according to the evidence, even thought about the possibility. There was no need, as it couldn't happen. Only now did I acknowledge that the unthinkable had, indeed, happened. We had lost the war. I still had only the haziest idea of what this was going to mean for the future, except that the rules, beliefs and social order I had grown up with, that I was part of and that were part of me, were about to be consigned to the dustbin. How could I possibly survive in any other world? Again, my mind went blank.

Another thought struck me. Now that we were defeated, the better a Nazi one had been, the more likely one was to be punished by whatever regime took over. That was why people were suddenly hiding, burning and burying tokens of their Nazi past. I went up to the attic and from the little treasure box that had accompanied me on all my travels I took the silver– as I thought– swastika badge that I had worn so proudly in my Mahlsdorf *Kindergruppe* days. I took it down to the garden and buried it. Like everyone else, I was learning to deny, or at least conceal, my principles.

Concealing them wasn't the same as giving them up, though. As I continued to brood on the prospect of the only life I knew being overturned, it occurred to me that even if I obeyed our new rulers outwardly they need never know what I was really thinking. Provided I kept it secret and didn't step out of line, I could carry on believing what I liked. That way I could keep my *Treue* and my *Ehre* and wouldn't need to become a *Feigling* or, perish the thought, a *Verräter* (traitor). That, I was sure, was what Papa would do. Nobody could ever make him give up his ideals; I could be sure of that.

Such thoughts comforted me and I began to feel less despairing. This would be my way of handling defeat. There and then I made my commitment to keeping the faith, always. Then I pushed it firmly, but securely, into mental storage and returned to my scrutiny of the ducklings, tadpoles and dragonflies on my pond.

II

COMINGS AND GOINGS

One day during this period of constant suspense I went up to the attic to fetch something; I opened the door and there was Papa sitting on the bed, deep in discussion with Mutti. I had last seen him less than a month ago, when he had been his normal charismatic self, immaculate in his smart uniform. Now he was transformed, barely recognisable. He was unshaved and had dark rings under his eyes; his face was lined and his expression one of humiliation and black despair. He was in civilian clothes, one trouser leg cut off at the knee to make room for a grubby bandage. I bounced into the room and started to run towards him, but then something made me feel like an intruder. Papa looked at me but his mind was elsewhere; I don't think he saw me. Mutti told me they had to discuss things in private and sent me away. She told me I mustn't let anyone know Papa was at Süppling.

He didn't stay for very long; Mutti later told me that she had begged him to leave. She was afraid that if the Americans came back and found them there together they would suspect she had been hiding him all along and had lied when she swore that she had no idea of his whereabouts. Then they might arrest her and take her away again, only this time indefinitely, on a charge. Then what would become of Udo and me?

They decided that Papa must give himself up to the Americans.

Mutti managed to get him food and clean clothes and to dress his
wound without, as she thought, anybody at Süppling finding out
he was there. Before dawn next morning we had to say goodbye
to him, but he could hardly bring himself to speak to us, or we to
him. Then Mutti and he crept downstairs to the car and Mutti
drove him off to the American headquarters, a route with which
she was by now thoroughly familiar. Even in those bizarre times,
I doubt if there were many prisoners who arrived in captivity in
their own cars, driven by their wife, or indeed, many wives whose
destination on their first serious outing at the wheel was
delivering their husband to his captors.

There is little doubt that if Papa had decided to avoid captivity
he could have done so. His SS officer brother and many others
like him managed it quite easily. My Onkel Jochen, we later
heard, shredded his identity papers and made his way to a relative
in a village where nobody else knew him. The old aunt took him
in and within a very short time he had become a pillar of the local
community. It seems that what persuaded Papa not to stay on the
run was Mutti's fears about what would happen to us children if
the Americans went on looking for him so urgently.

This whole episode is somewhat blurred in my memory. What
I have always remembered most clearly is the defeated, rueful
look in Papa's eyes when I first saw him in the attic. Another
memory is the plan that was made if – or rather, when – we lost
touch with one another: we agreed to make Tante Kätchen our
point of contact. Of all our acquaintances, her home in the Harz
Mountains was least likely to have been damaged by war and she
least likely to have moved away.

Seeing Papa looking so ill and dejected and knowing that he
was about to be a prisoner didn't depress me nearly as much as
the fact that we had lost the war. The fighting was over. Papa had
survived; I had seen him with my own eyes, alive and safe. OK,
being a prisoner wouldn't be very nice, but he couldn't get killed
any more and one day we would be reunited. What was more
difficult to cope with was trying to imagine Papa, and indeed our

whole family, living together again in some unspecified place and time in a Germany without Hitler and without Nazism. There my imagination failed me.

Throughout our stay at Süppling, Mutti had impressed on us the importance of not doing anything to annoy the forester and of staying out of his way as much as we could. Though I didn't understand the reason, I could sense he didn't like having us under his roof. In retrospect, the mystery is less why he didn't like having us there, as why he had ever agreed to take us in the first place and, having done so, why his family was so nice to us. As a dedicated socialist he had done his utmost to avoid all Nazis and anything to do with the war effort, yet at the very moment of liberation, here he was, harbouring the wife and children of the area's leading Nazi. As soon as the capitulation was official and a new order started to emerge we came under increasing pressure to leave. The question was, where to go?

It was now coming up to six months since Mutti had booked me into the Breslau children's hospital for my 'urgent' operation which, of course, had never happened. Since then she had become increasingly worried about my feet, noting that with every millimetre they grew they seemed to become more bunched up and twisted. This was when she decided that since, at that point in our lives, one destination was as good as any other, she might as well take me to the orthopaedic specialist, Dr Kleine, that she had heard about in Breslau – the one who was so good at treating club feet. Mutti consulted the notes she had made at the time and found that he was based in a town called Recklinghausen, on the edge of the Ruhr. This struck her as a most suitable destination for other reasons too: it was in the newly designated British zone of occupation and the sort of place where she could perhaps get a job to support us. A plan for our next move was gradually coming together.

There was a problem, however – a general curfew forbidding civilians to travel, especially into another military zone. To make the journey we would need a special travel pass that was only granted in extreme compassionate circumstances. Mutti decided that my feet could make themselves useful for once and applied to the American military governor's office for a permit on medical grounds. We had to appear in person at his headquarters and were directed into a panelled boardroom where a line of American officers were sitting at a table, scrutinising us. Mutti made me take off my shoes and socks and instructed me to parade up and down in front of them while she made an impassioned plea about the urgency of getting me to Dr Kleine. Our double act was clearly irresistible and we were granted our pass, dated a few days hence.

We prepared for departure. Mutti got out the faithful hand sewing machine that had accompanied us on every journey since we left Berlin two years before and, from a sheet and a remnant of red material, produced a Red Cross banner to fix on to the back window of the car, as extra safe conduct for our journey. We packed as much as we could get into the car, which was not very much, as we were taking an extra passenger: Hans, one of the Süppling deserters whose papers Mutti had forged and whom she had promised a lift home to the Ruhr in return for two valuable contributions to our trip. First, he could drive properly and, second, he could provide us with somewhere to stay. He assured us that if his parents were still alive and their home still standing, they would be delighted to give us hospitality until we found somewhere ourselves. The deal was struck. Mutti got out her forging kit for one last time and expertly added his name on to our travel pass. Everything was set for our departure on 22 May.

On our last evening at Süppling I was once again doing my favourite thing: lying face down by the pond, inspecting the tadpoles; some of them had by now developed little arms as well as legs and become the most adorable little frogs. There had been other changes, too. Water lilies had started to open and patches of kingcups and irises at the water's edge had made the pond a place of ever greater enchantment. As I got up to run round to the other side to check what had been happening there, my eye caught, deep in the forest on the Weissewarte side, a speck of bright red moving in my direction. Soon I could make out a face above the red speck, then a whole person. It was a little old lady and the colour came from her dazzling floral blouse. There was a little old man with her, wearing a crumpled-looking dark suit. He was pulling a wooden handcart containing a few bundles. After weeks when Süppling's only visitors had been men in uniform, speeding down the forest track in jeeps, the old couple made such an unexpected sight that I became uneasy and retreated towards the house. They came closer and I watched them peering round anxiously, as though they were looking for something. Then I recognised them. Oma and Opa. They had walked all the way from Berlin. It had taken them a month. I ran to hug them, but my greeting wasn't very kind. '*Oma, du bist alt geworden!*' (Oma, you've got old!)

12

OMA'S TRAMP

We had last seen Oma and Opa briefly on our stop-over in Berlin on the way from Silesia to Weissewarte, when they had been bombed out of their flat and were living in ours. Since then Mutti and Oma had exchanged letters almost daily, Mutti constantly urging them to join us while it was still possible to make the journey. It seems that Oma was willing to come but, as she wrote in a later account of the events that followed:

> The staunch old Opa could not be persuaded. The Nazi propaganda was very powerful and we were made to believe that they had a last minute 'something' which would save Germany and stop the Russians ever entering Berlin. This message was painted in big letters in all prominent places, but I will not say that many people believed it.

Judging by his behaviour, it appears that Opa was one of those who did. Yet Udo clearly remembers his dismay, quite early in the war, when he first heard Hitler had invaded Russia; already then he had expressed his doubts that Germany could win the war. By now he was sixty-seven and had, I think, invested too much in his commitment to Hitler as Germany's saviour to be able to abandon it and face reality. To admit that he had blindly supported a man who, far from saving, had destroyed Germany would be too humiliating to bear – and this, before the story of the concentration camps had even broken. I think Opa's instinct for mental self-preservation made him cling to his Nazi hopes far longer than common sense dictated and to insist on going dutifully to his office at the other end of Berlin, even when the transport system had collapsed.

He was not alone in maintaining his 'head in the sand' position. The population of Berlin were given no hint of the catastrophe in store for them. On 17 April 1945, three days before the artillery bombardment started, Hitler was still issuing statements to his soldiers that 'He who in this hour does not do his duty is a traitor'; the zoo was still open to the public and the Berlin Philharmonic played its last concert on 16 April, suitably including *Götterdämmerung* in its programme.

Oma starts her story with the terrific air-raids which, from the early part of April, were almost continuous:

> No one undressed or got into bed at night for at least a fortnight. We sat mostly in the cellar, often hand in hand, sure that our end had come. Then one morning, about 20 April, soldiers came along telling everyone to open all their windows – not that there was much glass left in them – they were going to blow up all their ammunition. They said the Russians were only half a mile away and anyone that wanted to get away must go now. We didn't know what to do. Some of the Fauststrasse people said, 'We must stop in our homes,' others packed what they could and ran. At last Opa did agree to go. Neither of us was altogether wholehearted about leaving everything and running away, we thought we'd very likely come back again but, anyway, we went.

Like most German families, we had a little handcart about the size of a large pram and the shape of an old-fashioned hay wagon with rails making up the sides.

Oma and Opa now packed into it strong shoes and warm clothes, a few valuables, like their cutlery, any tinned or packaged

Opa, my grandfather, in London, aged 23

Oma, my grandmother, on her engagement
visit to Germany, 1904

Opa and his brother, Max,
Berlin, 1904

Oma and Opa in London, 1905, probably
their wedding picture

My other grandfather, Fritz, taking my grandmother Olga and his coachman for a drive round the territory he administered for the Prussian Colonization Commission near Tremesno, Posnania, 1910

My father as a cadet at the Naumburg Military Academy, 1918

My mother with her parents in Hyde Park around 1912

Onkel Arno and Oma sight-seeing on a double-decker bus in London, 1911

Onkel Arno, Oma and Miss Connell with my mother on Hampstead Heath, 1911

Oma and my mother during the First
World War

Elsie Hope (Aunty Hopey) at around the
time she became Oma's friend

My mother on holiday in Kettering

'Mr George', Oma's Swiss employer in the
First World War, and his wife. Aunty Hopey
is on the right, his daughter Gabrielle sitting
in front

Aunty Hopey and my mother

Oma, just before she left England in 1919

My mother with Mr Hope *(left)*, landlord of the 'Wat Tyler', just before leaving England in 1919. Was this the coat that inspired my mother to make a similar one for me in 1946?

Oma with me as a baby

Papa, Udo and I on board a steamer bound for a holiday on the island of Rügen

'Papa and his little girl'

Our memorable watermelon experience

My first school photograph, in Fräulein Kesselring's class. I am instantly recognised by my non-conforming hairstyle

The Mahlsdorf unit of the *Kindergruppe*, the most junior arm of the Nazi Party, assembled for a visit to the bedside of wounded Spanish soldiers

An extract from my colourful picture book of anti-Jewish propaganda for six-year-olds – the vicious Jewish landlord evicts a poor German family

Grünstrasse, Köpenick. My grandparents' shop is the one in the middle

Aunty Hopey on a visit to Köpenick in 1922. In the background is Köpenick's best-known landmark, the brewery chimney, where a red flag was hoisted the day Hitler came to power

Onkel Arno, Aunty Hopey, my mother and Oma by the Müggelsee

The Druhm family on the Müggelsee in the *Yoho*

The Druhms in Köpenick, Christmas 1926

Opa on one of his motorbike trips to the Harz Mountains, June 1927

Papa, around the time my mother got to know him

My mother, around the time she got to know Papa

Kätchen Beume
(my future step-mother)
and my mother on a
visit to the Harz

Papa during the war

The Fauststrasse gang celebrating a birthday. We are
all still in touch

Onkel Arno

Jutta and Bernhard Diederichsen's wedding on 20 July 1944, the day of the Generals' Plot to assassinate Hitler

My big day as bridesmaid

The *Männekins*

Oma and Opa in Recklinghausen, shortly after their bolt from the Russian Zone, autumn 1945

My mother, Recklinghausen

Udo and me, Recklinghausen

Dr Kleine and his family

My idea of an English Christmas
(from *The Playbox Annual* 1919)

December 1946. Our last night on German soil, before my mother, Udo and I are 'repatriated' to England

Reg Hyne

Mrs Hyne with her 'company'. Behind them is 'Ni-krow', Reg's ingenious all-in-one studio bed-sitter

Bill Jater, soon to become my step-father

My mother in the uniform of the Control Commission for Germany, Hamburg 1947

Aunty Hopey in Staines High Street

Communicating with the Druids on the cliffs above St Ives

Oma and Opa, back in England, in peaceful retirement at last

My brother Udo as a medical student at Manchester University

At the age of 18 I spent a holiday in
Germany, a mirror image replay of my
mother's trip to England in 1928

Me, while a student at Oxford University

My mother's drawing of Opa,
October 1946

My mother, aged 83, at the
gravestone in memory of my
grandparents, Totnes,
September 1993

food they had left over and a long loaf. 'It was a drizzly morning, not nice for walking,' Oma recalled. 'Near Mahlsdorf we met cows wandering about at a loose end, horses too. Anyone could have had a cow for nothing.'

Their plan was to make for the home of Opa's brother, my great-uncle Max, who lived in Dahlem, a suburb on the south-west edge of Berlin, but they soon realised it was too far to reach in a day. It was at least twenty kilometres as the crow flies and their progress was slowed down by the fact that shells from distant guns had started whizzing overhead. They kept having to leave the cart and run for cover. Years later, looking at the history books I discovered that 11.30 a.m. on 21 April, the day they set off from Mahlsdorf, was the moment the Russian artillery began its bombardment of the capital.

That first day they decided to aim for half way, to a friend who could put them up for the night. They reached their first destination and the friend gladly took them in, but there was far too much war activity screaming overhead for anyone to think of going to bed. They went down to the air-raid cellar, which was just as well as in the night the building received a direct hit. Not only was their friend's flat smashed to a heap, but even the cellar was damaged. When they emerged the next morning they found a policeman standing by the door. Oma asked him if he thought they could get back to Mahlsdorf. 'He thought we had lost our senses. He said, "Between here and Mahlsdorf there is street fighting, Russians everywhere. Do you want to get your stomach ripped open?" So we decided we had better continue on our way to Dahlem.'

The streets were deserted but, as on the previous day, every now and then a shell whizzed past them and they had to take shelter in the entrance to a museum. When they got to Lustgar-ten, a big square in the centre of Berlin, they saw some senior-looking *Wehrmacht* officers standing by some guns, but no soldiers. The officers called them over and told them to get off the streets. 'We said we must get to Dahlem, so they let us go. What else could they do? When we got to the Tiergarten, we saw where the soldiers had been waiting; they were everywhere, hiding. They marvelled to see two old folk like us toddling along with our handcart and gave us some chocolate. The farther we went the eerier it got, with soldiers taking cover everywhere, armed with machine guns or the new German weapon, Panzer Faust.' Oma and Opa had unwittingly stumbled into the *Wehrmacht*'s final preparations for the Battle for Berlin.

They continued like this in a south-westerly direction all day and by about six p.m. were only a street away from Onkel Max. They passed a little wood, about 200 yards long, and there, too, noticed soldiers in hiding behind every tree. 'They shouted at us, "Get indoors, the Russians are nearly here." Russians after all! We had come to West Berlin hoping the invaders would be English or Americans, but now we discovered that the whole of Berlin was surrounded by Russians.' Oma and Opa could see that a last-ditch battle was about to be fought there any minute and heeded the advice. They were just by a brick wall and guessed there was a house behind so Opa bundled Oma over and scrambled over himself, leaving the cart on the pavement. The people who lived there took them into their basement for shelter but when they revealed their destination their hosts cried, 'It's only round the corner. Why don't you make a dash for it? It may be your last chance.' So, as everything seemed quiet for the moment, they got the cart and ran. The officers tried to turn them back again but they protested, 'It's only round the corner.'

The house next to Onkel Max's was the residence of the Japanese ambassador. There was no fence, so they dashed over his lawn and landed in Max's hallway. They didn't need to be let in, as there was no door – the front of the house, once all glass, was open to the elements. Onkel Max was amazed to see them. Besides him and Tante Martha, the old aunt in her eighties who lived with him, there were five other people in the house: Tante Martha's companion Meta, who was about forty and a bank manager, his wife and their two daughters, girls of twenty-six and twenty-three. They had made all the preparations to sit out a siege.

There were several rooms and corridors in the basement and about twelve inches of window above street level. They had brought down mattresses and blankets for themselves and now brought more for Oma and Opa. They had hardly been there an hour when Max came in and said, 'They are here!'

This is how Oma described her first encounter with the Red Army:

Down the stairs they came, four of them. There was a squeaky noise, I didn't know what it was, but the others told me; they had a kind of torch you have to squeeze all the time. They strode over to where we were sitting. The eldest girl had hidden herself in the coal cellar, covered over with a black fur coat. As soon as the Russians saw the other girl, they took hold of her and marched her off along the passage to a little bedroom. They were all four half drunk and had revolvers in their hands. What could we do? I think the next half-hour was the most painful that any of us ever lived through. The poor girl's father walked about with clasped hands, frantic. At last she arrived back to us and her first words were, 'Are you all right?' She wanted to know what we had suffered while she was away. She was so brave and tried to comfort her unhappy parents, but she was a wreck.

Then they were back. The worst kind were the ones with astrakhan busbies and long greeny blue coats. One was a Mongolian, really Asiatic-looking, but I must say he was the least awful of the four. One of them knocked down Tante Martha, then they started going round the house pinching anything they could get their hands on. They took Max's gold watch, shot their revolvers into the cupboards and smashed all the jars of conserves in the pantry. Then they demanded drink and to pacify them Max gave them his lovely wine and liqueur. Then they went away, squeaking their torches the while.

Within an hour another lot walked in and down the stairs. The two girls and Meta had all squeezed through a little trapdoor in the toilet and climbed into the loft. You couldn't really call it a loft as the house was a bungalow with a flat roof, but there was a space underneath, so low that they couldn't even sit up straight. Anyway, that's where they stopped. Every night and every day the soldiers came in, taking our food, tearing open handbags, throwing everything out of every cupboard and drawer. We hardly had time to put things straight before the next lot came. They would always hold their revolvers right up against our necks, or on our chests, while their other hand searched us.

When, in years to come, anything reminded Oma of this ordeal, she could never resist giving a demonstration of the Red Army's system for conducting body searches, especially the poking of their revolvers into their victims' flesh. Her account continues:

A Russian soldier was put on guard at the front door and we were forbidden to stir from the basement. We always trembled in case any of them saw the little trapdoor, for they would have shot the girls and us too, but they never did.

We noticed that at noon every day they changed the guard and there was often half an hour with no one there. That was all the time we had to put food up to the three girls. The little toilet was only about two yards from the front door and the anxiety of those five minutes – I don't think it took longer – cannot be imagined. This was how we did it. We had everything ready, coffee – I say coffee but it was of course that awful, bitter ersatz stuff made from acorns that we drank all through the war – and sandwiches as good as we could manage. As soon as the guard was gone, the men brought up a ladder, the father went up it, Uncle Max handed the food up to him and he put it through into the roof. Opa kept watch. We women were in pangs of fear lest the guard came back before they were finished. I'll never forget the tension, for the guards all had machine guns on their backs, as well as pistols in their hands at all times. This went on for a week. Day and night soldiers tramped down those stairs. If we were lying on our mattresses we had to get up and then the searching, with revolvers on our chests and necks would start again.

During that time in the basement poor old Tante Martha became suicidal. The first time she tried to sneak away with a rope; then I found her with her face, head and shoulders dripping wet, after she tried to drown herself in the bath but couldn't carry it through.

Then, after about a week, Opa saw people in the street for the first time. It had been completely deserted until now, nobody allowed out, no shops open and no bread baked. He also discovered that our guard had gone. Well, we thought, things have changed. We could make a dash for it. In a few minutes we had put our things in the cart, Opa went out to the garden to dig up his gold watch from where he had buried it in an empty condensed milk tin and we were gone. What a mercy, too, for we had no more food.

Before we left the three girls had come down from the roof. They didn't know that freedom had come, but hadn't been able to stay there any longer. They were as black as chimney sweeps and completely stiff through not being able to sit or stand up. We only just saw them, they looked ghastly and could hardly walk. They told us they had had a sharp razor with them and if they had been discovered, would have used that on themselves rather than submit to the Russians.

Oh dear! As we left the house I expected every moment a big filthy hand to grab my collar but we went as quickly as we could and soon found a little path in the bit of wood and then we were away. It was only about ninety miles to you and we thought we could manage it in a week, ten days at most, but we didn't know what hindrances we would meet.

First, in places there were still skirmishes going on. We heard shooting and often had to stop until it was quiet. In these remote parts the soldiers didn't realise that the war was over.

This was Oma's interpretation of the military situation, but it becomes clear from her account, as well as from the history books, that it was she, not the soldiers, who was mistaken. The war was obviously still 'on'. The day it officially ended, 8 May, was still ten days away so that, without realising it, Oma and Opa were legging it through the final scenes of one of its last theatres. At such a confused time it would have been impossible for them, or anyone else, to understand exactly what was happening around them, but it seems that their trek – begun on about 29 April – was roughly in step with the Russian advance towards the Elbe.

Oma's account focuses on the domestic aspects of their expedition, the scavenging and sleeping rough that enabled them to stay alive. It is her throwaway lines that leave no doubt about how close she and Opa were to the action, like her pleasure at finding 'packets of tea in a spot where the fighting had only recently stopped and dead soldiers were lying about', and her comment about them 'often finding useful things' on recent battlefields. Oma only referred to the grisliest sights – like a burned-out tank, with the charred bodies of its crew hanging out – where they had relevance to her own story of survival.

By the same token, Oma only mentions in passing the ransacked villages, not yet restored to order and the women in a village who were all in tears because they had just been raped. What they witnessed was not the war being 'over,' but the shock-waves of its violent climax:

> No shops or bakeries were open, it was a marvel how we managed to feed ourselves. One day we found potatoes all along a road. A cart must have dropped them. We picked up sixteen. Then we saw a woman looking out of her window and asked her if she would cook them for us. We had a lot of help like that.
>
> We came to a village where every shop was smashed and ransacked. Tins of meat were lying on the pavement, what

luck, we picked up seven! But we couldn't just eat tinned meat alone. Further along we saw a woman grovelling in a dry ditch by the wayside. She had found a few packets of biscuit stuff, like Ryvita. We went up to her and she gladly exchanged a few packets of that for two of our tins of meat. Then we went round to a quiet lane, opened a tin somehow with a penknife and some stones and had a really satisfying meal.

Once I saw a big Russian going along with a long German loaf under his arm. I went to him and made him understand that we had nothing to eat. He took a big knife from his pocket and cut the loaf in two and gave me one half. We often got help from the Russian soldiers, they were not all bad.

All this time we never knew where we were going to spend the night. Once we sat on chairs in a kind of summerhouse all night, twice people let us sleep in their air-raid cellars. Once we got such wonderful treatment, it was touching. We had found packets of tea in a spot where the fighting had only recently stopped and dead soldiers were lying about. We often found things like that where there had just been a battle. It was late afternoon, the weather cold and rainy and we were tired and hungry. We saw an old woman at her door and asked her if she would let us make a cup of tea. She invited us in and oh! she couldn't do enough for us. She lived with her two sisters, they were all round about eighty. They made us tea and opened tins of asparagus and fruit and made us a most lovely meal. Then they made us stay there the night. They had a spare bedroom and for the first time since leaving home we slept in a real, comfy bed. They must have felt sorry for us, two old people looking fairly bedraggled by now. Next morning they gave us a nice breakfast. They did it all with such pleasure, I'm sure their deeds were registered in heaven. They said it was their first night without Russians to worry them. We never forgot those three old dears.

After that the weather got bad and Oma and Opa had to sleep

in a field with only their coats to cover them. They had found some potatoes in a shed and an old enamel pot with a hole in it, so they made a fire and tried cooking themselves a potato supper. They couldn't stop the pot leaking and their supper took ages. It was a very cold night and next morning they were stiff and hungry, longing for a cup of tea.

That day turned out disastrously for them. They had gone through a very disturbed-looking village. They had no food left, only their tea, and they came to a house where the door was wide open so they went in. At the end of the passage was a little kitchen where a man was sitting so they asked if they could make themselves a cup of tea. He agreed, so they pulled the cart into the passage. The man had had a terrible night: the Russians had ransacked his house, his wife had run away in terror and still had not returned. But, before they had time to make their tea, a crowd of women came barging into the house; they were Poles who had been working on farms as forced labourers and were on their way home. Oma never got over her indignation at this part of her story:

> They pounced on our cart and took everything, all except my cutlery which was at the bottom in a sack. I saw one take my nice red umbrella and I tried to take it away from her. She pulled and I pulled. Then a young Russian soldier walked in. When he saw what was happening, he took out his big knife, opened it and held it up to my chest, quite close. Of course I had to let go and off they went, about six women, with all we possessed in the world. My fur jacket, Opa's suit, shoes, dresses, everything. After pulling that cart for about ten days there we stood with it empty.

One of Oma's favourite stories, which she had often told us in the Mahlsdorf days, was *David Copperfield*. The part she always dwelt on with extra feeling, so that it became for me the high point of the story, was the scene where the hero is robbed of his luggage and his money, just as he is setting off from London to

Dover, down the Kent Road. When I read the book myself many years later I was surprised to find that this is quite a minor incident in the story. Did Oma make so much of it because she had a premonition that the same thing would one day happen to her? Whether she did or not, I am sure that her and Opa's intimate acquaintance with the book helped them survive their four weeks living rough so well; for the story of David's 'tramp' (the very word Oma uses) – sleeping in haystacks, scavenging for food and meeting a colourful company of characters on the way – reads uncannily like theirs. Take this extract from *David Copperfield*: 'Very stiff and sore of foot I was in the morning, and quite dazed by the beating of drums and marching of troops, which seemed to hem me in on every side . . .' and Oma's 'It was an awful heatwave and so many troops were streaming in. Sometimes we had to sit by the wayside for hours on end to let them go by. They weren't marching but riding in those Russian vehicles drawn by one horse, hundreds and hundreds of them. Sometimes they were full of sleeping soldiers. The dust they made was awful.'

Oma and Opa seem to have taken to the vagrant life so naturally, that it is almost as if they were prepared for it and I can think of no more likely source of their know-how than Dickens. My final reason for believing that *David Copperfield* played a part in their survival is that when at last they had access to English books again, it was the first book they turned to.

Oma's story continues:

The next night we spent in a farmhouse. They gave us bread and *Weisskäse* (cottage cheese) and let us use a room upstairs with a tiny bed and a sofa. The woman warned us that Russians came in every night. She had a granddaughter living with her, aged about fifteen or sixteen. She had dressed this girl, who was luckily not very big, like a ten-year-old in a short dress to her knees and her hair tied up with ribbon. To me she looked queer but up to then it had saved her from the Russian soldiers. We were so tired we went to bed at seven o'clock, I on the sofa and Opa on the bed. We had only been in bed about an hour when we heard heavy steps coming up the stairs. The door opened with a bang and in walked a big soldier. He grinned and said in perfect German: '*Warum sind sie so früh zu Bett gegangen? Haben sie Angst?* (Why have you gone to bed so early, are you frightened?)' I said, 'No, we have walked a long way and are tired.' He grinned some more and went and we had no more intruders that night.

Well, from then on we found many useful things, so many houses had been ransacked by the Russians and their booty scattered over the countryside, perhaps when they realised they wouldn't be able to take it home with them. In the woods we saw sofas, mattresses, featherbeds and pillows, often burst or cut open and feathers all over the place, even on the trees. There were babies' prams, jars of bottled fruit, motor bikes, typewriters, cars, carts, bars of soap, a pile of penknives and what looked like shoes from a shop. Unfortunately, we couldn't find any two that made a pair, but we did find shirts, blouses and jerseys in the road, even a great wholesale 100-metre roll of white silk. We soon got our cart filled again. The roll of silk was a great help to us, we often managed to get food in exchange for a few yards of it.

Around that time we picked up a companion, a young German who lived right on the Dutch/German border and spoke with a strong Dutch accent. He had been in the German army and when it collapsed he just walked off. He got clothes from a farmer and was tramping home, getting out of many danger spots by saying he was Dutch and not letting anyone know he was a German soldier. We stayed together two or three days and he was very helpful to us. In one place we went through country roads where our cartwheels sank into the mud and without his help I don't know how we would have made headway. We were sorry when we had to part from him. But the whole time there were lots of people on the tramp like us.

Then the weather changed. After cold and drizzle we had a heatwave. I couldn't stand the heat in my own clothes and had to wear one of the blouses I had found. [That must have been the bright red one with large yellow and orange cabbage roses on it that Oma was wearing when I spied her moving towards me through the forest. It was so garish, and so out of character with her normally impeccable taste in sartorial matters that after my less-than-kind greeting, I hadn't been able to stop myself remarking on it. '*Oma, die Bluse lacht!* (Oma, your blouse laughs)']

We had many heart-breaking experiences, like trudging miles along a road that came to a dead end, where we couldn't get any further and had to go back, or where a bridge was gone, or a road so damaged that we had to find another route. Another time we were walking along quite a wide main road that was deserted. We saw a big board up with Russian writing and went past it, although we didn't feel very safe. Then we heard a shout. We couldn't see where it came from but all of a sudden a shot whizzed by my ear and scraped my collar. We were obviously not meant to be there and turned back, but we had to go many miles out of our way to find another route.

One little place we went through was rolling in food. The man who kept the grocery store was an active Nazi and had fled. The neighbours broke into the shop and carried off whole sacks of sugar, flour and cereals. We also managed to get a good supper that way. Walking through another village we had noticed a farmyard with Russians in possession. By then I knew the Russian for bread and, never missing a chance, I went in and asked for some. An officer standing by called a soldier and gave him an order. The soldier went into the house and came out with a beautiful silver dish full of what looked like old bread crusts but they were broken rusks. I tipped them into Opa's not very clean hanky but when we got to the place where the Nazi had run off, a kind woman we met added sugar and milk and made them into a lovely supper for us. Breakfast too, for they swelled up so much when they had hot milk on, there was enough. We slept in her air-raid cellar and started off next day feeling quite well. As you can see, I was always the one to take the lead in finding food or dealing with the Russians, never poor Opa.

There were also many people of all nationalities going in the opposite direction to us, mostly Polish forced labourers going home. Many of them had babies and they were just stealing anything they wanted, cooking utensils, horses and carts from the farmers, sometimes with a cow tied on behind. They looked like wild creatures, quite frightening. It was some of them who had stolen all our things.

At last, after nearly two weeks' tramping, we reached the Elbe and a place where we were told we could get a ferry to the other side, where the Americans were. This little place was not much bigger than a village and had only tiny primitive cottages. As we arrived we saw at nearly every door women or girls crying their eyes out. They had had such a terrible night with the Russian soldiers, it was awful to see them.

We had hardly stepped up on to the little landing quay when we were shouted at and ordered off. We tried to find a room for the night – we had money – but oh dear! not a hope. At the backs of the cottages were steps leading down to tiny bits of garden and a pump and, beyond that, a lane with a big barn at the end. Two young men were coming out and asked us if we were looking for somewhere to sleep. They said they had slept there a few nights and it wasn't bad at all; we could take their place, an offer we gladly accepted. The barn had a brick floor but they had put straw down and covered it with some kind of thick black paper they had found there. There was even some food hidden – tins of meat and packets of soup and tea – so we had dropped into luck. We hid our cart and made the acquaintance of a woman in one of the cottages. She was rather dirty and so was her kitchen but she really helped us. We used to give her tins of meat and she would make us nice dinners that we ate sitting on her steps. She even let us use her gas to make tea and that was how we lived for a week. Every day we went down to the quay to see if we could get across. One day a Russian told us we had to have a pass that could only be obtained from the Russian commandant at a place twelve kilometres back the way we had come.

Next day, in atrocious heat, we walked the twelve kilometres. We found the place but the man wouldn't give us a pass. He said they didn't want people to leave their zone. Well, I cried and put on such a moving act that he eventually gave us a pass. It was too late to walk back the same evening so we found someone to give us food and shelter. When we did get back the next day we went straight to the quay and showed the Russian our pass but he told us it was no good, not properly signed. Oh dear! We settled back in our barn. On our last expedition we had found a lot of soap; we hadn't had a change of underclothes for a long time, so in the heat of the day, we took the ones we were wearing off, washed them under the pump and hung them on a fence to dry. It went fine. Even Daddy's top shirts we washed. We couldn't iron them but that didn't matter.

The nights in that barn were dreadful because we were afraid that the Russians would find us. At nights they were always riding about on horseback. They had no idea of anything technical, couldn't ride a bike and many had never even seen a motorbike. They used to steal them from men in the street but then had no idea what to do with them. The one thing they could really do, though, was ride a horse. So in the quiet of the night we'd hear the clip-clop of horses' feet; it would stop at our gate and oh! we used to tremble. They often opened the door and even shone a torch in but they never saw us at the far end with all our black paper. Some nights that happened more than once. The danger was the greater because two young girls used to come and sleep up in the hay loft.

Well, we couldn't see any end to that life. Then, when we had been there about a week a boy told us that two Americans had been sleeping in a loft over the barber's shop for a few days. We went to look for them and found them. They were South Americans, very dark and swarthy. One had been playing in a dance band and he had found the other one just by chance and they had teamed up. They were both anxious to get back to South America and had heard that next day at midday a transport of French soldiers was going to be taken across the Elbe. They were determined to join the party and advised us to do the same.

Next day we had an early meal and went down the quay. Having dragged our cart so far we didn't want to leave it now, but if it was going to prevent us getting over the river we were prepared to leave it. The old woman who had been so good to us came with us and, if we couldn't take the cart, we were going to give it to her.

There we found a big steamer. The Elbe is so wide at this point that you could only just see the other side. We were told that every night some men were swimming over; they must have been very good swimmers. Well, there wasn't a soul about, not on the quay or on the steamer, only the two South Americans sitting behind a chimney. So we just walked on, cart and all, took a seat where we couldn't easily be seen and waited. We sat there for about four hours. Then two armies of French soldiers came on, so many that I didn't believe they could possibly all fit. Some had sacks on their shoulders, boxes, musical instruments tied on their backs with string, some even brought on bicycles. We were soon hidden to view, crammed in by hundreds of French soldiers. Then the ship moved off and the last stage of our journey had begun.

When we got off that boat we were heartily received by American soldiers. They crowded all the French soldiers on to army lorries, also us four civilians and our little cart. But after that we didn't fare very well. It was almost getting dark and, when the Americans found out we were English, they asked us to wait till they got everyone else put up, then they would find us special overnight accommodation. Instead of that, they forgot us and by the time we made our presence known there was no more accommodation to be had. They sent us to a school. We did get a grand supper there out of a field canteen, grand to us, anyway, but they had nowhere to sleep us and could only offer us a classroom with a few iron bedsteads with iron springs but no mattresses. That was where we passed the night.

By now we were only a few miles from you, but next morning when we got ready to look for you, we were given wrong directions and walked all day in vain. It was very hot and by evening we were exhausted. We saw a forester's house and asked for a bed. That was our most disgusting experience. He put us in a loft over a pig sty, with just a bit of straw. The floorboards were so wide apart we could see the pigs and they grunted all night; the smell and the heat were terrible. I did think it shameful of that man to put two respectable old people in such a place. But that was our last bad experience.

The next day we found you; it was 21 May and the first exclamation we got from Katrin was 'Oma, you have got old!'

13

RECKLINGHAUSEN

Seeing Oma and Opa popping out of the forest like that was just about the last thing we had expected. They looked old and battered, maybe, but at least they were alive and apparently in good health. Yet we could only stay together for a few hours. It had needed all Mutti's ingenuity to get our travel permit and she wasn't going to rock the boat by tampering with it any more than she had already.

We therefore held to our plan for leaving Süppling the morning after Oma and Opa arrived. Had they reached us only half a day later, we would have been gone – and without leaving a forwarding address, for the very good reason that we didn't know where we were going. We might well have lost contact with them for ever.

Thankfully that didn't happen and now the problem was quite the opposite: having found them, what were we going to do with them? They couldn't stay at Süppling and we couldn't take them with us. Even if we had a sensible destination and they were included on the permit, they wouldn't have fitted into the car.

Mutti commanded Hans to drive her parents and herself into Tangerhütte. She and Hans returned to Süppling just as it was getting dark; Mutti had located a flat for Oma and Opa to rent until they could join us, whenever and wherever we had established a new base further west. She had also hit on the idea of leaving Udo behind to keep them company. There had always been a special closeness between those three, no doubt as a counter to Mutti's preoccupation with me and my feet. They could use their time together profitably, teaching Udo English. Udo was conveyed to the new flat in Tangerhütte and Mutti said goodbye to them all, giving them strict instructions to stay put there until we re-established contact.

At dawn next morning the car with Mutti, me and as many of our things as would fit headed down the forest track for the last time, Hans at the wheel. My disquiet at leaving the other three behind and at severing the last tangible link with Papa was mixed with relief that something definite was at last happening after the uncertainties of the last few weeks, but also sadness at leaving a place I had come to love so much.

We set off in a westerly direction. Because of the bombed and pitted conditions of the roads and detours wherever bridges had been blown up it was a slow, stop-and-go journey. We drove through the town of Hamelin, I remember, joining a long queue of vehicles at a checkpoint controlling access to the bridge over the river Weser, the entry point to the British zone of occupation. As we approached the Ruhr we passed scenes of massive destruction, with whole towns reduced to rubble.

We were making for Hans's home in the coal-mining town of Buhr, near Gelsenkirchen. For all the changes that bombs and fighting had wrought in its geography, he had no difficulty navigating us to his street and identifying as still standing the block of flats where his family lived. His parents hadn't heard from him for months and had no idea what had become of him in the capitulation. He raced upstairs to present himself and returned minutes later with them in tow to welcome us. His father was a miner, early retired on health grounds. His skin was pale mauve and, even when beaming with pleasure, as now at Hans's safe return, there was something lugubrious about his appearance. Hans's little mother, too, for all her joy at having her son back, looked ill and exhausted.

As Hans had predicted, the pair of them now pressed upon us fulsome offers of hospitality, which Mutti at once accepted. There was a problem, though. Hans was one of five brothers and sisters, several of them married with children. Some of the brothers were also miners so they hadn't been called up and were either still living at home or else their homes had been destroyed in the war. Now they were all gathered at the only home in the family that was still standing, their parents'. I never quite managed to sort out who was who or to count up how many of us were living in the flat. What I do remember is that I – just coming up to my ninth birthday – was allocated to sleep in a toddler's drop-side cot in the flat's only bedroom, while the toddler was relegated to a drawer on the floor. One hot night when I couldn't sleep I counted six adults bundled together in the double bed, with several other bodies dotted about the floor. Mutti joined the party sprawled in armchairs in the sitting-room while another man occupied the bath.

Mutti lost no time in setting off on her first reconnaissance of Recklinghausen, leaving me in the care of Hans's extraordinarily open-hearted family. Within a week she was back, bursting with news. First, she had been snapped up by the British Military Commander of one of the new administrative areas who was screaming for a bilingual secretary. Secondly, so desperate was his plight, that he had even agreed to Mutti's request for a flat to go with the job, though this would take longer to arrange. Thirdly, she had tracked down Dr Kleine to a Catholic hospital in Herten, a few miles from Recklinghausen and had already made an appointment for him to see me.

The headquarters of Mutti's new boss were in Recklinghausen itself, an ancient walled town on the edge of the Ruhr. It had been less intensively industrialised and, perhaps for that reason, less heavily bombed than the Ruhr proper and, as a result, retained a good deal of its pre-war character. Until the promised flat materialised, Mutti had rented us a room in the home of a couple of sweet old ladies and that was where I celebrated my ninth birthday. Mutti managed to make it into a special occasion, too. She produced a bunch of pansies, my favourite flowers, a tiny cake with my name on it in paper and even a really nice present, an autograph book. How did she find something so suitable when she hadn't been near a proper shop for at least a year and commerce had, anyway, come to a complete standstill?

On the way to my appointment with Dr Kleine, Mutti told me what a famous doctor he was, so I didn't expect him to be quite so genial and cuddly as he turned out to be. He pushed my feet around, watched me walk and do my exercises and within a matter of minutes delivered the same opinion as the Breslau doctor. My left foot needed to be operated on urgently. This suited Mutti; she was supposed to be starting her job and having me safely looked after in hospital would give her a bit more time to make arrangements for my care.

A few days later I was delivered to the hospital's only children's ward. It stretched as far as the eye could see, with patients ranging in age from tiny babies to young adults and in diagnoses from enlarged tonsils to chronic palsies and severe deformities. A few beds away from mine lay a girl of seventeen suffering from, as she explained when I went to talk to her, a mysterious atrophy which had gradually deprived her of all movement. She talked about her condition with complete resignation.

The ward's most striking feature, though, was that the heads of at least half the patients were swathed in heavy bandages in the style of Florence Nightingale's patients at Scutari hospital, and it reeked of antiseptic. The reason was not, as one might suppose, a proliferation of head-wounds sustained in battle, but an outbreak of head-lice.

About the operation itself, all I remember is being helped on to a table in the operating theatre and made to lie down. A lot of people with masks over their faces peered down at me; I guessed that the one with particularly kind eyes was Dr Kleine. A pair of hands grabbed each of my arms and as a voice commanded me to start counting down from ten an ether pad was pressed over my nose. I counted ten, nine, eight ... the next thing I knew, I was back in the ward, with a fat, damp plaster on my leg.

I was lying there dozing, not fully conscious, when I overheard some unknown people talking somewhere near my bed. Suddenly, something one of them said shocked me into full consciousness. The speaker was explaining that the frontier between the American and Russian zones had, without warning, been altered. In return for a foothold in Berlin, the western Allies had given the Russians a strip of territory west of the Elbe. The people living there had gone to bed under American occupation and woken up to find the Russians in charge. I didn't need to be told that Süppling and the area around it were included in the swap. Oma and Opa were back under Russian captivity, and this time so was Udo.

I went numb. Until I heard that news I had been quite confident that the last plan we had all made in Süppling would eventually come to pass; we would get another home and one day would all be reunited, including Papa. That certainty enabled me to keep up my spirits. Now its collapse left me in despair.

The hospital was run by nuns. Visiting hours were for two hours in the afternoon of every third Sunday. Luckily – or perhaps unluckily – for me, my first Sunday as a patient was a third, visiting Sunday. Until that day, I had managed to keep a grip on myself and not disgrace myself in any way but now every ounce of my *Mut* (courage) deserted me. Like all the other children, I was agog, waiting for the moment the visitors were allowed in, but the moment I saw Mutti enter the ward I burst into tears and continued sobbing till visiting time was up. It wasn't long before Mutti was fighting back the tears herself. A nun came up to her and whispered that it was precisely this kind of behaviour, apparently not unknown on the ward, that made them doubt the wisdom of allowing any visitors at all, ever. I was certainly a bad case, for the moment I woke up the following morning I was off again, and the morning after that it was the same story. I didn't even know why I was doing it and on the rare occasions that, with enormous effort, I managed to control my tears, it only needed someone to speak to me, or to look at me kindly, to set me off again.

Every morning the commanding figure of the ward sister, negotiating her course in a billowing white habit like a ship in full sail, conducted Dr Kleine and his entourage on a ward-round; every morning as they passed my bed and Dr Kleine smiled at me, I dissolved into tears again.

I was supposed to stay in the hospital for four weeks, but can't have been much more than half way through my stretch when a new nun came up to my bed one day with an elephantine-looking leather shoe which she tried to fit over my plaster cast. Then she got me out of bed and had me hobbling up and down the ward. That evening she reappeared with a wheelchair. She told me to get dressed and started packing up my things. Then she made me get into the wheelchair, handed me my bag and pushed me out of the ward, down a lot of corridors to a lift, and then out of a side door into a courtyard. There an expensive-looking black car was waiting and the nun helped me, clutching my bag, into the back seat. What was going on? I had ceased to care and was just mechanically doing what I was told.

Suddenly Dr Kleine appeared. He thanked the nun, got into the car and drove out of the hospital gates. As we bowled along the roads towards Recklinghausen he explained that he was taking me to his home to complete my convalescence in the care of his wife. His tone was matter-of-fact, as though this was a normal part of the service. Numb and zombie-like though I had by now managed to make myself, just to stop crying all the time, it dawned on me that this escape must be part of a careful plot involving the nuns and Mutti as well. As usual, I was the last to be told.

The Kleines lived in a villa on the outskirts of Recklinghausen, only a ten-minute walk from the ladies where Mutti still had lodgings. It was set on a slope overlooking a beautiful garden. It was arranged in terraces, with rambler roses and other climbers trained in bowers and archways to connect the different levels and areas of cultivation. There were masses of roses and other kinds of flowers I hadn't seen before. In the orchard miniature espalier apple and pear trees promised an abundance of fruit at harvest-time. Everywhere in the house were flowers, arranged by Frau Kleine. The family had two daughters, Liselotte, a medical student, and Dorothea, studying for her *Abitur*. As Liselotte was away from home I was given her room, a large and grown-up looking bedsitter, perhaps not quite in the Jutta league, but a big improvement on some of the places I had slept in recently, particularly the drop-side cot and the Scutari-like hospital ward where, incidentally, I too had succumbed to the head-lice epidemic.

In such a soothing environment I stopped crying for good. The Kleines took me into their family so naturally, with so little fuss, that I quickly felt entirely comfortable with them. Their house-keeper, Leni, became my special friend and let me help her in the kitchen, the house and the garden. There was just one aspect of their arrangements I couldn't understand. Why did Leni have to eat her meals by herself in the kitchen, instead of in the dining-room with everyone else? I asked her about it but her explanation made no sense to me whatever.

I lived at the Kleines for several weeks, far longer than was necessary for my convalescence, but they kept me on so that Mutti could go to work. In August we were allocated a large furnished flat on Elperweg, in the same part of Recklinghausen, and I moved back with her to sleep and to spend the week-ends but stayed with the Kleines while she was at work.

When we were on our own together it was easy for Mutti and me to sink into depression, worrying about what was happening to the others in the family and frustrated that we had no way of contacting them. As we now had an agreeable home, Mutti decided to invite Tante Kätchen, whose home was also in the British zone, to come and cheer us up. With her effervescent

•

personality, she certainly helped take our minds off our troubles. A disastrous harvest throughout the British zone that year meant that we had less to eat than at any time in the war. Coming from the country where there was enough to eat, Tante Kätchen refused to accept our level of deprivation. One day she went for a long walk into the country on the outskirts of Recklinghausen and that evening asked me to accompany her on a return expedition to some of the more interesting spots she had discovered. As it got dark we set off into the countryside, each carrying an empty bag; when we reached the fields I watched in horror as Tante Kätchen, normally so *comme il faut*, metamorphosed into a shameless praedial larcenist, helping herself to potatoes, carrots, cauliflowers and turnips. She must have been very disappointed that I proved to be such a pathetic accomplice. Though I felt morally obliged to join in the stealing, I was much too frightened of getting caught to apply myself to the task in the spirit it required. To tell the truth, given the choice between starving and stealing, I would have every time have chosen to starve.

In September 1945, after a five-month break, I started going to school again. Considering how recent the capitulation still was, that several school buildings were still out of action due to war damage and the whole curriculum needed to be sanitised of Nazi content, the speed and efficiency with which the Recklinghausen education system started up again is remarkable.

For reasons I cannot now remember, I was initially enrolled at a Catholic school. Its ornate gilt and plaster entrance hall and corridors were cluttered with crucifixes and other religious statuary that meant nothing to me. In every classroom, the wall space above the teacher's desk, which had in all my previous experience been filled by portraits of the *Führer*, was here taken up by plaster statues of the Virgin Mary. Was this really a school? I felt like a fish out of water. I had my first introduction to the Lord's Prayer and the Creed and, though I learned to say them, parrot fashion, they made no sense to me either. Thankfully, I was transferred to a secular primary school as soon as it opened its doors again.

As the local senior school had been destroyed, it was arranged that our building should serve two schools simultaneously, Cox and Box fashion. The juniors had the building in the mornings, the seniors in the afternoons. Nothing was allowed to be left in any classroom when our session ended. If it was, by the following day even something like a jam jar of flowers had invariably disappeared or been destroyed.

Our classroom was packed; the girls all got seats, but the narrow space between the back row and the end wall became a promenade area for the overflow of boys. I once counted seventy-three of us, but within a few weeks the number was down to something in the fifties and everyone had a seat.

Our teacher was Fräulein Buchholz, another product from the Fräulein Vogt mould. She had strong features, freckles and straight, sandy-coloured hair pulled back into a bun. While keeping perfect order she offered – compared with other schools I had known, by now amounting to about eight – an interesting, even challenging education. To achieve her impressive discipline Fräulein Buchholz stalked around the classroom casually trailing a slim bunch of willow switches. Anyone seen talking or doing anything else out of order invited a nasty surprise in the form of a sudden sting across the back. Worse demeanours meant coming up to the front for a ritual swat on the palms of the hands. Even a thoroughly meek child like me came in for a share of *Kloppe* (wallops), leaving me with swollen hands or red weals across my back for several days afterwards. During my whole year in her class she did not miss a single day of school.

As in all my previous schools, most of our time was spent on the Three Rs, but Fräulein Buchholz also provided my first exposure to subjects like geography, local history, poetry, art and religious education, which she taught delightfully.

Under Nazism it was, of course, not unknown for people to

combine support for the church with support for Hitler. There were even attempts to forge an official link between the Protestant church and the Nazi Party, with the pastors who participated adopting a style of clerical garb that bore an unmistakable resemblance to a Nazi uniform. However, if there was one family that had made no attempt to combine the two traditions it was mine. Papa's distaste for religion bordered on the fanatical. He even made a point of collecting anti-clerical jokes which were, I suspect, blasphemous. It may have been his way of rebelling against the clerical relatives who helped to make his childhood such a misery after his parents died, but whatever the reason, I had been brainwashed into his prejudice, and now felt positively disloyal at enjoying Fräulein Buchholz's exposition of Bible stories so much. I had never heard of Noah's Ark, Moses in his basket or Joseph and his many-coloured coat before and couldn't get enough of them now.

Another enjoyable item on Fräulein Buchholz's timetable was singing. She taught us songs that were quite new to me and that made a nice change from the perennial diet of well-known *Volkslieder*. It was to be many years before I discovered they were choruses from Mozart operas.

The highlight of our morning at school came at break-time when Fräulein Buchholz went out of the room for a minute and returned trundling a large zinc churn with one hand and carrying a metal ladle with the other. This was our subsidised 'soup kitchen', organised by the occupation force to ensure school-children had a minimum nutritional intake. We each brought a metal cup to school and now queued up for our ladleful of whatever was going that day. It was incomprehensible to me that our conquerors were doing this – going out of their way to prevent us from starving. It didn't seem right or proper. You were supposed to slay your enemy, wipe him out, not take care of him. But whatever my moral scruples about accepting handouts – and they were quite genuine – they didn't prevent me doing my best to be first in line for my ladle of cold cocoa.

The greatest happiness by far associated with my excellent new school was making a friend, my first real one, other than Udo, since leaving Mahlsdorf more than two years before. Marie-Louise Friederichs had startling blue eyes, a big grin and lived just round the corner from me. We walked to school together, did our homework together and if there was any time left – not usually the case for any pupil of Fräulein Buchholz, who was a demon at setting homework – played together.

Throughout this time, the one problem permanently on Mutti's mind was how she was going to get Udo, Oma and Opa out from under the Russians. There were still no postal or telephone communications between the two zones and, from the end of May when we left the Tangerhütte area to the autumn of 1945, we had received no sign of life from them, or they from us. As secretary to the commanding officer of the local occupation force, Mutti was about as close to the corridors of power as it was possible for a German to be. Her boss and the other members of our local military government couldn't have been better disposed towards her yet, beyond giving Mutti an introduction to the Russian delegation to the British Military Zone, even they were unable to help. Mutti went to see the Russians and tried everything she could think of with them, from making a written application to attempting to bribe them with her jewellery, but she got nowhere on that front either. She discovered that it was a strict condition of the Potsdam Agreement between the Eastern and Western Allied powers that, once the map of post-war Europe was in place, there were to be no further population movements in either direction. None of the official delegations she approached was about to risk new political ructions by breaking the agreement and there seemed no prospect of ever, legally, getting them to join us.

Then Mutti heard of a neighbour called Herr Drenhaus, a teacher who was in a similar position to ours, with a wife and son stuck in East Berlin. He was preparing himself for the only method that appeared to have the slightest chance of success in getting them out, self-help. He proposed to enter the Russian zone underground and to smuggle them back over the border with him. Mutti got an introduction and asked him if he would make contact with our three in Tangerhütte, not far out of his way, and if possible, bring them back. She offered him all her jewellery and money in return. Herr Drenhaus promised to do his best but refused a reward, whether he succeeded or not.

By the time Herr Drenhaus set off on his expedition, we and millions of other Germans had been forced to accept that our country's cold-war division into two had become an irreversible fact of life. Although Herr Drenhaus was our only hope, neither of us could feel very optimistic about his chances of success and, as we gave him our farewell wishes, we had grave doubts that we would ever see him again, let alone his family and, least of all, ours.

14

COPING WITH DEFEAT

At this time, when my fears for the safety of the other members of the family were never far below the surface, another worry was continually gnawing away at the back of my mind. We had lost the war and were living under enemy occupation. It was humiliating. It was important to me that I should be able to go on thinking well of myself, but under our new circumstances, I didn't know how to set about it, what to think or how to behave.

In many ways, losing the war hadn't turned out as terrible as expected. The worst defeat scenario I had visualised, that we would all be wiped out, hadn't happened; the occupation forces I had seen were restrained and civilised to a fault. We may have had little to eat, but the rubbish was being collected, trains were running and schools had reopened. With a few exceptions, like the disappearance of Nazi paraphernalia from all public – and more especially, all private – places, life in Recklinghausen was probably more normal and orderly than since the first year or two of the war.

Our first American 'liberators' had hardly triumphed over us or rubbed our noses in our defeat at all; they were friendly and easy-going, they smiled at us, as though bearing us no grudge. Being conquered by them was baffling, but one could get used to it.

At around the time we arrived at the Ruhr, the division of

Germany into distinct military and administrative zones of occupation was being finalised and, overnight, the Americans pulled out of Recklinghausen. The British liberators who took over were much more as we had expected conquerors to be. They were tight-lipped and snappy, as if struggling to control their anger against us. Yet in their own way they were even more mystifying than the 'Amis'. For example, take their parades in central Recklinghausen. You could hardly call them 'shows of strength', when the centrepiece was a column of soldiers in skirts, with bandsmen dressed in Neanderthal-style animal skins and an officer striding out in front for a display of baton-twirling about as menacing as a circus-master's. How could our iron-hearted *Wehrmacht* have been brought to its knees by such a bunch of cissies? They didn't even seem embarrassed to let us see how unmanly they were, on the contrary, they were positively showing off! They must be *verrückt*.

Whenever I saw them marching around Recklinghausen with their relaxed, unhurrried strides, skirts or no, I compared them with the parades at the *WE Lagers*, with Papa taking the salute. 'Call that marching!' I would say to myself. 'They're not even *zackig* (smart).'

Though I found them so perplexing, I concluded that there must be more to the British than first appearances suggested. They certainly weren't all bad. It must be they who were supplying our daily 'soup kitchen' at school, I thought. As for the only member of their force with whom I became personally acquainted, there couldn't be a nicer man, for all his shyness and reserve. Captain Chapman was a twenty-four year-old commando and, despite his extraordinary dark-green beret with what looked like a shaving-brush sticking out at the side, very good looking. He had been to Germany before the war on a bicycling holiday and, when he got to know Mutti at work, asked her to introduce him to a family where he could practise his German. Mutti didn't know anybody else, so invited him to practise on us, including, while she was in Recklinghausen, Tante Kätchen. Seeing how we were living made him so concerned about the lack of vitamins in my diet that when he went to England on leave he brought me back a bottle of Ribena.

Thus, a new worry for me was that if the enemy was really okay, as seemed to be the case, odd, perhaps, but not monsters, then why had we been fighting them? Did it, could it, mean that our war effort had been a mistake? That our crusade to spread Germany's superior culture around Europe, fighting everyone in sight, had been silly?

I frightened myself thinking such outrageous thoughts. Of course there must have been reasons why we had tried to conquer Europe, reasons I was too young to understand, but that Papa and people like him knew about. But in that case, why had *das Schicksal*, destiny, not come up with the promised victory? And if I now started having doubts about some aspects of Nazi ideology, and found myself wanting to be friends with our enemies, was I being a *Verräter*? A traitor? Selling out on my *Deutsche Treue*? I couldn't begin to fathom answers to such questions.

The decision I had made at Süppling at the moment of defeat – that I would outwardly do what our new masters wanted, but inwardly go on thinking my own (Nazi) thoughts – certainly helped me cope with my problem, but only up to a point. It protected me from total humiliation, but provided no guidance at all on how to tackle the daily problems of life under enemy occupation.

While I can't have been the only child in Germany grappling with such thoughts, they weren't being brought out into the open. I never heard anyone discuss them. And there wouldn't have been any point asking Mutti what to think; a pragmatist to her fingertips, her mind didn't work like mine, brooding and thinking about right and wrong all the time. She just got on with life, making the best of every situation as it came along.

I wished I could dismiss my worries, or that they would go away. Instead, I was having to confront them every day in very direct ways. For example, I was living in a comfortable flat, courtesy of the military government; Mutti's salary came from the same source. I was having my bread buttered, handsomely, by people whom I still felt obliged to categorise as my enemies, though I didn't feel that way about them at all.

Mutti had told her prospective employers most of the truth about herself, but to make sure of getting – and keeping – her job she had changed just a few little details, like the timing of some key events. She had, for example, changed the time since her last contact with Papa from 'three weeks' to 'three years'. She said that was when he had been reported missing in Russia. She impressed on me that I must stick to this story too, that I must never mention to anyone the *WE Lager* episode, Papa's Nazi Party and Hitler Youth connection, or her – or indeed, my own – radio work with the *Kurze Welle*.

I doubt if, in those chaotic first weeks after the war ended, Mutti's boss had any way of checking up on her story. Even if he had, I doubt that he would have bothered. Everybody was lying about their past and he was probably far too relieved at finding a competent – and attractive – bilingual assistant who could help him in his task of ruling a large chunk of Germany, most of it in ruins, to make difficulties for himself by excessive prying. Mutti wasn't to know that, however. She was convinced that if the truth came out she would lose her job and home and be arrested for having actively supported Nazism. Those interrogations by the American military police had really frightened her. Papa had not told her much about what he was doing in the war and the interrogation had made her fear it could have been something irregular. Whatever it was, she was determined to dissociate the rest of the family from it – and therefore from Papa. The knowledge that I had a share in the responsibility for our safety – and my fear that I might let the truth slip out – weighed heavily on me.

We were of course not the only Germans at the time trying to shed an embarrassing past. Most people had something to conceal. It was remarkable how, in a population that had given every appearance of being unanimous in supporting Hitler and Nazism, you could, almost overnight, no longer find a former

Nazi, for love or money. They had disappeared off the face of the earth. Had they been lying all along, or were they lying now?

Apart from some big show trials, like the ones at Nürnberg, official policy was to round up the most important and fanatical Nazis – if they hadn't made it to South America – and put them in prison for a spell. Even after their release they had to pass a 'denazification board', which ranked them into categories, according to their seniority in the Nazi Party and the seriousness of their misdemeanors, and then deprived them of certain privileges until they were deemed to have been reformed. But were these perhaps not the lucky ones, forced to confront their Nazi beliefs and be exposed to alternative views of society? That must have helped them no end to adjust to the new order. But what about the rest of us? Children like me, for example? We got no help at all with understanding why what we had been told to believe before was suddenly wrong. Why, overnight, the Hitler supporters who had been 'goodies' under the old regime had suddenly become the most despicable 'baddies'.

I could have done with a spell of 'denazification', but it wasn't forthcoming. Hitler and Nazism had become taboo subjects, there was nobody I could talk to about them. They weren't even mentioned at school. However, until I had a better reason than expediency for renouncing my beliefs, I decided to stick to the policy I had adopted in Süppling, conforming outwardly, but inwardly continuing to 'keep the faith'. It was already becoming clear, however, that there would have to be a few adjustments, here and there, in what I believed.

Only Papa could have released me from this obligation. He had been the authority in our family and had imposed Nazism on us as part of that authority. Udo had refused to swallow it and in so doing had jeopardised his relationship with his father. I had lapped it up and as a result our relationship was perfect. But unless I had his permission to throw it overboard, I was going to be stuck with it in some form or other for the rest of my life.

One day Marie-Louise and I were dong errands for our

mothers, including a visit to the post office. As we came out we noticed a horrific poster stuck on to the door. It showed a heap of emaciated bodies, their heads looking more like naked skulls covered only with skin, and holes where there should have been eyes. How could anyone put up something so repellent in public? Then we read the text. The pictures claimed to show what the Allied forces had found when they reached a camp somewhere in Germany, where Jews had been imprisoned, starved and gassed to death. The poster stated that several millions had been treated in this way.

I cast my mind back over what I knew about Jews. The only one I had ever known, Udo's friend Günter in Mahlsdorf, had been a nice, gentle little boy; Udo had liked him better than any of the other children around the *Hof* and had never again had such a satisfactory friend. Apart form Günter, I had occasionally seen people with yellow stars sewn on to their clothes, mostly when I went into Berlin to go to the Charité or the *Rundfunk* to broadcast. They usually looked ragged and run-down and tended to creep about as though trying not to draw attention to themselves, but I never gave them much thought; they weren't anything to do with me. I knew that Jews were 'baddies' that I wasn't supposed to like, but I didn't understand why and when Papa gave us that horrible book that was meant to provide an explanation, I didn't even finish it. It didn't seem relevant to anything else going on in my life, including the Nazism I embraced.

Nothing I had heard about Jews had prepared me for what these posters were saying and I searched desperately for another explanation of the pictures. Had our conquerors, who appeared so mild and kind, really been much more cunning than we had given them credit for? Were they putting out this story to break our spirit and make us hate ourselves? To make the rest of the world hate us? It didn't sound very convincing. The pictures were photographs. Those were real bodies, not actors, Yet I couldn't think of a better explanation. Someone, somewhere had treated people like that. Who could it possibly have been?

15

UDO'S STORY

One afternoon at the end of that September, I was on my way home from the Kleines, playing 'Lines and Squares' on the highly suitable Elperweg pavement. I noticed a little group of people with scruffy-looking luggage loitering uncertainly outside our building. Even for those deprived times they looked particularly down-and-out; I hoped they were nothing to do with me. Then I saw who they were – Udo, Oma and Opa! I raced up the road to throw my arms round them in turn and hug and kiss them. Herr Drenhaus had brought them – and his own family – and they hadn't long arrived. I let them into the flat. Mutti was due home from work any minute and got her first inkling of the news when she saw Udo tearing down the road towards her. We went on celebrating our reunion until late into the night, listening to the tribulations which had begun for them within hours of our leaving Süppling. Herr Drenhaus popped in to introduce his wife and little son to us. He had bruises and a nasty wound on his face where a Russian soldier had struck him during one of their many abortive attempts to cross the border, but nothing could conceal his joy. As before, Herr Drenhaus refused any reward for what he had done for us.

That night Udo and I had to share a bed. We fought and kicked each other for most of the night, but what happiness to have him back to fight with! Next day I got out the *Männekins* and we started putting them through what had happened to each of us during the months of our separation. Compared to Udo's adventures, my life had been pathetically tame.

The little flat that Mutti had rented for them in Tangerhütte before we left was really nice, Udo told me, quite modern by local standards and they soon got themselves organised for living there. They had only been there for a few days when, to their astonishment, they received a letter from Papa; they had no idea how it had found its way to them. It came from the hospital of an American-prisoner-of-war camp in Wolmirstedt, a town about forty kilometres away, and in it Papa asked one or all of us to visit him. He can't have known that Mutti and I had gone, or Oma and Opa arrived. Anyway, Udo was the obvious person to go.

There was only one way to get there, by a makeshift kind of public transport that was running between various towns in the area; it consisted of a tractor towing a farm wagon fitted with primitive seats. A few days later, equipped with sandwiches and a letter from Oma and Opa, Udo was put on to this contraption in the direction of Wolmirstedt. It chugged along extremely slowly and the trip took several hours.

Udo managed to track Papa down in his hospital and spent part of the day with him. 'It was a strange meeting,' he recalled years later. 'Papa wasn't in bed but he had his leg in a big bandage. He had no idea what was going to happen to him. He was no longer so frightening and I felt a lot of loyalty towards him. He gave me the address of some German people he knew in Milwaukee, Wisconsin, in case we all got separated and the Tante Kätchen rendezvous didn't work out; he also gave me a letter for Oma and Opa.' Udo couldn't remember much more than that.

On the way back to Tangerhütte he noticed that the tractor/bus was being shadowed by a German policeman on a motorbike. He hadn't been home long when there was a knock at the door and this same policemen and some others came into the flat. They demanded to know where Udo had been and if any of them knew the whereabouts of Oberleutnant Thiele. Though Udo can't remember the exact lie he told them, he didn't reveal to them where Papa was and also managed to find an opportunity to flush Papa's letter – unread – down the lavatory. They were all three very frightened at the discovery that they were being watched like this, especially as they didn't have the faintest idea why. It just didn't make sense for the German police, working under the auspices of the American occupation force, to be looking for Papa when he had already been in their custody for at least a month.

The mystery deepened the following day when they had arranged to go to Süppling with a rented horse and cart to fetch the rest of our belongings. They found everything in order, but 'there was a very strange atmosphere at Süppling,' Udo recalled. 'None of the people there would talk to us. Everyone just stared at us in hostility. There was something so sinister in the air, I didn't understand it, but I have never forgotten it.'

On their way back to town another policeman on a motorcycle suddenly appeared behind them:

We were going along, clip-clop, clip-clop in this horse and cart, so slowly that he had to keep making U-turns and go off and then come back again. We were really mystified but also scared. When we got into Tangerhütte he told us to go directly to the police station, where they took all our stuff from us, saying they had to search it. Fortunately, we had thrown away the remains of Mutti's forgery kit.

The next day three or four policemen came and started interrogating us again about Papa's whereabouts. Their leader was a horrible-looking fellow in civilian clothes, called Koch – I've always remembered that name; he must have been something like a CID man. Again we said we didn't know, but then they suddenly arrested Opa and took him away with them. We had no idea why, and you can imagine how scared Oma and I were feeling by now. Then this Koch man came back and told us to get out of the flat. He said we must move into a place across the road. When we went to look at it with him our hearts sank. It consisted of one very small room, about half the size of an ordinary bedroom with a single bed, a cupboard, a small table and chair and a little sofa with high curved sides, like a Victorian settee, that could just about seat two dolls. Oma protested and asked, 'Where am I going to cook for my grandson?' Herr Koch took us outside to a *Waschküche* (boiler room) off the yard and pointed to a huge vat with a wood oven underneath, big enough to cook for a regiment. That was it. There was nothing we could do.

Their new quarters turned out to be the end room of a private flat, whose owners weren't best pleased at the intrusion forced on them. 'It was really unpleasant living there,' Udo told me, 'a primitive old house, outside privy and no running water. I had to sleep bunched up on that little settee and for the whole time we lived there, at least four months, the people never spoke to us.'

Oma managed to make friends with a nice family living a few doors away. Downstairs lived an old couple and upstairs their daughter, who had lost her husband in the war, and her two children. They kept house together in the parents' kitchen and let Oma use the daughter's upstairs one. Udo couldn't remember whether Oma paid them or bartered something in return, but anyway, they went there every day to cook their meal and, because there was mutual good will, the arrangement worked well.

Udo later discovered that throughout this period with no word of Opa, Oma had been in such despair that she was contemplating suicide. Her plan was to somehow convey Udo to Tante Kätchen and then drown herself in the local river. However, one day, before she had a chance to implement this plan, there was a knock on the window of the little room. They looked up and, to their delight, saw Opa peering through. He was looking much thinner. Udo can't say for how long he had been away but thinks it was the best part of six weeks.

Opa was no wiser than before about why he had been taken away and imprisoned in Stendal, Tangerhütte's nearest city. Ostensibly it was to help the police find his son-in-law. Yet the most curious aspect of the whole affair was that, while Opa was doing his stretch there, whom should he bump into one day in the exercise yard, but Papa himself. Whenever I try to visualise the scene of them spotting one another in that setting the only reaction that would seem to be appropriate would have been to burst out laughing, but they were both too frightened to indulge in such spontaneity and pretended not to know one another. Oma and Opa never discovered the reason for this whole curious episode and it was to take another forty-eight years before, in the course of my research for this book, I came up with a possible explanation.

Once Opa reappeared from his stint in Stendal jail, life in Tangerhütte improved. He started teaching Udo English, a two-hour lesson every day. Opa had somehow got hold of an English school book called *The Island Realm*, by Francis Webster. It told the story of a German boy who goes to an English boarding school, learns English sports and is invited home for the holidays by one of the other boys. Udo says they went over the text word for word:

> By the end, I knew that book off by heart. Then Opa made up a story for me about a boy called Percy who goes to sea as a cabin boy, travels all over the world and has all sorts of adventures. He started in Hamburg, then stopped in London, Gibraltar, Brindisi, Alexandria and other ports in the Mediterranean, taking in the Pyramids and other sights on his travels. As he told it to me in English, I had to write it all down in a notebook. Oma taught me English songs and poems.

As Oma and Opa only ever spoke English to one another, Udo's conditions for learning English could hardly have been more ideal, a combination of background 'immersion' and intensive formal teaching. 'Within a very few weeks I was quite fluent.'

No doubt Percy's adventures owed quite a lot to *Treasure Island* and the other books Oma, Opa and Mutti had read together in Köpenick, but Opa had always been something of a bookworm. Years later, when Udo was a medical student, he spent a holiday travelling round the Mediterranean on a tramp steamer that also, by pure chance, set out from Brindisi. 'I remembered everything he had told me about the places I was visiting and it was uncanny how accurate he had been, seeing that the furthest he ever got himself was the Matterhorn.'

As they had no idea how long it might be before they heard from Mutti, they prepared themselves for a long stay. They would need firewood, so Opa bought some big logs and he and Udo started sawing and splitting them up with an axe. According to local practice, there was only one correct way to store one's firewood, in a big round stack in one's yard, and even Opa and Udo succeeded in putting up one of these constructions. 'One started from the centre, gradually working out to a circle about eight feet across. Then one built it up in layers to about eight feet, going into a cone on top so that water could run off. Every day we spent a couple of hours chopping and stacking wood, Opa and I. I really enjoyed that, it was fun and I became very adept at it,' Udo recalled. Their friendly neighbours had a big plot of land and let Opa start growing vegetables there, as well as his favourite crop, tobacco.

They were just starting to make the best of their circumstances, trying not to be too depressed, when they woke up one day to a lot of noise, troops marching and tanks rumbling. They noticed great red flags up everywhere. Overnight, without a word of warning, the Americans had withdrawn and the Russians marched in. It must have been the day that the post-war division of Europe agreed between Stalin, Roosevelt and Churchill at the Yalta Conference, and later finalised at Potsdam, was put into effect. Regardless of whose army had first occupied the area, it had been designated for the Russian sphere of influence. If the people living there had been warned of their fate they would have panicked and stampeded to the West, so the switch was done surreptitiously.

While the sudden appearance of Russian soldiers on the street obviously came as a shock, it was a relief to discover that they were perfectly behaved. 'One saw them striding about, but there was no interference of any kind,' Udo recalled. The contrast between these Russians and their brothers with whom Oma and Opa had their encounter in our great-uncle Max's Berlin cellar is easily explained. As the invasion and conquest of Germany was coming to its climax, the Red Army, one of the most disciplined in the world, was given the green light to run riot, rape and pillage. Once the war was over, discipline gradually returned to normal, when soldiers found guilty of misbehaviour, including rape, were shot.

One of the first things the Russians did in Tangerhütte, as in other places, was to put up memorials to fallen comrades, each one individually named and decorated with a red star. As these were the first Russians of any sort sighted in the area, let alone any involved in fighting, the monuments were more a symbolic statement of Russian power than a shrine to local casualties. 'The town looked ridiculous covered in red flags, hammers and sickles and all these memorials,' Udo remembered.

The only truly menacing aspect of having Russians in control was that the three of them were now separated from Mutti and me by a frontier – soon to become the Iron Curtain – through which no transport, goods, mail or personnel of any kind were allowed. Oma and Opa were thoroughly alarmed by the situation but Udo, just twelve at the time, did not remember being unduly anxious or unhappy; he just carried on with his life, quite prepared to spend the winter there.

After a while they started making daily visits to the police station to try to get back the luggage that had been confiscated when they collected it from Süppling. Eventually they did get most of it but the item Udo had looked forward to more than any other, that Mutti had left for him in one of the boxes as a special treat, had disappeared. It was a tin of hard chocolate, the kind given to fighting soldiers as their iron ration.

Life went on peacefully with their daily routine of English lessons, chopping wood and walks into the forest. One day the local swimming pool opened up and, as none of them had had a bath for several months, they got in for a good wash. 'It felt wonderful!'

On the whole they had enough to eat but Udo remembered eating strange food, like *Himmel und Erde* (heaven and earth), a concoction of mashed potatoes and apple sauce. Once they got hold of a huge joint of pork that had been condemned at the slaughterhouse. They were told it was still safe to cook, so they invited their neighbours, the old couple, their daughter and two granddaughters to join them for a big feast of roast pork with all the trimmings, English style, cooked by Oma. Condemned meat or not, everyone survived.

Then one day in the middle of September there was a knock at the door; it was Herr Drenhaus. He gave them Mutti's letter and told them he was going to help them cross the border to the West. First he had to go to Berlin to fetch his wife and son but then they would all meet up together in the town of Neuhaldensleben, close to the border. He had an aunt living there, so had chosen that crossing for his outward journey. It had been pretty easy, through countryside and forest and not too many Russians around. He gave them a date for his planned return, which left them about a week to prepare themselves for the journey. All three were overjoyed.

They gave the family who had been so kind to them everything they couldn't take with them, including their food, firewood and, for the family's grandpa, Opa's precious tobacco crop, some of it already cured, cut and ready to smoke. Then they traded the Thiele family's three bicycles – God knows how they ended up in Tangerhütte – for rucksacks and the handcart Oma and Opa had pulled from Berlin for tins of food. They packed their rucksacks with bread, tinned meat and other food and as much else as would fit. More clothes were packed into a suitcase which Opa and Udo were to carry between them, each taking one side of a stick wedged under the handle.

On the appropriate day they said their farewells and took a train – the railways were running again – to Magdeburg and from there another small one to Neuhaldensleben. When they arrived in the evening they discovered that there was an even lesser train from Neuhaldensleben to somewhere called Zuckerfabrik – where there was, indeed, a sugar factory – even closer to the border, where people were said to be getting across. They found Herr Drenhaus's aunt's house but he hadn't yet arrived, so they left a message for him saying that they were going to try to get across on their own. Then they took the little Zuckerfabrik train.

The scene that greeted them was not encouraging. They had planned to be anonymous, just three little people sneaking across the border at nightfall, but others – many, many others – had had the same idea. In the course of the next few years, several million Germans were to cross illegally into the West, and thereafter, several hundred more would be shot in the attempt. Anyway, that night alone, an enormous crowd of passengers got off the little train at Zuckerfabrik, all refugees with rucksacks, bags and bundles. 'There was a whole contingent of released German prisoners,' Udo remembers. 'They must have come from Russia because they looked so emaciated, like skeletons. Then there were some young boys, too; they looked like inmates just released from a concentration camp. They were a terrible sight.'

It was getting dark as they struck out in a westerly direction into some fields and then along a railway embankment. They had no idea how far they still had to go, when a shadow suddenly appeared from behind some bushes – a Russian soldier with a rifle, shouting '*Stoi!* (stop)' and gesturing that they were to go back to where they had come from. 'As I thought we must be almost across,' Udo continued, 'I foolishly said to Opa, '*Gib ihm doch deine Urh'* (Why don't you give him your watch?) The Russian must have caught the word *Uhr* (watch) as he started demanding '*Uhr! Uhr!*' It was the Russians' favourite German word. Opa had two gold watches on him, heirlooms from his family. He gave one of them to the soldier, well, he more or less had to after what I had said, but also in the hope that he would let us across the border. He did let us continue, but just a little further another Russian soldier accosted us and he turned us back.'

They made several more attempts that night but had no luck and ended up spending the night in a little shelter at the railway station, cold and surrounded by the mass of emaciated-looking released prisoners. 'It was an utterly depressing scene, on top of which I was feeling really bad about the watch. It's the kind of mistake you remember all your life, but do you know, Opa never once reproached me. That shows the kind of person he was.'

Next morning, feeling very depressed, they took the train back to Neuhaldensleben and made their way to Herr Drenhaus's aunt's house. She was very kind, gave them something to eat and promised to let them sleep there. In the course of the day Herr Drenhaus arrived with his wife and son, so the aunt was putting up six extra people in her little flat, and feeding them from her single ration card. Oma shared out some of their food and the following morning they made another attempt with Herr Drenhaus in the lead. They left the extra suitcase behind and repacked their stuff so that they had everything they needed on their backs.

Once more they boarded the little train, but this time travelled a bit beyond Zuckerfabrik. Once again there were hundreds of refugees on the train, who also got off at their chosen station. Udo resumed his tale:

Sure enough, as we left the station and started uphill across some fields in the general direction of the West, Russian soldiers appeared and started herding us back. One of them had a stick in his hand and started hitting people. He hit Herr

Drenhaus right in the mouth, and we saw blood spurting out. Anyway, we started to run for it, Oma and Opa and I; we just ran in a sort of diagonal direction away from all these people and soldiers and for some reason they didn't chase us. Perhaps they thought it better to herd the mass of people rather than bother about us three. We were going uphill, though, across a ploughed filed and carrying our rucksacks. When we got to a little piece of woodland, a typically German one with trees planted in orderly rows, all the same height, we were exhausted and threw ourselves on to the ground to recuperate. Opa was gasping for breath and I started crying, I thought he was going to die. He was so short of breath and there was this loud gasping coming from him, he really looked as though he was going to die.

Eventually he recovered his breath and we lay low for a while; then we had a bite to eat and recovered ourselves pretty well and started walking westwards again through this little forest. After a while we came to a clearing where we met some people who told us, 'You're almost across'. Then we came to a quarry with a fence around it; there was a hole in the fence and people were climbing through, saying, 'The other side is England!' Everyone was calling the English zone 'England'. Well, we climbed through the fence but the other side wasn't England. We found ourselves in the midst of a group of people who were once again being herded by Russian soldiers back in the direction they had come from.

They started marching us along a little country lane to a place where there were still more refugees and more soldiers, a kind of collection point where they had accumulated at least a couple of hundred people. Two or three of the soldiers started marching the whole lot of us back towards the East, away from where we wanted to go. Being the weakest of the bunch, two old people and a young kid, we were right at the back of the column, but our desire to get away must have been really strong.

We had no plan for what we were going to do, but the next thing I remember is that while we were being marched off I noticed that a soldier behind me was busy talking to another one who had come from the opposite direction. Without thinking, I threw myself out of the column of people into the little ditch by the side of the lane that had thick ferns growing round it. Naturally, when Oma and Opa saw what I did they followed suit and, believe it or not, we were the only ones out of all those people who got away. It was amazing. We could see the column of people being marched away into the distance and we had escaped.

We stayed there until the coast was clear and then walked back into the woods. We sat down for a rest and a bite. Suddenly we saw a man coming towards us, whistling. He was wearing a Tyrolean hat and greeted us very cheerfully. '*Bin ich in Russland?* (Am I in Russia?)' he asked and we told him he was. He had just come from the English zone and told us it was easy. 'You continue in this direction till you come to a big area of ferns, tall ferns. In amongst them there are some little animal tracks going in a westerly direction. Just keep going.' We thanked him and found this area of very tall ferns; they must have been five feet high. Right in the middle we found a little track a couple of feet wide, irregular and undulating, you could tell it had been made by animals. Anyway, it was going in a westerly direction, so we went along it in single file, me first and Oma and Opa behind, with our rucksacks. We walked and walked. Then the ferns ended and we came to a dried river bed, with a narrow little stream and ferns growing high up on either side. We walked along the stream bed for a while, until we asked ourselves, 'Where on earth are we?' So I decided to have a look. I climbed up the bank and to my amazement found myself face to face with a signpost made of two poles painted blue and in between them there was a board with the words: ENTERING BRITISH ZONE. We were ecstatic.

Just to make sure, absolutely sure, that we were entering the

British zone and didn't make a mistake, we each stepped between the two poles and under the sign board; when we got to the other side we sat down and had a break. A man came towards us with a horse and a little cart, picking up firewood. He asked us, '*Kommt ihr von Russland?* (Have you come from Russia?)' We said we had. He told us, 'Sometimes the Russians come across and nab people back again,' so we got up quickly and walked on until we came to a country road. We saw a jeep with some English soldiers on it, so Oma hailed them and talked to them in English. They were very pleased to see us and gave us a lift and some chewing gum and chocolate and took us to the nearest village which was called Grasleben. From there we caught a little train to Helmstedt and from Helmstedt another one to Braunschweig.

As there wasn't another train to Recklinghausen till the next day we spent the night in the waiting room, with lots of other people. Like many stations it had been bombed and was just an empty shell without a roof. I was wearing an old air-force cap and it was so cold that I tucked the peak into the top of my jacket, so I was huddled in. That's how I stayed all night, sitting on my rucksack.

Early next morning we went to the platform from which our train was supposed to leave and found there were already hundreds of people waiting. All of a sudden, next to us, we heard a woman screaming; *Mein Kind ist tot! Mein Kind ist tot!* (My child is dead)' as she held up her dead baby. It was so terrible to see that; she was with an old man a bit like Opa, and he looked utterly bewildered, that old man. I'll never forget the scene as long as I live. I suppose the child died of malnutrition.

Then, while we were still waiting for the train, we saw Herr Drenhaus and his family. He was as happy to see us as we were relieved that they had made it. His face was a bit battered and bruised, but not as bad as I expected. Then the train came. By that time I had become an expert at getting on to trains and as usual was the first one on, saving seats for the others. It was a funny old train designed for local travel, without a corridor, just separate compartments. We sat in this compartment all day, at least eight hours, travelling slowly towards Recklinghausen. In the course of the afternoon I was getting desperate for a pee, but there wasn't anywhere to go. When we were just pulling out of a station a man in the compartment said to me, 'Go on, I'll hold the door open for you before the train gets up speed', so I had my pee in the general direction of the town. What a relief. Not long after that, by late afternoon, we got to Recklinghausen and Herr Drenhaus took us to Elperweg. There was nobody at home, so we settled down to wait for somebody to come. We hadn't been there very long when you came skipping up the hill.

16

OMA REBORN

The autumn of 1945 was a bleak time in Germany, and Recklinghausen was no exception. Families were mourning those they had lost in the war – two million of them killed or missing. The economy had collapsed and the Marshall Plan was yet to be introduced. Apart from our food rations – now way below what they were at any point in the war – there was nothing in the shops. For the first time in my life I went to bed hungry and to school badly dressed. Mutti couldn't get her hands on any more cast-off clothes to alter for me. She made me a dirndl dress out of an ancient swastika flag. Age and wear had darkened the material to the colour – and texture – of dried blood. It was hideous and scratchy but I had to wear it; I'd outgrown everything else.

At an even deeper level than the personal tragedies and material hardships that survivors of the war now had to endure lay their helplessness and bewilderment at the disintegration of their society. After the chaos and depression of the 1920s, Hitler had helped them build it up and given them self-respect and hope. For more than a decade now Hitler's propaganda had hammered into them that they were the greatest and that it was not just their duty, but their destiny to triumph in the war. The reality of defeat was traumatic for everyone.

People retreated into themselves, turning to the crudest self-interest as the only guide to behaviour. Long-neglected country cousins suddenly found themselves popular; if they had any land, they were likely to find themselves playing host to their personal refugee camp. Some town-dwellers kept their heads down, depressed and withdrawn; others stayed watchful, knowing they must keep their wits about them to survive, striving to develop the talents that now brought the greatest reward – expertise at barter and the black market. It was a time of quiet despair.

But while, all around, morale was at rock bottom, the mood at Elperweg 33 was close to euphoria. I watched the three adults in my family undergo a remarkable renaissance.

Within days of their arrival, Oma and Opa had cast off for ever their demeanour as a pair of battered, geriatric refugees on their last legs and emerged, reborn, as a sprightly old couple in a permanent flush of excitement. Mutti, too, shed her strained, haunted look of the last few months; her narrowed shoulders relaxed; she appeared to have grown several inches in height. Her personality became more bubbly and assured than I had ever seen it.

What had sparked off this rebirth in the three of them? With Oma and Opa there was more to it than escaping from the Russians for a second time, and being reunited with us. It was their delight at making contact, unexpectedly and directly, with their English roots; having the opportunity to talk to comprehending listeners about their English past and so reliving the one period of their lives that could qualify as any kind of 'golden age'; picking up, after six years without a letter, the threads of their lives in England.

Until our reunion in Recklinghausen I had only experienced my grandmother as part of my Mahlsdorf life. There she had suffered the same bombs and deprivations as everyone else and done her best to conform, going so far as to support the German war effort against her own people. Yet, though this certainly protected her from persecution as a foreigner, it did nothing at all

to get her taken seriously, accepted as an equal. The neighbourhood had cast her, irrevocably, into the role of comic though
lovable oddball, tolerated out of the goodness of people's hearts,
not because it was her right. Under Nazism, being laughed at
was, however, your only way of getting away with being in the
slightest bit different and Oma was certainly different.

Now, more than two years later, I had to revise my impression
of my Oma, rapidly and radically. Within just days of her arrival
in Recklinghausen the curiosity and failed *Reichsmutter* of the
Mahlsdorf days had metamorphosed into a self-assured, cheerful,
cosmopolitan, not exactly matriarch, but let us say senior citizen,
held in respect, even awe, by a large circle of new admirers. They
were a strange assortment, these admirers, with only two things
in common; they were members of the occupation force and they
were English.

True to character, Oma's first priority on arriving in Recklinghausen had been to do her nails, get Opa to do her hair and
generally organise her toilette. She conspired with Mutti to
rejuvenate her residual wardrobe and soon nobody could have
believed that just a few days ago this elegant little person of sixty-
five had been chased by Russian soldiers across the rough fields
of the Iron Curtain's no-man's land, carrying a heavy rucksack on
her back. She assumed command of the housekeeping while
Mutti was at work and began to flourish as I had never seen her,
full of energy, optimism and good humour.

This was the first time since Mutti got married fourteen years
before that she and her parents were living under the same roof
again. Effortlessly they slipped back into the exiles' intimate
lifestyle that had bound them together so closely while Mutti was
growing up in Köpenick. In those days speaking English together
and thinking of themselves as English had inevitably isolated
them somewhat from the rest of society, but this time there was
no question of isolation.

The flat in which we were living had been confiscated by the
military government for 'political' reasons. We never found out

who the previous owners were, or whose fine furniture and household equipment we were using – any more, I suppose, than whoever was using our things in Berlin knew about us. Whoever they were, they couldn't have had more appreciative usurpers. If we hadn't had such an agreeable home there is no way that the year that followed could have been such an enriching one for each of us, in our own ways.

Mutti had been promoted to personal assistant to Major Dunsmore, the Canadian military commander in charge of Recklinghausen's area of occupation. She was now the principal point of contact between the occupation force and the local German population, sitting in the front office of the administrative headquarters, processing applications, complaints and requests that people brought for Major Dunsmore's attention. She wrote reports and letters for him in whatever language was required and acted as his personal interpreter at all briefings and meetings between the military government and the civilian population.

Her job brought her into contact with all kinds of military personnel. There wasn't supposed to be any fraternisation with the natives, but many of her British colleagues were bored and lonely and made no attempt to conceal their impatience for the day when they could get about and meet a few Germans – especially some that could speak good English. Mutti felt herself coming under pressure to produce such people but, as she didn't know any apart from herself and Oma and Opa, it was the natural thing to invite them home. Even her status had its problems, though. She may have become the king-pin of the military government, but technically speaking she remained as much a 'native' as any other German, including the rest of our family. Nevertheless, a demarcation dispute that I can imagine overwhelming a German bureaucrat yielded easily to British pragmatism. Very soon after Oma and Opa's arrival, a trickle – rapidly building up to a stream – of Mutti's English colleagues and acquaintances began to appear at Elperweg 33. The fact that the address was officially out of bounds gave Oma's 'salon', which now came into being, a faintly conspiratorial air that could well have been part of its attraction.

The participants I remember best are Major Dunsmore himself and his British assistant, the rotund, red-haired and moustachioed Major Gadd (yes, really!), Sergeant Pedley, who came from the Black Country and, appropriately, had the most smouldering black eyes under even blacker eyebrows, and the Misses Green and Brown, a pair of robust Salvationists in charge of the Recklinghausen NAAFI. I can't remember the names of any of the others. To my disappointment our very first friend, Captain Chapman, the only one who could speak any German, was also the first one to be demobbed. He always stayed in touch with us, though, became a teacher and sent me the first English book I ever owned. I still have it.

The hospitality we offered didn't usually include anything to eat or drink, unless the visitors brought it themselves. Even if we'd had enough to share, I doubt if our guests would have thanked us for the taste of our leaden bread, artificial, watery jam or our mouth-numbingly bitter ersatz coffee. In fact, eating with us could be quite embarrassing, as Captain Chapman revealed to me years later. As he had so often brought us contributions, Mutti invited him to a meal and, being a well-mannered young man, he offered to help. Mutti asked him to carry a bowl of potatoes into the dining-room and he was already on his way to collect the main dish when it dawned on him that he had just done so. That must have been when he got the idea of bringing back the Ribena for me next time he went to England, and a book of soup recipes from hedgerow delicacies like nettles and dandelions, recently published by the WRVS, for Mutti.

Our visitors came for the company and were clearly taken aback the first time they called to have the door opened by a diminutive grey-haired lady, so English that she could easily have been their mother or aunt. She was a real character, too, and they quickly succumbed to her lively personality, quick wit and funny stories. After twenty-five years of being regarded as a curiosity,

Oma was being admired and appreciated for herself, and she basked in the experience.

They started having noisy card evenings, playing games unknown to Udo and me; at other times Mutti entertained their new friends on the piano. As I still couldn't speak English, I didn't understand very much of what was going on, but there was no doubt that everyone was having a good time.

Occasionally their friends took the three of them on outings, including once to an amphitheatre to watch a full-scale military tattoo. It was the closest Oma ever came again to taking in the *Chu Chin Chow* type of spectacle to which she had been so addicted in her youth. She returned flushed with pleasure and did her best to describe – and demonstrate – to us the wonders she had seen.

Her greatest moment, though, came during a time she was in hospital. 'I was sitting up in bed when I heard a brass band playing English tunes like "Greensleeves" and "The Lord is my Shepherd, I'll not want". I looked out and there was Daddy marching down the drive with Captain Crainer [a new Salvation Army friend] and the whole Salvation Army band marching behind. They had to have Daddy to show them my room. When they got to me they stood in a circle and went on playing for at least half an hour. Every window was thrown open to see what was going on. Captain Crainer waved to me. Then to end up with, they played "Abide with Me". It was beautiful.' She was tickled to death by this incident, the only occasion in her life that I know of when she was ever celebrated for herself.

Opa, too, quickly organised an agreeable life for himself. One day a brass plate appeared on our front door announcing that this was the residence of Herr Richard Druhm, *Englischlehrer*. The Germans of Recklinghausen were desperate to learn English and Opa soon had a full teaching schedule, including a sprinkling of British soldiers wanting to get a head start with German in readiness for the day when fraternisation became legal. I still couldn't speak any English other than the politenesses, but that was quite enough to make me feel superior the day I opened the door to a new German pupil who, stepping into the hall, greeted me with a cheery 'Goodbye!'

Opa's next scheme was to acquire an allotment where he mystified the neighbouring gardeners by cultivating a plant they had never seen before. They hadn't spent three-and-a-half years in that university of hard-times-survival know-how, an English First World War internment camp. That was where Opa had picked up not only his expertise in growing and processing tobacco but other esoteric skills, for example, giving eternal life to his last razor blade by rubbing it in a special way with a piece of glass from a broken beer bottle.

There was as yet no postal service between the two countries and military personnel were under strict instructions not to carry letters for German civilians. Miss Green, our Salvationist friend, pooh-poohed this regulation and put herself at Oma's disposal as a go-between for finding out how her English family and friends had fared in the war. The first casualty she heard about was her mother Bessie, who had died in its first year, aged eighty-six. Oma now spent many hours on correspondence with her two sisters and her English hairdressing friends, receiving back fat letters in unfamiliar, sloping scripts. We had by now heard a lot about Aunty Hopey and came to recognise her letters from their envelopes. She always wrote in green ink, the ultimate in decadence by Udo's and my standards.

With hardly any English, I had little to do with any of this new social scene. Udo became something of a favourite, though – except for his name. Sergeant Pedley and a few other soldiers bluntly announced one day that 'Udo' was too unacceptably German and that from henceforth they intended to call him 'Jack'. They did and the name stuck.

No regular English lessons were arranged for me; Mutti must have assumed that through hearing the language being spoken around me all the time, I would just pick it up. I didn't, though. It wasn't deliberate non-co-operation, I was just too busy with my own life, school, Fräulein Buchholz's piles of homework, the piano lessons I had recently started and my various friends like the Kleines, Marie-Louise and, the latest addition, my fox cub. I had made friends with the zoo-keeper at our *Stadtpark*. He let me help feed the animals and had now given me responsibility for taking the cub for an exercise run on a lead every afternoon; heady stuff! As far as I was concerned, the English thing happening in the family wasn't anything to do with me. Except for Captain Chapman, I couldn't talk to any of them and, much to my chagrin, he was the first to be sent home. It was the grown-ups' scene, Oma and Opa's and of course, Mutti's.

The only times I did all I could to get in on the English act was when Miss Brown brought round one of the NAAFI's Monopoly sets and I discovered that I didn't need to speak English to play it. Nor was I too proud to take an interest in the NAAFI delicacies Miss Green and Miss Brown sometimes brought us. We were so starved for anything sweet that we could envisage no greater luxury than a plate of doughnuts or sandwiches made from soggy English white bread and golden syrup. Whether either of these could seriously be called food was another matter. They were so sticky, so mushy, there was nothing to chew. Irresistible yes, food no, was the general verdict. As for the other offerings that our visitors often brought for Oma, Opa and Mutti and which so excited them, like English books, magazines and packets of tea, they didn't interest me in the slightest. Anyway, because of me the family had to stay bilingual.

Out of the five of us who now made up the family, there is no doubt that Mutti was the one who thrived most in our new circumstances. She seemed to have discovered in herself powers that nobody had ever suspected, least of all she herself. There was about her a confidence and animation I hadn't seen before. She was looking more beautiful than I could remember, too, and even I could tell, from the way their eyes followed her every movement, that more than one of our new friends had become her slave.

It was the first time since leaving Berlin that we had a piano, which she was now playing with extra flair; then she got the urge to take up painting again. It wasn't easy to get hold of the necessary materials, but she persevered and in the course of the year produced a set of large watercolours, easily her best work yet, and her charcoal portrait of Opa.

Thinking about it now, it's not difficult to see what made her blossom like that. For the first time she was fully in charge of her life. Until the age of twenty-one she had lived at home, the supportive daughter, exceptionally close to her parents and never rebelling in any way. Getting married, in that male-dominated society, had got her no closer to independence, particularly not with a husband like Papa, with his highly conventional ideas about a woman's place in the family. Even though he was away for so much of their married life, he never relinquished his authority and even when he was hundreds of miles away Mutti wouldn't dream of taking an important decision without consulting him. The closest she ever got to doing her own thing had been her radio programme, but even that had been arranged by Papa. Now there was no Papa to lean on, to tell her what to do. She was in charge and, by all appearances, liked it.

Then there was her job as a high-powered, bilingual secretary, exactly what she had dreamed of as a teenager, before Onkel Arno persuaded her to concentrate on her art. It was a challenge, but one of very few jobs in the world in which nearly all her abilities could be put to use. She wasn't just translating from language to language, but from culture to culture and making creative use of her potentially problematic status as an Anglo-German *Zwischending* (tweenie). What's more, she was making a first-class job of it and gaining enormous appreciation.

Last but not least was her decision to organise us into a new extended family with herself as the head. In those pre-women's liberation days having to act as the head of a family was still seen as something of an unfair burden for a woman; misfortune might force her into it, but she would never choose it if there was an alternative. In contrast to these stereotypes, Mutti had taken on full responsibility for the four of us as though it was the most natural thing in the world. Being the breadwinner and providing us with a home gave her a real sense of achievement. She felt successful and fulfilled and it showed.

The star of only one member of our family was seriously on decline, and that was Papa's. As Mutti's stature grew, his diminished. None of the others ever seemed to mention him and when I did I was fobbed off. It was almost as though he had ceased to exist.

There were, of course, excellent reasons for not talking about him in public. The one shadow hanging over our lives the whole time we lived in Recklinghausen was our belief that we owed our good fortune to a fraud, to the lie that Papa had been an ordinary soldier, missing in Russia. If his active Nazi past became known and the fact that our most recent contact with him, Udo's visit, had taken place while Mutti was already working for the military government, Mutti would be fired on the spot and our flat taken away, or so we thought. An even more frightening prospect, though, was that Mutti would get into trouble, not just for lying about Papa, but because of her own dangerous past. Her propaganda work with the *Kurze Welle* (short wave) radio station had become a major worry for her, especially when she heard that Lord Haw-Haw was being charged with treason and about to be hanged. He and Mutti had worked in the same department and she had even been to tea at his house. 'A complete nonentity,' was Mutti's verdict on him, when I asked her about the occasion. 'He made no impression on me whatever. His wife was there; she had more personality.'

With hindsight, our anxieties at the time were exaggerated. Most people had skeletons in their cupboards; if the authorities were going to punish all Nazis, they would have had to take on most of the population. We weren't to know any of that, however, and conspired to conceal anything about our past that could prove an embarrassment – the main one, of course, being Papa himself.

I could see all that and was quite prepared to co-operate with the others. What I couldn't fathom was why we had to carry on in the same way, as if Papa didn't exist any more, when we were alone among ourselves. As I had so recently seen him alive and reasonably well, I took it for granted that it was only a matter of time before he was back with us. Yet when I asked Mutti, interminably, questions like where she thought he might be now, and how long she thought it would be till we heard from him, I was getting noncommittal, guarded replies, even hints here and there that he might actually not come back at all. Was she suggesting that he had been executed for something dreadful he had done? That was the only interpretation I could put on the innuendo in her answers. Though I didn't know what praying was, as nobody had ever taught it to me, I found myself spontaneously saying a fervent prayer every night for Papa's safety and his return to the family.

But I was deluding myself. Had I been able to confront the reality before me, I would have been forced to acknowledge that there was no longer a place for Papa in this new family we had become. Mutti had become its head. The role suited her; she flourished in it. Returning her to being Papa's little woman would be like cutting off her limbs. And I couldn't see Papa changing either, giving up his natural authority, sharing responsibility and decisions equally with her. He didn't have it in him. And then there were Oma and Opa. During our time together in Reck-linghausen Opa celebrated his sixty-eighth birthday, Oma her sixty-sixth. Mutti had obviously committed herself totally to taking care of them. It was difficult to envisage a future for a family in which their welfare was given such high priority, that also had a place for Papa. Even if I recognised what was happening to us – and I think I could have, if I had wanted to – I couldn't bear to draw the obvious conclusion. I didn't want to see the truth and, pushing aside any doubts, returned to daydreaming about some indeterminate time and place in which Papa was reinstated into his rightful place in the family.

17

To England

I can't remember when I first heard of the possibility that we might all go to live in England. It was a time when it wasn't usual for adults to discuss serious matters with children and as I, anyway, couldn't understand very much of what the adults in my family were saying amongst themselves because it was usually in English, the idea could well have been in the air for quite a while before it was mentioned to me. At that stage, some time towards the end of the summer of 1946, it was still being discussed more as a 'wouldn't it be lovely' idea than a serious proposition. We had recently met a family that dreamed of emigrating to Argentina. They had jokingly suggested that we team up with them in their fanciful scheme and the going-to-England idea struck me as in much the same realm of fantasy. I didn't take it seriously.

Life in Recklinghausen had by now swung into a busy, cheerful routine for all five of us. Mutti, one sometimes got the impression, was governing Recklinghausen and its environs single-handed. Yet she was also a regular interpreter at meetings and constitutional conferences being held to prepare for the eventual hand-back of power from the military occupation to a new, democratic, civilian government. She interpreted speeches for aspiring German politicians like Konrad Adenauer, just then resuming the pre-war political career that was to culminate with his becoming Germany's first post-war chancellor in 1949.

Udo, meanwhile, was happy at the Boys' Gymnasium and had a best friend. Opa's English lessons were going well and the English social scene at home was flourishing. By September 1946, soon after my tenth birthday, I had graduated from Fräulein Buchholz's class in the elementary school and, along with Marie-Louise and a few other classmates, transferred to the Sexta of the Girls *Gymnasium*. It was a very different atmosphere, a class of only thirty-five or thirty-six girls in our own classroom, no more willowswitches and several new subjects, including English. It was amazing how helpful just a few formal lessons were in making me able to use the bits of English, mostly domestic vocabulary, that I already knew. I made rapid progress and soon had the courage to try out a sentence or two on Miss Green and other members of the English salon. 'Oxford English!' was the immediate reaction of Sergeant Pedley, our Black Country friend, when he heard my first English utterance. I didn't know what he was talking about.

Throughout the year there had been no sign of any improvement in our food supplies. Every day Mutti brought home most of her canteen lunch to share with the rest of us. Ration cards of the time show that adults were entitled to a kilo of bread per week, 100 grams each of meat and starches and 62.5 grams of fat. There were additional fortnightly stamps for half a pound of sugar and 62.5 grams of cheese. For ersatz coffee the ration was 200 grams for the whole month. There wasn't a stamp for eggs and for quite a while we only received an egg each once every three months. I remember intense discussions at family mealtimes about what each of us was going to do with our next egg. Would we eat it boiled, fried, scrambled, whisked up into a drink, or would we be the hero that sacrificed our birthright by donating it for a communal cake?

The idea that Mutti should apply for us all to be 'repatriated' to the United Kingdom had come from her work colleagues. It clearly bothered them to have a nice English woman like her work with them by day and then, like Cinderella after the ball, return at six o'clock every evening to the deprivations of life as a German civilian. They told her that, in contrast to its practice after the First World War, the British Government was operating a generous repatriation scheme. The flimsiest claim to being British appeared to qualify people for entry into the country, provided they had someone to sponsor them at the other end.

Mutti needed no persuasion to make the application. Nor did Oma and Opa. As they saw it, history was set to repeat itself. Germany was in for at least another decade of poverty and hardship, just like after the last war, only this time the recovery was starting from a far worse position than before; Germany was in ruins. Last time there had not even been bombs or fighting on German soil, only civil strife and vandalism. Mutti and Oma thought back to their visits to England in the 1920s and the contrast in living standards between the two countries. On those grounds alone they thought we would be crazy not to have ourselves repatriated, if we had the chance. Yet for all three of them other reasons were, I think, even more important.

Millions of disillusioned and disgusted Germans were dreaming of emigrating to Australia, Canada, Argentina, anywhere where they could start a new life and pretend the last twelve years had never happened. Mutti, Oma and Opa, I am sure, shared that feeling. I never heard them discussing how they now felt about having supported Hitler for all those years; they were no doubt too shocked and stunned by all that had happened to be able to think objectively about it. I doubt if Oma and Opa, anyway, were aware of any feelings on the subject, other than relief at having survived intact and not become permanently separated from the rest of us. What could they have found to say to one another about having been Nazis, about the fact that the support of people like themselves had enabled Hitler to wage genocide against Jews, lay waste whole countries and populations and lead millions of Germans to their destruction? Should they have known that the man who so magically got rid of unemployment, put goods in the shops and made the trains run on time and who, after years of gloom, had made them glad to be German, would bring all this upon them? Sophisticated historians and political thinkers may have been able to predict where Hitler's nationalism would lead, but Mutti, Oma and Opa were political innocents. The only way they, like millions of others, could now deal with having been Nazis was to exorcise the experience from their memories and what better way of doing so than getting out of the country?

Furthermore, after all they had been through, Oma and Opa's renewed contact with England had raised their spirits more than one would have believed possible. It had not only given them optimism and hope, but also made them nostalgic for the place where they had spent the most enjoyable years of their lives, before everything became soured by the unprecedented hysteria against Germans.

For Mutti, too, there was a further reason for being desperate to get to England. I couldn't make it out exactly, but I could tell it had to do with Papa. She had become more and more cagey when I broached my same old question, where was he, when were we going to see him? Every day we were hearing of other children's fathers returning home from the war or contacting their families by letter. Almost the only men still out of touch were the ones in Russian captivity and we knew that Papa wasn't one of them. Tante Kätchen, our designated go-between, came to stay again but she still had nothing to report. Why had we not heard? I couldn't understand it.

None of the others in the family seemed to share my permanent concern about Papa. Almost the only context in which they now mentioned him was how important it was to keep up our story that he was missing in Russia. I became aware that my questions were making them uncomfortable and I started feeling guilty when I raised the subject. Much as Mutti's attitude to Papa disturbed me, I had such faith in her that it wouldn't have occurred to me to doubt or question what she was doing. There must be good reasons, she just couldn't tell me what they were.

What I couldn't bring myself to face was that our family had reached a point of no return between two utterly conflicting futures. We had a straightforward choice between England and Papa. If we chose England, there would never again be a place in our family for him. If we chose to wait for him, or even so much as publicly acknowledge his existence, the England option was ruled out. There was no middle way.

It was obvious that the three adults in the family had made their choice. They were in love with the idea of being repatriated and Udo instinctively shared their preference. For as long as he could remember, Papa had been hovering over him, putting pressure on him to make him be something he wasn't, making him feel a failure. During the last eighteen months that he had spent out of Papa's reach, gentle, wise old Opa, who never bullied or shouted but only explained and encouraged, had become his mentor. Udo had started to come out of his shell and to thrive. Now, as a head of steam built up in favour of the England option, Papa seemed to dematerialise from the family altogether.

But just because Mutti and the others had become indifferent to him was no reason why I should. On the contrary, if they were now abandoning him, it was up to me to hang in and remember him. It wasn't just because I loved him, but also because of *Treue* and all the other ideals drilled into me so effectively by my *Führer*. When I had made the decision at Süppling to remain a closet Nazi, I had, unwittingly, set myself a standard of behaviour that would turn out to be not only extremely demanding but impossible ever to give up. As Papa's presence receded from the family and I learned to keep my thoughts about him to myself, my commitment to him became ever stronger.

Once the idea of us all going to England had taken hold, there followed some intense discussions between the adults, followed by sessions of letter-writing to England. As we were most unlikely to find anyone to take on all five of us together the plan was that Mutti and we children would go first and Oma and Opa follow as soon as we had a home where they could join us. Even finding someone to sponsor just us three was going to be a problem. The family's closest friend, Aunty Hopey, was ineligible for a start. She was a woman – and single.

At last, in the middle of October 1946, the critical letter that Oma and Mutti had been waiting for so eagerly arrived. It was from our great-aunt Gertie and her husband Harry. They had agreed to receive us in their home in Eastbourne and had signed the sponsor form. Mutti sent it off with her application and after less than a month got an answer. We had all passed muster as sufficiently British to be repatriated to the United Kingdom. What had started off as a pipedream was now sprung on us as a definite plan, ready to be implemented almost immediately. We had been put on to a waiting list for seats on a train to Calais and a cross-Channel passage and could expect to go in two or three weeks' time. We were to hold ourselves in readiness, as once our travel papers arrived we would only have a few days before departure.

As each hurdle was overcome, the level of excitement in the family grew. Had I been asked, at any stage of the preparation, if I wanted to go to England and how I felt about the whole idea, I would have found it very difficult to answer. I hadn't been brought up to have likes and dislikes, make choices or have views, but to fall in with whatever the adults around me expected. When I heard that our departure was imminent, I did what came naturally, letting myself be swept along by the glamour of it and by the excitement around me. I told my friends and my teacher. She was so impressed, she made a formal statement to the whole class. Everyone turned to look at me and gawped. They had never met a child who had travelled abroad. Nor had I. In the year and a half I had spent in Recklinghausen I had never got much further than a couple of streets beyond Elperweg.

Oma now started to have little chats with Udo and me about how to present ourselves in England. Her principal theme was that we must on no account, ever, tell anyone we were German. Unless we took this message to heart we were just asking to be bullied, beaten up and otherwise discriminated against wherever we went. Oma's advice sounded entirely reasonable. Ill-treatment by victors of their defeated made a lot more sense than what we were getting from our occupation force in Recklinghausen. They were so nice to us, it wasn't natural! I therefore co-operated keenly with Oma's grooming for my forthcoming entry into English society.

The first requirement, Oma told us, was to have names that didn't raise suspicions about our German origins. We would therefore either have to take new English names, or anglicise our existing ones. All our various names were scrutinised in detail. Oma and Opa agreed that Thiele had better go. It was too difficult to anglicise. The only English surname in the family, Oma's maiden name, had served her well in the First World War, much better than Droome, the anglicised version of Druhm. It was therefore agreed that we, too, would become Norris. As for our Christian names, that was easier for Udo than for me. He had always hated his name and Sergeant Pedley's 'Jack' had really caught on. Even the family had started to use it when they were speaking to him in English. No problem there. Of his three middle names, Fritz and Konrad were obviously far too aggressively Teutonic to survive, which left him with just one, inoffensive middle name, Richard, after Opa.

My names were more difficult. Katrin was at the time just as rare in Germany as in England. I had still never met another, but I badly wanted to keep it. Oma toyed with Kathleen and Katherine but finally conceded that so long as I anglicised it by adding a final 'e', making it into Katrine, it would just about do. Of my middle names, Ethel was approved but Olga out.

Next Oma drilled us in manners. She advised us to abandon for ever that *sine qua non* of German good manners, shaking hands and *beugen* (bowing) or *knicksen* (curtsying) whenever we met a friend, acquaintance, relative, even a member of our own household. As for that essential of German table manners, keeping your hands firmly on the table throughout the meal (introduced, it is said, to stop people molesting or stealing from one another under the cover of the table), Oma told us that it was one of the rudest things one could do during an English meal. Finally, she told us about the royal family and taught us to sing 'God Save the King'.

While Oma worked on our behaviour and presentation, Mutti got down to the issue of dress. Udo's clothes were the most problematic. The shabby air-force jacket he had arrived in from the Russian zone a year before was still his sole outdoor garment and he only had one pair of trousers, those German-style shorts at least nine inches higher than the knee-length trousers being worn by English schoolboys of the day. They had already been too small for him for months. Mutti was, for once, forced to give up on the problem. Even if she had any suitable materials, she doubted whether her style of home dressmaking was appropriate for the trousers of a boy of thirteen.

There was at least hope of making me look respectable, so she put her all into making me a new coat. Was she perhaps remembering the beautiful coat Aunty Hopey had given her to travel in on her first journey to Germany, nearly thirty years before? She had been much the same age as I was now, about to set off in the opposite direction.

Mutti worked hard to produce a pattern that would do justice to the sumptuous materials she had somehow got hold of – a beige blanket, quite thick and rough, and a matching piece of sheep skin. The design she came up with was in a bold Cossack style, with a flared skirt and sleeves out of the blanket material, and a fur bodice and Cossack hat trimmed with blanket material tassels. A fur-trimmed muff added a final exotic touch. The result was so spectacular that everyone agreed it must be recorded for posterity. A neighbour with a camera had agreed to come and take a last picture of the five of us together on German soil, but when he arrived I was first made to pose for a separate photograph, dressed up in my coat, hat and muff. Then the photographer lined us all up on the sitting-room sofa for our group photo. As he was arranging us I noticed him peering from Oma to Mutti, Mutti to me and back again to Oma. then he shrugged his shoulders and said, '*Drei Frauen, ein Gesicht* (three women, one face)'. Everyone was always saying how alike we were.

By the end of November we were all ready and packed, just waiting for our tickets and our travel day. On 1 December they arrived, with instructions to travel on the 6th.

It wasn't till our final evening when we had said our last good-byes that the enormity of what was happening hit me. Oma, Opa and Udo were talking excitedly, Mutti has having a final for-tissimo fling on the piano. I suddenly felt as if a bomb had exploded in my head. What was all this about? What did it mean? Was I really not going to see Marie-Louise any more, or my nice school, or the Kleines, or my zoo-keeper friend and the animals I loved so much? And if we left Germany, what was going to happen to Papa: what would he do when he came out of imprisonment and found we had gone? He would go mad; it would kill him and it would kill me, too. And anyway, I loved Germany and had always liked – still did like – being German. I liked being Katrin Thiele. How could I go round for the rest of my life pretending to be somebody I wasn't, telling lies and denying that everything that had happened to me so far, most of which I had thoroughly enjoyed, hadn't really happened? If I started off like that in England, living a lie, how would I ever get out of it again, get back to being the me that I was now, that I liked being?

Thoughts like these were racing through my brain. Suddenly I realised what was about to happen and also that there was nothing I could do to stop it. The tears were welling up and then I was sobbing, sobbing, sobbing uncontrollably. The others were mystified. Why on earth was I collapsing in tears on the day that should have been the happiest of my life? It certainly was of theirs. They looked at me indulgently, as if to say, poor kid, she can't handle the excitement. When I gave no sign of drying up but, on the contrary, became almost hysterical, Mutti got quite upset herself, but she couldn't comfort me. How could she find the words when neither she, nor any of the others, had the faintest understanding of how I was feeling? I was certainly spoiling their pleasure. When I finally collapsed into bed, my face red and swollen, I still couldn't bring myself to speak.

Early next morning a military car drew up outside to take us to the station. We handed our luggage to the uniformed driver and put on our coats. My Cossack creation was certainly eye-catching. I doubt if there was another like it in the whole of Germany, let alone Eastbourne. Oma helped me into it. 'Oh, you do look nice, dearie', she told me, doing up the furry buttons. 'Now remember, when people ask you where you were born tell them London, tell them you're a Londoner, like your mother. You can't go wrong with that.' I gave her and Opa goodbye hugs and when Oma had finished adjusting by Cossack hat to her satisfaction and handed me my muff, I climbed mechanically into the car. We were off on the first stage of our journey to England.

Part 2

ENGLAND

18

EASTBOURNE

Our so-called repatriation began disastrously. My mother's most recent experience of England, gained in the 1920s as a teenager on holiday, was of little use to her returning in 1946, destitute and with two pre-pubertal German children in tow. The relatives on whose support she had fixed her hopes took one look and rejected us.

We arrived in style, travelling in the officer class of military transport, but we were literally penniless. Post-war German marks had little value inside and none at all outside Germany, so we couldn't change any into sterling. On the boat train from Dover we shared a compartment with a major from the FANYs (First Aid Nursing Yeomanry). She got talking to my mother and when she grasped our situation became so alarmed that, as the train approached Victoria, she reached into her handbag and insisted on giving my mother a ten-shilling note. That was the sum of our liquid assets when, dazed and exhausted from the most violent channel crossing any of us have ever experienced, we emerged from our train at Eastbourne, shortly before midnight.

My great-aunt Gertie and her husband Harry were there to meet us. She had last seen us on her visit to Mahlsdorf in 1939 when I was three and Udo six. I had seen photographs of the visit and recognised her at once, as she stood at the barrier, peering at the passengers alighting from the train. She was short and plump, with a very pale, puffy complexion, quite unlike our daintily built, brightly complexioned Oma. Her hat, too, in navy blue felt and with a military-style peak, was unlikely to have found a place in our stylish Oma's wardrobe. Then she caught sight of us – Udo in his outgrown, skin-tight shorts and bomber jacket and me in my Cossack outfit – and I could see that there was something seriously wrong. Her face was working oddly, struggling with some powerful emotion that wasn't pleasure. There was no hint of a welcoming smile.

There was clearly more to Aunty Gertie's dismay than our unmistakably German appearance. Throughout their youth, she and Oma had been entangled in a turbulent love/hate relationship, apparently fuelled by Gertie's jealousy of Oma's superior looks and talents. Yet, between their rows, there must have been some measure of affection between them; even Uncle Harry and Opa had become friends. All this came to an abrupt end in 1914 when Gertie and Harry became infected with the anti-German hysteria that took over the country in the run-up to the First World War. The only support they gave Oma after that was when she had to dispose of her home and the shop on Haverstock Hill and turned to Uncle Harry in his professional capacity as an auctioneer and valuer. In the twenty-eight years since Oma went to Germany, the sisters only met on two occasions, first in 1928 when Oma made her only return visit to England and then in 1939, when Aunty Gertie, dangerously, visited us all in Mahlsdorf.

Sometime in the mid-1920s, when she was only thirteen, their only daughter Betty died of diabetes. They never got over the loss and Oma often told us how Aunty Gertie continued to communicate with her daughter through a spiritualist medium. Betty's long red ringlets had been her mother's pride and joy and after more than twenty years still occupied a central position in her parents' bedroom; though framed in silver, they looked lugubriously like a Red Indian's prize scalp. At least one faded sepia photograph of Betty hung in every room of the house. With all that in the background, I suspect that Aunty Gertie would have found entertaining Oma's daughter and grandchildren a strain, even without the extra insult of their being Germans.

It was on this aspect, however, that she now focused her highly charged, barely concealed emotions. On his own Uncle Harry, tall and silver-haired, was charming to us. He chatted and joked, told us about his adventures with Opa when they were young men and about his bicycling holiday to Germany where he had got along famously with just three phrases: *Ein Glas Lager, bitte, Zwei Glas Lager, bitte* and *Drei Glas Lager, bitte.* Yet he knew better than to try to curb his wife's zeal in the mission she had set herself. I couldn't understand much of what she was saying, but there was no mistaking her message. She had a duty to make us understand that everything German was despicable, including, by implication, ourselves. She must make us recognise how fortunate we were to have relatives like her and Uncle Harry, so ridiculously sentimental as to give us the chance to start life afresh as British.

Her attitude didn't surprise us in the slightest. It was what Oma had led us to expect in England and why she had insisted so vehemently on us concealing our origins. Nevertheless, Udo and I wished we could keep out of our aunt's way, but it wasn't easy. The house offered few opportunities for escape and we were far too frightened to go outside to explore our new surroundings by ourselves.

Up to now we had nearly always lived in standard urban flats, never in anything remotely like this twee stockbroker's Tudor cottage down a winding lane in a village called Willingdon on the edge of the Sussex Downs. With its leaded checkerboard windows and studded oak front door it looked enchanting from the outside, like something out of a fairy story. Who would believe the inside could be so uncomfortable, with everything fussy and pokey, the stairs narrow and twisty and a profusion of doors and little hallways not leading anywhere in particular.

My biggest disappointment was the fireplaces. In my English

books, the *Playbox Annuals* with their illustrated adventures of the Bruin Boys, rooms with blazing open fires always looked so cosy and inviting. None of the pictures ever showed a grate that was empty. Yet here, though each room in the house had a perfectly nice fireplace, all but one were concealed behind ugly screens, without a fire even laid, let alone burning. Though it was the famously cold winter of 1946–47 Aunty Gertie – no doubt on account of the critical coal shortage – attempted to heat only one room in the house, starting so late in the day that it stood no chance of becoming even moderately *gemütlich*, by our standards, before bedtime.

Having never before experienced a cold indoors of any kind, not a cold bedroom or bathroom, not even in the worst days of the war or the post-war collapse, I was now permanently frozen and for ever hanging round the one and only fire, trying to crawl inside the fender. Once I even grasped the poker and tried to stoke up the fire, but Aunty Gertie stopped me short; she told me that touching somebody else's fire – like so much else that came naturally to me – 'wasn't done in England'. Fireplace etiquette had clearly been a sad omission from Oma's crash course in English manners.

Other things we noticed about the house were the way none of the doors and windows fitted properly into their frames, or locks into their catches. In our icy bedroom, even with everything closed, there was often still such a draught that the curtains and counterpanes flapped. At last we understood how expressions like *auf englischer Art*, 'English-style', meaning 'cackhanded' and *Englisch-rum*, meaning 'skew-whiff', had found their way into the German language.

Udo and I spent much time in our overcoats upstairs playing cards. Though we were thirteen and ten respectively, we once or twice got out the *Männekins* and tried to continue the game we had played with them for as long as either of us could remember. For some reason, they refused to come to life; the *Männekins* were clearly German and we gave up the attempt for good.

For our aunt, having us hanging around the house all day must have been a severe trial. Sometimes she sent us on errands to the shops and post office at the end of her lane, no doubt hoping that we would go for a walk, explore the village, climb on to the downs or just get lost. It wouldn't have occurred to us to show any such initiative; we were much too frightened to stray from the one route we knew and as soon as our task was accomplished we would hurry back and wait to be told what to do next.

One blustery afternoon Uncle Harry drove us to a cinema in Eastbourne to see *Pinocchio*. I found the little of it I could understand, the roguish actors leading the little boy astray and his nose growing grotesquely long, improbable and frightening. It wasn't the film that made the outing memorable, nor our walk along the promenade afterwards, watching the waves being whipped up into thousands of white horses. It was buying our first ice-cream cone; after a bit of an argument about the best way to share it, we settled happily for alternate licks.

My mother was as disoriented as Udo and I. On her first expedition to Sainsbury's in Eastbourne, at that time an ordinary grocer's shop, the sight of all those shelves stacked with foods she hadn't seen for years made her quite faint. She had left Germany with only the vaguest plans for what to do with us all in England. As her aunt and uncle had officially accepted responsibility for us, she took it for granted that they would take an active part in helping us get established, but that wasn't their plan. As they saw it, just enabling us to enter the country had been daringly improper, bordering on the unpatriotic; making life too easy for us thereafter would be practically treason. They didn't give Mutti even the most basic information about living in England and made only one suggestion: that she should find herself a residential job where there would also be accommodation for us. They wanted this plan to be put into operation immediately after Christmas, in just over two weeks' time.

Harry and Gertie always spent the holiday with my mother's

cousin Ethel's family, the daughter of Gertie's and Oma's other sister Nellie (the bigamist living in Australia), taking it in turns to be host. This year it was Ethel's turn and she invited us to join the Christmas family party at her home in Uxbridge. Well, she couldn't really get out of it.

Our great-aunt and uncle did their best to prepare Udo and me, not only for our first English Christmas, but also for our first encounter with our second cousin Roland. He was a year or two older than Udo and, according to his great-aunt and uncle, represented everything that was perfection in British boyhood. The qualifications they advanced to support this claim were that he attended a public school and that he played cricket, neither of which meant anything to us. What impressed us rather more, when we were shown a photograph, was the size – and angle – of his ears.

Once again, my principal sources of information about what to expect from an English Christmas had been the 1919 *Playbox Annual* and the adventures of the Bruin boys. What with those amazing-looking plum puddings with holly sticking out of the top, crackers, funny hats and games of Blind Man's Buff on Boxing Day, it looked so merry and convivial, quite as good, in its own way, as the more sedate and atmospheric German festival. Now, as Uncle Harry drove us to Uxbridge in his Wolsey, Aunty Gertie added further important details, like the King's Christmas broadcast and standing up when the national anthem was played at the end. By the time we reached our relatives' riverside bungalow I was quite excited about the novelties in store.

As children, my mother and Ethel had known each other well. During the First World War when, for different reasons, neither of their mothers was able to look after them, they had both lived with their grandmother Bessie in Brondesbury, for at least a year. Any warmth that might have existed between the two cousins, however, had not survived the war and Ethel's welcome was deeply chilling. As for Roland, though Udo and I were greatly looking forward to meeting the first English member of our own generation, especially such a paragon, the feeling obviously wasn't mutual. For most of the festive season he stayed out of sight in his den, into which we were never invited and when he couldn't avoid being in the same room, he ignored us.

It wasn't long into the festivities – five minutes, perhaps – before we again got the message that even at Christmas, if one was German, there was nothing one could do to redeem oneself.

In terms of plum pudding, crackers, funny hats and so on, everything about our first Christmas in England turned out as I had been led to expect. However, as none of it produced a ripple of jolliness or Christmas spirit in any of those present, I kept wondering what was the point of it all. The sight of the artificial Christmas tree decorated with hideous electric lights made me homesick for the special aroma of the only kind of tree I had ever known, a pine tree lit with candles. The King's Christmas message was no compensation. I couldn't understand a word and, throughout, our relatives were casting accusing glances at us. Then, when the national anthem was played, they leapt to their feet and, with their eyes, dared us not to follow suit.

At last it was over and we packed up to leave. The plan for the return journey had been for Uncle Harry to make a short detour via Staines to drop the three of us off at the home of Aunty Hopey, which was to be my mother's job-and-home-hunting base. At the last minute they relented and made the offer to take Udo back with them for a little longer, which my mother gratefully accepted. Then they dropped Mutti and me off on the pavement outside Aunty Hopey's flat and sped off back to Eastbourne with Udo in the back seat.

Thinking back now, I am still deeply puzzled by our relatives' attitude towards us that winter. Most mysterious is the fact that, feeling the way they did, they had agreed to sponsor our repatriation. Yet at the time I accepted their behaviour as what was to be expected; I didn't take it personally or let it upset me. It was exactly how, if the situation had been reversed and

Germany had won the war, uppity English arrivals would have been treated in a victorious Germany. What I found much more mystifying was that nobody else we came across in the weeks and months to come treated us in a remotely similar way. Everyone was so kind and sympathetic, so keen to help, we couldn't understand it. This was something Oma hadn't prepared us for and I found it thoroughly confusing.

Part of this phenomenon was, of course, the gentler style of everyday social intercourse in England, compared with wartime and immediately post-war Germany. In my previous experience, officials dealing with members of the public, whether on the railways or in a post office, and even many shopkeepers, were invariably rude and dictatorial, especially to children. I assumed it was part of their job. Yet here in our aunt's village we were astonished to see shoppers and sales assistants smile and chat together like equals; the lady in the post office was positively eager to help her customers . . . even when they were children with thick guttural accents.

Then, after Christmas, when we started contacting other people we knew or with whom we had a connection, they welcomed us with open arms. Members of our Recklinghausen social circle, now demobbed and living back in England, and even friends of Oma and Opa's from a quarter of a century ago expressed delight that we were in England and made us welcome in their homes. We were invited to the wedding of Miss Brown, one of our original NAAFI Salvationists, and were made a special fuss of by her parents. As soon as he heard we were in England, Captain Chapman, now at college and studying to become a teacher, came to Willingdon to see us. All of these people had either forgotten we were German, or didn't care.

Though their goodwill and concern for us made all the difference to our morale, at a time of critical post-war housing shortage no one could come up with solutions to our most urgent needs: somewhere to live and something to live on. Of our closest friends Aunty Hopey, my mother's second mother, lived in a tiny bachelor flat; Miss Connell, Oma's apprentice in the Haverstock Hill shop and our new 'Aunty Kath', lived in a desperately overcrowded terrace house with her family of recently demobbed sons, their wives and babies. They could always be relied on for a sofa or a mattress on the floor in an emergency, but only at the cost of our being a nuisance.

The only people we knew who had space and resources were our relatives, but after that first Christmas in England they never invited us back, neither to the mock-Tudor cottage at the edge of the Downs nor to the riverside bungalow in Uxbridge.

19

LONDON

I had never met anyone like my new Aunty Hopey – so individual in appearance, personality or style. In her mid-fifties, bespectacled and none too slim, she might have been considered plain but for two attributes that dominated her presence. The first thing that struck me was her elegance; I was ready to be overawed by that when I became aware that peeping from behind the heavy spectacles were eyes with such a twinkle that there could be no doubt about their owner's warmth and humour. In everything practical Aunty Hopey turned out to be a perfectionist; her flat, her clothes, hair and every aspect of grooming were immaculate. No wonder she needed an hour in the bathroom every morning and she wore beautifully tailored suits even when doing her housework. Though, living alone, she had only herself to consider, her daily, monthly and annual routines operated like clockwork and yet she exercised all this self-discipline effortlessly and projected a tolerant, kind and gregarious personality that was full of fun.

Aunty Hopey's Mayfair salon must have done well since, by the time we appeared on the scene, she and her partner had sold it several years before and were living in comfortable retirement on the proceeds. Aunty Hopey had moved into a small block of 1930s-style flats overlooking Staines Moor. In keeping with Mrs

Beeton's advice about 'a place for everything and everything in its place', her flat was perfectly organised around her strongly individual lifestyle. Putting up my mother and me for more than a month must have been a major disruption to her life, but she gave no hint that she was not delighted to have us squatting there.

Until we moved in with Aunty Hopey, my English had progressed little since coming to England; there had not been much chance to practise. Among ourselves the three of us were still speaking German and the relatives had not rushed to engage me in conversation. Now all this changed. Though Mutti and Aunty Hopey had years of catching up to do and were chattering and laughing away together non-stop, they made me join in whenever possible. Then Aunty Hopey showed me how to tune her radio and introduced me to *Children's Hour*. I loved it and soon discovered other programmes that I could more or less follow. My rapid progress in English from now on, despite spending quite a lot of time in the flat alone, owed as much to listening to BBC programmes like *Twenty Questions* and *Have a Go!* as to direct conversation.

Within a few days Mutti had found a temporary job on the Euston Road in London, in the office of a warehouse for plumbing equipment. She started commuting there. Though officially retired, Aunty Hopey had a busy schedule, including home visits to some of her long-standing customers. She found plenty of time for me, however, and took me along on visits to her friends and on her *de rigueur* daily walks along the Thames towpath. Best of all were the special trips she planned for my entertainment, for example to Kew Gardens and to Windsor Castle to see Queen Mary's doll's house. I studied it in minute detail and finally, very grudgingly, had to admit to myself that it was nearly, almost, just about, as nice as the one I had abandoned in Silesia two years previously.

My mother found her job heavy going. She hated her compli-cated journeys from Staines to King's Cross and back, having to set off in the dark and spend hours waiting for trains on icy platforms. She couldn't make sense of the work and had the greatest difficulty communicating with her workmates, especially in the matter of understanding their jokes. Her boss must have been very disappointed to discover that, for all her beautifully spoken English, his new employee should prove so incompetent at arranging for the delivery of consignments of ballcocks or lavatory seats. By mutual agreement, they soon parted company.

The whole of this time my mother was endeavouring to follow Uncle Harry's advice, looking for a residential job which would accept children. Before January was out she received an offer. It was as an assistant manageress at the Harrington Hall Hotel in Harrington Gardens, South Kensington. There must have been a staff crisis at the hotel, for the two of us moved in there at virtually no notice. We were allocated an attic bedroom on the staff corridor and told to have our meals downstairs, in the main dining-room, alongside the guests. The hotel's public rooms with their thick carpets, innumerable gilt-framed mirrors and many chandeliers struck me as extremely grand yet, as far as I can remember, I had the complete run of the place.

Many of the guests were permanent residents and the atmosphere between them and the staff was very friendly. One old gentleman living there must have had a serious passion for pantomimes, which he was too embarrassed to indulge on his own. As I was the only child around, he asked my mother if she would allow me to chaperone him to not one, but five of the pantos showing that season in the West End. Nearly every time we sat in the front row, inches away from Bud Flanagan, Ted Ray and the rest of the stars. For most of the shows, while the old boy was rolling about in ecstasy, laughing, I would be hard at work trying to make sense of what the crazy English were up to this time. For example, having been invited to see *Little Red Riding Hood*, I naturally expected to see the familiar story acted out, as would have been the case in Germany, realistically and to the letter. All the available resources would have gone into making the botanical and anatomical details of the forest and the wolf as accurate as possible. Instead of that, the glitz, pie-slinging, pyrotechnics, transvestism and flying ballet had me bedazzled, but also discomforted. To make the show funny, the actors were breaking a fundamental principle instilled into me throughout my German education, the supremacy of literalness and precision over everything else. Much as I relished the result, I couldn't entirely approve.

As soon as we were settled at the hotel, Mutti enrolled me at the nearest primary school. I could now understand quite a lot, but my spoken English was still limited and it was already well into the term. Everything conspired to make me stand out and attract attention to myself, exactly what I dreaded. Yet, when I was introduced to my class and my teacher as coming from Germany, I was amazed by everybody's kindness and special caringness towards me. I returned to the hotel for lunch, convinced that my morning had been a surprising success.

My mother asked me what it had been like. I told her that the classroom was very crowded and the children mostly dirty, smelt of pee and ran about throughout the lessons, talking. When the noise got too much, the teacher started shouting and told them to put their hands on their heads. Though they complied with this instruction, nothing else was any different. The work being done in English was grammar of the kind I had done with Fräulein Vogt in Luckenwalde nearly three years ago and the maths, fractions as taught me by Fräulein Buchholz more than a year ago. I wasn't complaining, just describing but, if truth be told, I had found the chaos and lack of discipline in the class seriously unnerving. Whether my mother picked up my anxiety or acted on educational grounds I cannot say but she told me that I wouldn't be going back to that school any more. Such was the goodwill towards me that when I didn't return for the afternoon the teacher telephoned the hotel to make sure I hadn't got lost on the way back. I couldn't imagine that happening in any of my German schools.

That evening my mother must have done some pretty intensive research, because at the same time the next morning she led me out of the hotel in the opposite direction, to another school. This time it was the Virgo Fidelis convent on the corner of the Brompton Road and The Boltons. Had she been inspired to approach it by the memory of the nuns who had come to her and Oma's rescue in the First World War? If so, she had no reason to be disappointed. The Mother Superior was expecting us and welcomed me with extraordinary sweetness. She led me into a class of about eight girls in dark green gymslips and introduced me to them individually. They all had names like Auriol, Vanessa and Annabel that I hadn't heard before. Afterwards she whispered to me that one of the girls I had met, the slim one with blonde hair called Marianne, was the daughter of the wartime resistance heroine, Odette. She seemed to expect me to feel a particular bond with this girl. I felt deeply embarrassed and more confused than ever about what to make of the response I was receiving to being German.

In that memorably cold winter of 1946–47 when snow was piled high on the pavements, just like in a German winter, I enjoyed my walks to and from my new school through Kensington's most elegant streets and squares. My mother and I had no idea that, by accident, I had landed in one of the most exclusive schools in the smartest parts of town. The nuns weren't even concerned about collecting my fees.

The class I joined had just started on a project to compile an ABC of the Catholic church. As the teacher took us through each letter of the alphabet we were supposed to suggest suitable items for inclusion and then to draw and write about them in our books. As I had not come across concepts like 'C for Chalice' or 'H for Host' even in German, I wasn't able to contribute much to this exercise.

A few days after my arrival, the whole school was to attend a special matinée of a Shakespeare play and I was instructed to ask my mother for permission to join the party. By the time I got home and tried to pass on the request I had forgotten the name of the play, 'Something about *Speck* (ham)', I told my mother. She laughed and said it must be *Hamlet*. She warned me that I was about to be as confused as she had been at my age, on her first day in a German school, when the very first lesson in which she participated turned out to be French. She was right. I joined the theatre excursion, but the only scene that made the slightest sense to me was the play within a play, when the actors performed the murder of Hamlet's father in mime.

Music was the subject I enjoyed most at the convent. The nuns' beautiful choir made the obligatory church attendances just about bearable for me and I learned many nice songs, including some from Shakespeare plays, like 'There was a lover and his lass' and 'Where the bee sucks there suck I'. My favourite, however, was a song called 'God be in my head and in my understanding'. It was obviously a grown-up song with a serious meaning, yet the words were so simple that, for once, even I could understand everything they were trying to say.

In nearly a term at the Virgo Fidelis convent I didn't make a friend or form a relationship, not with another pupil or a member of the staff. I considered it a freak stroke of luck that everyone was being so nice to me and continued to live in fear that Oma's dire warnings would come to pass. I needed every ounce of my energies for working on my image as a 'Londoner, born and bred', conforming to my surroundings and not standing out in any way. Soon I was fairly confident that I was not in danger of making the grossest lapses Oma had warned me about, like mentioning Papa or talking about my experiences and allegiances during the war. However, with so much going on around me that I couldn't understand, there was always a risk that I might ask questions that would alert people to the fact that I wasn't what I pretended to be and that might lead to my exposure. For the time being, making sure that didn't happen had to be my priority, but it wasn't conducive to making friends.

I had been given the impression that if I kept up my pretence of being a Londoner for long enough I would in due course actually become one; my embarrassing German identity would wither away and there would no longer be a need to pretend. I could certainly visualise the day when the last trace of my German accent had gone and I was so familiar with everything that leading a double life would no longer be quite such hard work. That day couldn't come soon enough for me and in the hope of hurrying it up I was following Oma's instructions to the letter.

I was much too preoccupied with getting through each day, and too obedient, to question Oma's and my mother's plan for my metamorphosis; it didn't occur to me to wonder if I wanted to become, permanently, someone else or if it was even possible. Yet one problem about the plan was only too apparent: Papa. I still thought about him every day and prayed for his safety and for the day our family would be reunited. When I tried to place that dream into any sort of context, my mind either went blank, or we were back in Mahlsdorf.

One day during this time, in a voice devoid of emotion, my mother broke the news that she had heard from Papa. I knew it! Of course he wasn't dead and of course he was always going to turn up again.

'Really? When? Where? How? Where has he been all this time? When will we see him?' I was overjoyed and, though I sensed my mother's reserve, I couldn't conceal my delight. I knew that, deep down, she was as relieved as I at the news, only putting on this controlled manner because of the practical difficulties that Papa's reappearance brought with it.

'We're not going to see him.' Mutti spoke steadily and deliberately, in a voice sounding like someone else's. 'With his past, he can't come to England and we're not going back to Germany. The country is ruined; it has no future. It's better for us to stay here and for you children to make your lives in England.'

Her words horrified me, but my love for her and my reluctance to add to the despair she was, I knew, permanently feeling prevented me from arguing. I had such faith in her judgement and her habit of always putting Udo's and my well-being before her own that I told myself, 'she would obviously prefer to be with Papa again. She is sacrificing her real wishes for our sakes.'

Mutti told me that Papa had been a prisoner of war of the British all this time. She had no idea how that had come about, seeing he was last seen giving himself up to the Americans. 'He is well. When he was released he went to look for us at Tante Kätchen's and he is still living there.'

'It's very important that we get divorced immediately,' she continued, 'otherwise we are in England illegally. Papa can't understand what risks we are running here so long as we are married. He's refusing to co-operate. We're corresponding through Oma and Opa and he doesn't have our address. I've had to tell him that he can't start writing to you until the divorce is through.' Despite her threat, she handed me a little letter of greeting in Papa's unmistakable handwriting.

She must have been aware of the shock and misery her words produced in me, but there was no mistaking the steely determination to go through with her plan.

I tried to imagine Papa living in Tante Kätchen's house in Lautenthal, but again my imagination went blank. It was a nice enough family home, but another family's, not Papa's. His devotion and commitment to my mother, Udo and me had been total, rivalled only by that to his *Führer* and his *Vaterland*. Now, with all his ideals shattered, everyone he loved gone, I couldn't imagine him as a person at all. What was there left for him to live for? I couldn't imagine him, but I could imagine how he felt and my heart ached for him.

20

CORNWALL

As Easter approached, Aunty Hopey came up with a bright idea. She was planning to spend the holiday with her cousins in Kettering, the ones my mother had so often stayed with in the First World War, and asked me if I would like to go with her, to repeat the pattern established thirty years before. She pointed out that this way Udo could come up from Eastbourne and take my place at the hotel for a while. So that the two of us could also see each other, she invited him to stay with her for the first few days of the holiday and sent him into London to meet me each day. Everyone was delighted with the plan.

Udo appeared at the hotel in the same clothes he had worn on arrival from Germany, including the aggressively short trousers, now more ill-fitting than ever. He was still wearing a pair of underpants my mother had made him in Recklinghausen to replace an earlier pair that had terminally fallen apart. He had been attending a secondary modern school in Eastbourne and, though he must have cut a spectacular figure in a playground peopled with several hundred other adolescent boys in identical grey flannels, he too had experienced nothing but friendly tolerance. His classmates competed with one another to teach him things they thought he should know about England, including the game of cricket. He and Uncle Harry had become good friends and altogether his time in Eastbourne had not been nearly as awful as might have been expected.

Now when he joined us in London Udo had his big moment. Mutti bought him some new clothes, including his first pair of long trousers. During our time at the hotel she and I had tended to spend all her free time visiting Aunty Hopey and other friends living scattered in various London suburbs, spending many hours on buses and on the Underground. Udo was more interested in seeing the sights and he and I now spent several happy days exploring the capital together. What stopped us ever feeling completely lost in unknown territory was finding ourselves in places whose names we recognised from our beloved games of Monopoly. In Leicester Square we made our most exciting discovery, a cartoon cinema called the Cameo. We had of course heard of Mickey Mouse and Donald Duck but never seen them on screen, or heard of other characters like Goofy and Dumbo. Now we became addicts and could easily have spent all and every day in the Cameo. We would have enjoyed nothing better than seeing the same films over and over again, but it wouldn't have occurred to us to sit through the show more than once without paying. 'Continuous performance' cinemas like the Cameo were unknown to us and we were shocked to discover how easy it would be to cheat. Another absurdity in the same class we noticed was the newsvendors' honesty boxes. How could people lay themselves open to being cheated and robbed like this? we asked ourselves. The only explanation we came up with was that they were, like so much else in England, *verrückt*.

My Kettering expedition with Aunty Hopey added yet another strand to the range of my cultural education since coming to England. Dot and Freda, two of my mother's erstwhile play-fellows, now had families of their own but still lived near their parents. Their children, though a little older than me, made me as welcome as the previous generation had made my mother. Dot showed me old photographs of them all playing in their orchard during the First World War and of her wedding in 1923, with a youthful Aunty Hopey and my teenage mother among the guests. Since those days Dot had established a School of Drama and Elocution and I arrived just in time for her students' end-of-term production. They were mostly adults and the items of the programme I remember best are their sketches from well-known classics. In a single afternoon I became acquainted with Lady Catherine de Bourgh, Eliza Doolittle and Heathcliff.

I returned from Kettering to find Udo still in residence at the hotel. My mother was supposed to have only one of us living there at a time, so why wasn't he back in Eastbourne? It seems that a day or two after I left a little parcel had arrived from Eastbourne, with all his possessions and a note from Aunty Gertie saying that he wasn't to return.

There followed a chaotic few days when Udo and I took it in turns to stay at the hotel, while the other one squatted with whichever of our friends could offer a bed. Mutti was still keeping up her habit of not discussing her worries with us, but it was obvious that she, normally so positive and capable, whatever the challenge, was in despair. Seeing her all hunched up, with no appetite and sometimes surreptitiously crying, distressed me terribly. She still never hinted at any regret that we had left our secure life in Recklinghausen but, on the contrary, continued to insist on how lucky we were to be in England. She was spending a lot of time working on legal documents, trying to sort out our nationality status and also to get Oma and Opa to join us in England.

As had happened so often in the history of our family, it was Aunty Hopey who saved the situation. The obvious solution, she declared, was to send Udo to a boarding school and for as long as necessary she would lend the fees. She even produced a school that satisfied the only criterion any of us was interested in – that it was cheap and near enough for her to keep an eye on him. Udo was duly enrolled at a ramshackle establishment called Staines Grammar School and another crisis had been weathered.

It was, however, only a temporary solution. My mother realised that she would never be able to afford Udo's boarding fees while she remained in her low-paid hotel job and, even if she could, there was the problem of what to do with him in the holidays. She started desperately looking for better-paid work where she could perhaps use her special linguistic skills. She found there were plenty of opportunities but, unfortunately, not in England. She would have to go back to Germany to work with the Control Commission in charge of the British occupation, so that option was ruled out.

Then, at last, she was offered a job that seemed almost too good to be true. One of the hotel residents was preparing to move into semi-retirement to his country house in Cornwall and offered Mutti a job as his personal assistant. A greater attraction than the handsome salary, by far, was the flat that came with the job. It was, in fact, exactly the solution Uncle Harry had advised my mother to seek and which she had long concluded didn't exist.

It must have been about the beginning of May when we left the hotel. Mutti's first task was to get her new employer's house ready for his move and the two of us set off on a sleeper to Penzance to start yet another new life. Mutti felt so sorry for me, the way I was being shunted around from place to place that, on the spur of the moment, she bought me the one present she could be sure would make me entirely happy for ever more – my very own puppy. Ecstatic though this purchase made me, in the light of the circumstances under which we were living it wasn't the most practical present. It wasn't even house-trained and spent the whole night of our train journey to Cornwall making puddles and squealing and barking, keeping the other passengers awake.

It soon emerged that for the first month or so of her new employment Mutti would have to be travelling up and down to London all the time and she didn't know what to do with me. How did I feel about a boarding school, like Udo, just for the rest of the summer term? She had found a school nearby that was prepared to take me at such an odd time of the year, where I could start as a boarder and then become a day girl. One of the gardeners was even prepared to give my puppy a permanent home.

As it happened, the idea appealed to me very much. My Christmas present from my Aunty Ethel had been an Enid Blyton paperback called *The Twins at St Clare's*. At first I had found it too difficult to read but by now I had just about struggled to the end and it had been well worth the effort. Children's books had been such a rarity in Germany that before coming to England I had read at most only half a dozen, nearly all fairy stories. The exception, and my favourite, was *Heidi*, and I had read it at least five times. Any book about girls of roughly my age would have been a treat, but one set in something as familiar as a school, with the exotic extra of it being a boarding school, had me enthralled. I could imagine nothing more idyllic than the lives of the twins and their friends and now my mother proposed to send me to a similar establishment that, miraculously but quite coincidentally, was also called St Clare's! My first sight of the handsome stone building set in grounds with rhododendrons, lawns and tennis courts thrown in surpassed all expectation.

Unusually for me, I remember little about my first term at St Clare's, no names or faces of any other girls or teachers. I suspect that I was in a permanent state of bewilderment, trying to make sense of the high-pitched, semi-hysterical dormitory culture at the school. In my ill-fitting secondhand uniform, speaking with a strong German accent and with a permanently glazed look, I must have cut a curious figure. When people asked me where I came from, which they often did in the beginning, I rigidly followed my instructions. They obviously didn't believe my claims to being a Londoner but I didn't care so long as it stopped them prying.

I was convinced that I had succeeded in hiding my origins when disaster struck. It was in a geography lesson and the teacher was trying to teach the class the concept of a 'native'. When they continued to look unconvinced she suddenly pounced on me as a typical example of a 'native of Germany'. How could she do that to me, when I had obeyed my orders to the letter? I dreaded what would happen after the lesson but nothing did. Were my classmates just lying low, preparing to lynch me at some later date, when I was off my guard? It seemed inconceivable to me that they didn't particularly care where I came from and that, having had their efforts to be friendly rebuffed, they had simply written me off as a hopeless case, German or no.

Though I remember so little about it, being a pupil at St Clare's was clearly less fun for me than for the fictional twins. I was missing my mother terribly but I was determined not to let it show. From my first days in England I was finding my Nazi training, the habit of striving with every fibre of my being to conform to what was expected of me, without question or complaint, a most effective support for getting me through difficult times, including this one.

In the corridor outside my dormitory were many shelves of books, including dozens by my new favourite author. I discovered that most of them were for younger children and much easier than my book about the twins. My English was now so good that I could positively race through the adventures of Noddy, Big Ears and other fantasy characters. I also discovered *Winnie the Pooh* and, though it was so silly, was enchanted by *Alice in Wonderland*.

My big moment came when I had been at the school for perhaps six or eight weeks and it was time for the end-of-year examinations. I had never come across the concept of exams and my only indication of what to expect was the obvious terror the very mention of them struck in everyone around me. Then, the minute I was handed my first paper, a flash of insight struck me. This was what the Fräuleins Vogt, Buchholz and all my other German teachers had been preparing me for when they drilled me so ferociously and nit-pickingly in spelling, grammar and other technical aspects of the Three Rs. I found most of the exams child's play, especially English grammar. It was so easy compared with the German variety. Having never before stood out at school in any way – at least, not in a proper school, all-in-one village schools like Podewilshausen and Wilkau didn't count – I now came top of the class in several subjects, including maths and English language in which I scored a distinction, with 87 per cent. My downfall was subjects requiring factual knowledge, like nature study, which I had never been taught in any form. For a question requiring me to draw a mushroom, I produced not just one, but a whole plantation of beautiful red and white spotted mushrooms in an attractive woodland setting, with a family of rabbits and some birds thrown in. My picture was so fine, I couldn't understand why, when I had done so well in everything else, my effort there didn't earn me a single mark.

Through my phenomenal exam results I acquired a new status in the school as 'brainy'. I didn't take it seriously, though. I knew I had an unfair advantage. I had by now come to realise that English and German schools weren't remotely about the same thing. English ones were for being interesting, for reading stories and poems and talking about their meaning, for choosing topics one wanted to learn more about. One was even encouraged to imagine and invent, activities severely frowned upon in any German classroom of my experience. German schools, as I saw it, had only one purpose, *pauken* – swotting, drilling, learning by heart, until the whole class could perform the task in hand, no more and no less. In England the German-type skills were almost a side-issue that one picked up while doing other things. What was so illogical – and therefore so typically English – was the weight placed on exams, which seemed to test skills not otherwise seriously taught or valued. Anyway, it meant that by doing what came naturally to a German child I was bound to succeed. I felt that I had somehow cheated, an impression confirmed by my form-teacher's comment at the bottom of my end-of-year report. She had written 'A determined little worker'. It was clearly a reproach.

Late one afternoon my mother appeared at the school, unannounced. She looked thoroughly agitated, which was hardly surprising after what had happened to her earlier that day.

She was working with her employer in her new office when some policemen burst in. She was in such a general state of anxiety that she took it for granted they had come for her; something must have gone wrong with her immigration papers or about Papa. To her astonishment, they marched off her boss who, it turned out, was a well-known swindler on the run under an alias. That was the moment she decided to give up her struggle to support us and find a home for us in England. Until then she had always ruled out the option of returning to Germany, where she could earn a good salary using her languages. Now there was no longer any doubt that it was the only way out of the mess she was in. She had tried everything else, but nothing had worked.

She had come to my school to explain what had happened and to warn Miss Johns, the headmistress, that I wouldn't be returning after the holidays. To her astonishment Miss Johns not only begged her to let me stay, but as an extra incentive offered me a scholarship. I would love to know her reasoning for this surprising gesture. I don't know what my mother had told her about my background when she had brought me – she must have explained my thick German accent somehow, for I doubt if another like it had been heard in the corridors of St Clare's. With hindsight I suspect that she saw me as a deserving refugee child, a 'good' German of the kind one had a moral obligation to help; once again, we ourselves couldn't understand why she was being so helpful.

My mother's next plan was to go to London immediately to get in her application to the Foreign Office for joining the Control Commission. It would take several months to be processed, so she had no time to waste. Until her posting came through she would have to return to taking temporary residential jobs.

By the time she fully extricated herself from her disastrous job she had missed the last train to London. She needed somewhere to stay the night and on the outskirts of St Ives found a neat white bungalow displaying a large Bed and Breakfast sign. The proprietress was a stout elderly widow with a head of thick white curls and an outgoing, quirky personality. That evening as she served my mother a delicious supper and again next morning over the biggest breakfast she had ever seen, Mrs Hyne entertained my mother with lively tales of the local happenings. My mother noticed that every one of her stories somehow led back to the same favourite topic, her contribution to the war effort. She had provided a home to four evacuee children from the East End of London, her 'Little Women'. She had clearly relished this role and confided to Mutti that her spirits had never recovered after they returned to London, they had been such good company and now she was all alone. Before she knew what she was doing, my mother heard herself asking, 'Would you like another little girl?' After that, she was always convinced that her guardian angel had led her to knock at the door of that neat white bungalow that evening.

21

Mrs Hyne's 'Company'

Shortly before the end of my first term at St Clare's, sometime in July, my mother arranged for me to make an exploratory visit to Mrs Hyne in her bungalow. Then she offered me the choice of either returning to the school as a boarder or moving in with Mrs Hyne and becoming a day girl. I chose the latter.

My mother's first priority on arriving in England had been to get our papers in order, making sure that we couldn't be deported again in a repeat of what had happened in 1919. She applied to have her British nationality restored, with Udo and me written into the document and all of our surnames changed to Oma's maiden name. As it happened, the British Nationality and Status of Aliens Act of 1914 – still in force – contained a clause that had been specially designed to enable British-born wives like Oma get rid of their German husbands, or, as the act described them, 'subjects of a State at war with His Majesty'. As my mother *did* want to part from Papa, who was also a 'subject of a State at war with His Majesty', she successfully invoked this clause and some time during our first summer in England the naturalisation papers arrived. This was also the time when my mother noticed that I had lost my last trace of a German accent. She decided that my metamorphosis from a German to an English child was now complete. Katrin Thiele could cease to exist and Katrine – soon to become Kay – Norris take over.

When my mother offered her Cornish Bed and Breakfast landlady her new foster-child, she must have revealed something about our German background, but they evidently agreed that the least said about it in the neighbourhood the better. Thus the girl who arrived in St Ives ready to start the autumn term as a day girl at St Clare's was Kay Norris and, like Mrs Hyne's previous Little Women, a Londoner. This was the cover under which 'Aunty', as I was instructed to call her, presented me to her friends and relations and they welcomed me into their community. They may have found it mildly odd that I never mentioned anything that happened to me before I appeared in their midst, including having a father, but for the whole time I lived in St Ives nobody, including 'Aunty' herself, ever asked me awkward questions.

In Mrs Hyne's kindly household I had no difficulty acting the part of the person I was supposed to be. I had still spent no time to speak of living in a normal English home and my ignorance of everyday domestic and national institutions remained total. I had never heard of Guy Fawkes, Hallowe'en, Remembrance Day and the two-minute silence, Pancake Day, the Boat Race, the Cup Final, the Trooping the Colour, Wimbledon or August Bank Holiday. I didn't know the names of the most common dishes, utensils, brand names, trees or garden flowers; I didn't know nursery rhymes, sayings and proverbs, jokes, popular songs or Christmas carols, or what to do with a Christmas stocking. Though I had just had my eleventh birthday, I couldn't make a cup of tea. To conceal my ignorance of what was going on, I developed a technique for playing dumb and making myself invisible, while at the same time watching and listening hard until I had the gist. I suspect that Aunty Hyne usually picked up my embarrassments and helped me out by repeating and explaining.

It would have been only too easy to catch me out but nobody cared about my background. Their only interest in me was as 'Mrs

Hyne's company'; provided I came up to scratch in that respect
– and by all accounts I did – I could do no wrong. It was hardly
a demanding position. All that was required was to allow myself
to be the centre of attention, to be waited on hand and foot and
fed – rather too much – delicious home-cooked food. For the first
time in my life I became chubby. For all this care Mrs Hyne
charged my mother £1 per week, plus the Family Allowance, no
great sacrifice, as that was the first my mother had heard of it. Mrs
Hyne, a veteran at dealing with bureaucracy from her time with
the evacuees, soon tackled the task of getting me signed up for it
with relish. It must have been around halfway through the
summer holidays when I presented myself in St Ives to begin my
new life.

I had spent the first part of the holiday with my mother in yet
another of the temporary jobs she took to see her through until
her Control Commission posting was confirmed. Her first such
assignment had been as temporary nanny to the children of Lord
Lucan, whose son and heir, aged about twelve at the time, was
later to gain notoriety fleeing from justice as the suspected
murderer of *his* children's nanny.

Her next job, where I was allowed to join her for a while, was
in a haunted Elizabethan manor house on the edge of Exmoor.
There was said to be a curse on the house, responsible for no end
of tragedies in the family of the ancestral owners who had, as a
result, moved out and turned the place into a holiday home for
children with parents overseas. Several of the family's ghosts
were still regularly on the prowl and every morning over breakfast
the staff would swap stories about the previous night's sightings;
even my mother claimed she had spotted a soldier in armour
lurking in an alcove. I dreaded a similar encounter but, after the
night a bat flew into our bedroom and attempted to settle in my
hair, I decided that, given the choice between the two, show me
a ghost every time.

One morning near the end of my stay there, my mother and I

got up at dawn for a last *Wanderung* on Exmoor together. I have a clear memory of that expedition, how we surprised – or rather, were surprised by – a magnificent stag and of our enjoyment of the still, misty morning and the stunning surroundings, the whole thing given an extra edge by the knowledge that we were about to be parted again and this time for even longer.

Then I was taken to Taunton and put on the Penzance train. At St Erth I changed to the branch line to St Ives where I was expecting Mrs Hyne to meet me, but she was nowhere to be seen. Then a good-looking young man sauntered up to me and asked if I was Kay. He introduced himself as Reg, Mrs Hyne's son, and led me through the narrow, winding streets of Downalong St Ives and up some steps to the bus for Upalong, the newer part of the town that stretches back up the hills, away from the old fishing village and the sea.

Reg was a student in London, home for the holidays. I could tell straight away that he was an unusual person, so confident, well spoken and with such a natural air of authority, yet so unassuming, relaxed and casually dressed. In my previous experience of England, those characteristics didn't go together. In the days to come I was to discover a great deal more that was exceptional about Reg. I only had to admire a painting or a piece of pottery in the house to be told, 'Reg done it!' There seemed to be nothing at which he didn't excel, from playing the piano to painting, pottery, carpentry, even cooking. Best of all, he was wonderful company.

Reg was the only one of Mrs Hyne's three children who still lived at home. They were devoted to one another but they made an odd pair, he such a natural sophisticate, she such an unrepentant countrywoman. In the months to come I was to hear many stories about Mrs Hyne's early life, how she came from a remote part of the Lizard Peninsula where her father was a tin miner and the family so poor that she left school when she was only ten to start work as a milkmaid. She used to have a long walk to work through the fields, in the winters when it was dark and scary. Then she went into service and eventually married a coastguard. She and her husband Tom spent more than thirty years living in clifftop cottages, miles from civilisation. Tom's last posting was to Gurnard's Head, between St Ives and Land's End; when his health forced him to take early retirement Aunty Hyne bought Chy-an-Mor, her bungalow, and moved the family to the comparatively bright lights of Upalong St Ives. When Tom died in 1942, Aunty was very lonely and the opportunity to look after four little evacuees couldn't have come at a better time.

Though I appeared on the scene when Aunty Hyne had already lived at Chy-an-Mor for the best part of ten years, she had still not altogether abandoned the pre-industrial lifestyle that had obviously served her well for sixty years. Her bedtime ritual still included lighting an oil lamp in her kitchen, switching off all the electric lights in the bungalow and crossing the five feet of hall to her bedroom, bearing the lamp aloft. Her washday was conducted in an outhouse with a copper boiler, zinc tubs, a washboard and a hand-mangle. As for her ironing – the most perfect I have ever seen – that was done with a pair of cast-iron smoothing-irons, heated up, alternately, either on her gas-rings or the top of a Primus stove.

One of the most heart-rending stories from her past concerned the trials of being the mother of a child like Reg. For what was a woman living on the farthest clifftop of the Cornish coast supposed to do with an infant prodigy who, from the moment he could hold a stick or a piece of coal in his little fingers, was using the beaches and rocks around Gurnard's Head as his canvas? Eventually she articled him to a firm of architects in Penzance and he was just beginning to develop his talent there when the war started and he was called up. He went into the navy, was commissioned and on 6 June 1944, as navigator of the minesweeper HMS *Boston*, led the D-Day fleet across the Channel to the beaches of Normandy. Then, at the end of the war, came the chance to study for his ARIBA diploma in London, where he was turning out to be an outstanding student.

Reg's first architectural design was already up and in use, an eye-catching adornment to Aunty Hyne's garden. Built as a perfect hexagon, in clapboard and with a pagoda roof, it could have passed for an ordinary, if especially attractive, summer-house. However, as the name above the door, Nikrow, ('Work-in' spelled backwards) suggested, it was really an all-in-one studio/bedsitter, accommodating a bed, various fitted drawers and cupboards and a huge drawing board, all in a space not much bigger than a telephone box.

From the day I joined their household, mother and son treated me as though I had always been part of their family and as though their home was my home. It was an arrangement into which I was, apparently, more than ready to enter. Aunty Hyne allocated a corner of her bedroom as my territory. I would normally have been embarrassed at being thrust into such intimacy with someone I hardly knew, but in this family it felt natural and acceptable. Reg became my second much-loved older brother; it was always a black day for me when he had to go back to London.

In her own way Mrs Hyne was just as striking a character as her son, intuitive, resourceful and competent at everything she touched. Yet, for all her abilities, she could only function properly when she had somebody to look after, or, as she called it, 'do for'. That was where I came in, the unsuspecting beneficiary of several years' deprivation and one that offered endless scope for her frustrated energies.

Her first initiative on my behalf was to appoint a piano teacher for me. This was her friend, Miss Haydon, a seriously short-sighted retired governess in her mid-eighties who lived in a bedsitter nearby. My musical education now became Miss Haydon's over-riding commitment and I enjoyed my lessons with her, for which Aunty instructed me to pay her sixpence a week out of my shilling's pocket money.

An even more remarkable achievement was her recruitment of a thoroughly suitable friend for me, my first in England. She only had to signal word of my arrival into her grapevine and the very next day a tall, smiling girl called Mary Edwards appeared at the bungalow and invited me to tea.

Mary was nearly thirteen, more than a year older than me, and a pupil at the grammar school in Penzance; she had a calm, confident personality and was frighteningly clever and knowledgeable on every subject. For what remained of the holidays she took me on walks along the cliffs, expeditions to the beach and forays to the local recreation ground to join in the non-stop game of cricket happening there. I was delighted with my new friend but puzzled that she, who had lived here all her life, was apparently quite pleased to find me. Then the autumn term started and as I made my way to join a little crowd of uniformed children waiting for the school bus to Penzance I noticed a possible reason. Mary was the only girl.

The forty-five-minute journey to and from school now became the high point of my day. Mary and I sat together chatting, playing paper and pencil games and larking about with the other travellers. Except for me they were all grammar school pupils and how different from the children I had known in Germany or at the giggly, snobbish St Clare's. They were so confident, so full of jokes and so awesomely disrespectful of authority. Two of the most waggish boys, Tommy and Barry, became our special friends. One day after school they boarded the bus with a test tube, various chemical substances and a box of matches concealed in their satchels and let off a stink bomb. I was hugely impressed by their daring.

None of my new friends had a clue that they were associating with a German, which was just as well, since Germans were the butt of their most outrageous humour and mimicry. Tommy's German officer was, in fact, an uncannily accurate imitation of Papa. I didn't know whether to laugh or cry.

Though life in St Ives was turning out to be surprisingly agreeable, it felt as far removed from everything I had known before as if it was on another planet. Then, as the winter evenings drew in, something happened to connect me to my previous life, my real one, where I was still living in my head. I discovered that my new friends were Monopoly addicts. After that, for my first winter in St Ives, happiness was a fireside game of Monopoly with Mary, Tommy and Barry.

I had now lived in England for nine months but in my mind the past was all mixed up together in a chaotic ragbag, regardless of weeks, months and years. What a contrast with this new life where everything was finely tuned to seasonal routines and where order and forward planning ruled.

In termtime the focal point of Aunty's week was the arrival every Tuesday of Reg's parcel of dirty washing. That afternoon the same carton would be repacked with clean laundry, a fruitcake, a special giant-sized Cornish pasty and a letter and sent back to London. The timing of washday, ironing day, baking day, letter-writing day and post office/pension day, in fact, Aunty's programme for the whole week was fitted round this high point. Yet, controlling the domestic round was a still superior force previously unknown to me, the seasonal cycle that rules the lives of country people.

Arriving in St Ives towards the end of August, I was just in time to join what was to become my favourite of Aunty's seasonal rituals. On a morning when she judged conditions suitable we set off from the bungalow armed with buckets, jugs and a couple of pasties to board the country bus to Zennor. We got off in what appeared to be the middle of nowhere and made our way to a particular field that Aunty remembered from the time she lived on the nearby clifftops as an outstanding place for blackberries. We picked all day until all our containers were full, stopping only to eat our pasties and drink from a stream. As there was still time before our bus back we called in at the farm of one of aunty's old neighbours. She was delighted to see us, produced a huge tea and, while the two of them settled down to an intense gossip, sent me off to explore the farm. In every way, it was a thoroughly enjoyable expedition. The next few days were taken up with bottling the blackberries, making jam and baking pies for ourselves and the neighbours.

Easter saw another 'hunting and gathering' ritual, this time with Reg in the lead and Udo, who always spent that holiday with me, a keen participant. Once again we returned to the Hyne family's familiar haunts around Gurnard's Head, this time to collect a special kind of seaweed that was supposed to be a great delicacy. We spent the day in a cove beneath the headland, pulling transparent, rubbery strips of seaweed, that had to be carefully distinguished from other kinds, off the rocks. They were so slippery and squashy that several armfuls could be condensed into a small shopping bag. Back home, released from their containers, they would spring up into mountains of tangled mackintosh that we had to rinse in bathfuls of fresh water. When the last grains of sand were sluiced off the whole mass was pushed into a vat with vinegar and boiled down to practically nothing. It looked like ready-to-pour tar, but when fried in dripping, was supposed to be a special breakfast treat. Much as I loved every stage of the preparation, I could never bring myself to taste it. The smell put me right off but everyone else raved about it.

During the spring and summer Aunty Hyne was busy with her Bed and Breakfast visitors; at the end of September her board was brought in and the bungalow rearranged for its off-season mode. Aunty counted her profits and worked out how much to spend on repairs and redecoration. She mended her sheets, prepared her garden for winter and replaced her gingham summer curtains with heavy velour. At around this time, when I had been with her for just a few weeks, she suddenly asked me how many Christmas presents I would be needing to make. Eh? What was she talking about? She made me list all my family and friends and helped me choose a suitable item to make for each of them. The only point not up for discussion was that everyone's present would be handmade and finished in time for Christmas. For the rest of the autumn the two of us spent most evenings sitting on either side of the kitchen fire, listening to the radio and, while her knitting needles flew in and out at dizzying speed, I would be struggling with Opa's knitted slippers, Oma's ingeniously folding crocheted string bag or my mother's cushion-cover, made from a floor-cloth and bits of brightly coloured wool remnants. For all my lack of talent, I emerged from three seasons of this routine as a WI bazaar organiser's dream.

Happily Aunty's routines were never an end in themselves, but her way of being efficient and having time for the real stuff of her life, which was social. She didn't go out much but received a steady flow of colourful visitors. They may have started off as three distinct groups but, given her gregarious nature and the size of her kitchen, they had merged into an easy mix of family and neighbours, bed and breakfast clientele and what I can only describe as her 'artistic circle'.

Her immediate local 'kitchen Cabinet' called in at least daily; they conferred in powerful Cornish accents about the subject dearest to their hearts, the ups and downs of the tourist industry. They had their own technical jargon, according to which 'Do 'er do?' meant 'Does she take in visitors?' and ''Ers got three in' meant 'She has three visitors staying'. Then there were her old friends from Zennor and her B & B guests, many of whom returned for their holidays year after year and had become friends. They must have congratulated themselves on discovering a landlady who not only pampered them disgracefully but who provided so much local colour, for in her case the classic Cornish tales of smugglers, shipwrecks and salvage were, for once, based on personal experience. Aunty was, in fact, so authentic that in the latest round of the Dancing Round Knill's Monument festival, that only happens once in five years, she had been picked as one of the principal characters, one of the two widows who lead seven little maids dressed in white in the Helston floral dance.

The arty-looking individuals who drifted in and out of the bungalow must once have had a connection with Reg but by the time I appeared on the scene they had long ago merged in with the rest of Aunty's personal circle. Some popped in to say hello in passing, others came to stay for a week or two and one stayed for a whole winter; she was waiting for builders to complete her new home in Downalong St Ives, a former fish-salting loft, being converted into a studio to one of Reg's most ingenious designs. The women from this group were inclined to be dressed in sandals, masses of beads, drooping shawls and handwoven skirts a foot longer than anyone else was wearing at the time. Their hair, too, long and straight with a fringe that obstructed vision, was an affront to the curlers-and-hairpins fashion of the day. Oma would have been appalled.

My early training in conformity had reached too deep for me to appreciate these characters as they deserved. Why did they go out of their way to draw attention to themselves and make themselves look so ridiculous? I would ask myself over and over again. It was such a pity, when they were otherwise such nice people. My only way of coping with their eccentricities was to dismiss them as *verrückt* and laugh at them behind their backs, as I assumed everyone else, including Reg and Aunty, were doing too, though they were too polite to let it show.

One reliable source of Aunty's house guests was the famous St Ives Leach Pottery, situated so close to the bungalow that seeing Bernard Leach at work became for me an everyday sight. Pottery was Reg's overriding passion and he had managed to insinuate himself into the pottery as a disciple and friend of the Leach family. That contact naturally led to requests for Aunty Hyne to put up visitors to the pottery, many of them students from overseas. I especially remember a Jamaican called Cecil Baugh, Aunty's first black house guest. Though he was the mildest of men, Aunty wasn't taking any chances and while he was in residence she always made sure to lock her bedroom door. He has since become that island's leading potter, with a worldwide reputation.

Every Christmas Reg and his mother gave a splendid party for all their – and soon my – friends; they invited the neighbours, the

Zennor farmers, Miss Haydon, the arty crowd, Mary, Tommy and Barry. I didn't realise how unusual it was to find such a social mix in England, then or now – it would have been normal in Germany. I was put in charge of the decorations, Aunty of the food and Reg of the entertainments, including quizzes, charades and party pieces. The star turn was always Mr Vibert, the Leach Pottery manager, a brilliant conjurer and a member of the Magic Circle. Compared with my awful first Christmas in England, my second was every bit as jolly as I had been led to expect from reading about the Bruin Boys' Christmas in my *Playbox Annual*. Just to confirm the point I asked Reg to include some rounds of Blind Man's Buff in his party programme. A further pleasure was Aunty Hyne's Christmas present to me – a copy of her favourite book, *Little Women*.

One Saturday evening soon after this a girl called Kitty from one of the farms dropped in to see Aunty on her way to a dance in St Ives. She had ridden in from Zennor on her bicycle and in the confident expectation of getting a lift home asked if she could leave her bike, which she would collect later in the week. I hadn't ridden a bicycle since I was last in Berlin and the sight of Kitty's, propped up against the back of the house for several days became an irresistible temptation. Aunty wouldn't hear of my riding it but on the last morning of the school holidays temptation proved too strong, even for me. I took the bicycle without permission and set off on a trip.

All my previous bicycling experience had been gained on the north German plain and on German bicycles, with brakes attached to the pedals. The moment I was astride Kitty's the difference to cycling in Cornwall became alarmingly clear. First, Chy-an-Mor was at the very top of a long hill that winds up from the town and as I had set out on my expedition pointing the bike in the downhill direction, it had already begun to gain momentum before my feet had even touched the pedals. Then, being used to foot brakes, I pedalled furiously backwards, but the bicycle continued to gather speed. I tried the hand-brake, but to no effect. I know I panicked but I cannot remember what followed.

The next thing I knew I was lying on a very hard surface in a dark room with bright spotlights shining on me. Directly above me hung a huge chrome lamp, in which a ghastly mess of blood and grit was reflected. I wondered vaguely what it could be. Around me people were talking in soft voices. Then I smelt that revolting ether again – but not for long, as I immediately lost consciousness once more.

I was in the theatre of the St Ives Cottage Hospital, having my knee, my face and various other parts of my anatomy stitched up. I wasn't in pain because I had severed some nerves that would take a very long time to heal again. A grocery delivery man had found me and Kitty's battered bicycle lying in a side road. He emptied his groceries, fetched blankets and cushions from a nearby house and brought me straight here. Someone must have identified me, God knows how, for it was already evening when I regained consciousness. Aunty Hyne and Reg – emergency-summoned back from London – had been hovering at the hospital for hours. I will never forget the relief on their faces when they were shown to my bedside and saw for themselves that I was not only alive but not damaged beyond repair. Until that moment they hadn't dared to notify my mother.

Next morning, on his way to the train back to London, Reg popped in to see me for the last time. My leg was by now encased in a most exotic rubber dressing, a spaghetti junction of hoses, tubes and drains hooked up to a water tap that channelled swirling jets of water over my gruesome-looking, but fairly superficial, wound. The doctor told me he had learned this method of treatment during the war, in the air force, treating plane-crash survivors. Reg must see this remarkable sight, I decided. I lifted up my bedclothes and invited him to have a look. He was just peering in when a voice behind him thundered, 'How dare you examine the bed!' It was matron. Reg fled in terror, the only time I have ever seen him lost for words. Afterwards, matron interviewed me minutely about the identity of the scruffy young man who had taken such liberties on her ward.

I spent three enjoyable weeks at the hospital, the only child patient and more fussed over than ever in my life. Even Kitty came to see me and, instead of giving me the telling off I dreaded, apologised for the condition of her brakes.

One day not long after I was well enough to return to school, Aunty Hyne told me not to catch the school bus to Penzance the following day. I was to go instead to the St Ives Primary School where she had entered me for a special examination. I presented myself as instructed and, having by now become addicted to exams, spent a happy day working my way through various strange maths and English papers. A few weeks later a postcard arrived to say that I had passed the 11 Plus. Aunt Hyne explained that I would be changing to the grammar school after the summer holidays and that I must inform my mother in my next letter. It seems that Aunty Hyne had penetrated the mysteries of getting a child through the 'scholarship exam', as she called it, with one of her wartime Little Women. Suspecting that she had another suitable candidate on her hands, she had no intention of letting her expertise in that department go to waste.

I was delighted that I would be joining Mary and the rest of my travelling companions at the grammar school. I was the only St Clare's girl in my part of St Ives and had remained a complete loner at the school. Now Aunty Hyne instructed me to inform Miss Johns, the headmistress, that I would be leaving her school at the end of the year. When I knocked on her door and went in to tell her the news, her face flushed dark purple from what looked alarmingly like rage. She spluttered out something to the effect that my mother was under an obligation to leave me at her school for the rest of my school career. I had to explain that my mother didn't know anything about this, it had all been arranged by Mrs Hyne. Her face fell. She had the sense to realise she was beaten game, set and match.

22

My Secret Life

While the London-born-and-bred foster-child I was impersonating quickly settled into the daily round at Chy-an-Mor, the real me was otherwise engaged. For my first few months in England living out my assumed identity had been hard work but in the ideal conditions of St Ives it required only the shortest period for me to perfect my act.

I had longed for this day, when my metamorphosis would be complete. Oma and my mother had always given me to understand that once I became a typical English schoolgirl on the outside I would also feel like one and would be able to stop pretending, relax and be myself again, even if a different self. Yet when my transformation was so total that I sometimes caught myself speaking – even thinking – about Germans as my enemies I discovered that inside me nothing had changed. I was still the same Katrin Thiele as ever. My masquerade may have become second nature, but it remained a masquerade.

I could, I suppose, have convinced myself that my new script was the right one, that I really was an English girl and that the German episode in my life had been an unfortunate mistake, best forgotten, but it never occurred to me to take this way out of my dilemma. That would be *untreu* (not keeping the faith), a prospect more horrible to me than either of the others on offer, continuing my double life or exposure as a German.

I now needed all the energies previously devoted to cultivating my Kay Norris identity to keeping Katrin Thiele alive. She belonged to another world, a world that didn't exist any more, but for the sake of my sanity I had to hang on to her. I kept up my nightly ritual of thinking about Papa, confident that, wherever he was, he too was thinking of me. I imagined to myself what he might be doing and feeling and sometimes found myself suffering his loss and disillusion as acutely as if they were happening to me; I tried picturing him as the prisoner he had been for two years, or as one of the unemployed ex-prisoners I had seen drifting about Recklinghausen, stripped of the confidence and authority over others which, for me, defined his personality. With everything he had lived for lost, how could he retain a shred of hope or self-respect? Such thoughts reduced me to despair and I still couldn't accept that the divorce my mother had spoken about so determinedly would really happen.

In another part of my mind I was trying to make sense of everything to do with the war, especially the Nazi beliefs that everyone around me had at first supported so passionately, then disavowed. Not me, though. Nobody was going to catch me being a *Verräter*, a traitor. I continued to cling to my Nazi ethic to guide my life, albeit an increasingly revisionist version.

There were now few occasions when my inner and my outer worlds connected up together, mostly when something to do with Germany, Hitler or Nazism came up for discussion at school, on the radio or in a film. I always gave it all my attention and never ceased to feel a shock when I heard yet another, to me, die-hard fact being contradicted. Thus I had known for as long as I could remember how the war started: warmongering England had declared war on peace-loving Germany. The first time I heard that England only did this to protect other little countries Germany had invaded I couldn't believe my ears. Worse was to come.

As with my first sight of the concentration-camp picture at the post office in Recklinghausen, my initial reaction to every new atrocity story was to hope that they were merely anti-German propaganda. They couldn't have happened. If they were true, we must have known, but nobody did. I refused to believe that ordinary, high-minded Nazis were really the despicable monsters now being portrayed. But if these crimes had happened – as I came to accept – who had done them? I concluded that a special, secret, military squad had been responsible, without anybody else knowing. Papa, for certain, had had no part in it. Nothing was going to stop me thinking well of him, but I was terribly confused.

While, in time, I came to accept the conventional English view of the Second World War, I managed, with mental gymnastics on a Herculean scale, simultaneously to hold on to large chunks of German wartime ideology. It was the only way I could cope with my conflicting emotions: horror, disgust and guilt by association at Germany's crimes, love and respect for my family and friends and last, but not least, the need to hang on to my own integrity.

Condemning these terrible things that had happened was, however, not the same as condemning everything I had experienced in Germany and, with a few little adjustments here and there, I continued to find the Nazi ethic of my early childhood as exemplary as ever. I could, for example, find no fault with the basic principle that everyone had a *Pflicht* (duty) to put one's *Volk* before oneself. Admittedly, our wartime definition of *Volk*, much the same as *Vaterland*, had been confined to Germans, but my revisionist version was equally suited to other nationalities and communities, wherever one happened to be living, even St Ives. Other Nazi virtues I still supported were *Opfer* (sacrifice), *Tapferkeit* (bravery) and *Mut* (fortitude). *Ehre* (honour) I was less sure about. What was it for? How did it help? As for *Schicksal* (destiny), that lacked any merit. After all we had heard about it in the war, just look at the result! I still liked *Treue* (keeping the faith) though, and *Willen* (resolve or determination). If you had that, you were sure to follow your plans through to the end and not give up when things got difficult. Though my revisionism would have been enough to make Hitler turn in his grave, he would have approved of my fervour.

It irked me that nobody in England seemed to grasp that Nazism had been about building a new world order based on the noble ideals I still found so satisfying. For it had not taken me many weeks in the country to discover that the English definition of Nazi could be summed up in a single word, 'Jew-gasser'. That was so misguided, such a mistake. Yes, we were taught to despise Jews, but what English people didn't seem to appreciate was that for Nazis like me everything to do with Jews had been a minor issue, that one could be a Nazi without ever seeing or thinking about Jews.

One of the worst problems about trying to make sense of my previous life in England was not having anyone around to talk to about my confusion. Living incognito in St Ives made the subject unmentionable among my new friends and on the rare occasions that I saw my family it was clear that they didn't want to discuss it either.

For my first Easter holiday in St Ives my mother and Udo came to stay with me. My mother had brought with her Bill, a friend and colleague from her Control Commission posting in Hamburg. It was typically Cornish April weather, bright and blustery. We walked on the clifftops and beaches, took country buses to scenic fishing villages and went on expeditions to St Michael's Mount, Land's End and other local landmarks. Bill was a widower, very youthful in outlook and, though he had no children of his own, excellent at everything to do with sport and games. Udo and I enjoyed his contribution to a thoroughly enjoyable holiday for us all.

My mother and my brother had plunged wholeheartedly into their new lives and I could see that outwardly, at least, they had adjusted to our new circumstances more successfully than I. They could, of course, have thought the same about me, for we never did get round to comparing our techniques for, and relative success in dealing with, our embarrassing past.

Udo who, like me, had never distinguished himself in any way in German schools had settled into Staines Grammar School much better than might have been expected. Aunty Hopey usually had him over for part of the weekend and a close bond had developed between them. No doubt thanks to his training for the *Hitlerjugend Sportsabzeichen*, he was even making a name for himself as an athlete. He had, apparently, made a clean break with his German self and was fully engaged in the present.

My mother had the strongest reasons for forgetting her previous life. On top of her determination to cut off all contact with Papa, she was acutely aware of the risk of losing the job on which all our survival depended if her career as a Nazi supporter came to light. One of her techniques for handling the situation was to block anything that no longer fitted from her mind. Discussing our previous lives with me was not only the last thing she wanted for herself. She also believed it was in my best interest to forget the whole episode and assumed that the best way of achieving this was never to mention the subject.

On the one occasion I took the bull by the horns and confronted her with my doubts her answer left me more confused than ever about what to think. 'Of course we didn't know about the existence of gas chambers. One did hear rumours that Jews were being badly treated and put into camps. I heard them, anyway, because of Papa, even though other people may not have. Your father did hate Jews and was all in favour of what was going on. You ask why people like me didn't do anything to stop it. What could we do? It wasn't a society where anyone could ask questions or protest about anything, not like it is here. Who could one ask? It just wasn't done. Anybody who even so much as hinted that they didn't approve of something the regime was doing was considered *untreu*, morally reprehensible and a public enemy. The only way to show that one was a decent, public-spirited citizen was by supporting the Nazi ideal and not rocking the boat.'

That creed must have packed a powerful punch, for it had

made an indelible mark on me. Here I was, years after the German collapse, living in St Ives, without any outside reinforcement, on the contrary, under every possible family and social pressure to renounce it, but still clinging to some vestige of my past life. Not only that, I knew that if I let it go altogether, I wouldn't be able to live with myself any more.

23

DRUIDS TO THE RESCUE

The lack of anyone in St Ives with whom to discuss my Nazi past was only to be expected, yet two return trips to Germany to visit my mother produced no opportunities either; not even the time I spent a weekend with Papa.

The first trip came in the summer of 1948, when I was twelve and just about to change schools. It started with my first visit to London since coming to Cornwall more than a year before and I can recall my excitement as I sat on the train, looking out for my favourite landmarks – the two red sandstone ladies in crinoline dresses, rising out of the sea near Dawlish in Devon and the white horses carved into the chalk of no less than three hillsides on the Wiltshire downs. The biggest excitement of the journey, however, was the knowledge of who would be meeting me off the train at Paddington – Oma and Opa.

Within less than a year of our own arrival and nearly thirty after they were deported from England, my mother had organised their repatriation. After our departure from Recklinghausen they had been forced to leave our flat; living conditions in Germany had continued to deteriorate and they had become increasingly dependent on their English friends. Then, after months of bureaucratic wrangling, in the autumn of 1947 their authorisation came through and they were brought back to England by the Red Cross. Their travel documents were dated for 7 November, the same day as my mother's orders to take up her long-awaited Control Commission post. They worked out afterwards that their ships, travelling in opposite directions, passed one another in mid-Channel.

Compared with the uniformly overweight people I now lived among in St Ives, Oma and Opa struck me as pathetically shrunken and little when I caught sight of them looking out for me from the back of the platform. They were in excellent spirits, however. They loved being back in England, speaking English all the time, drinking tea, travelling on buses and on the Underground, reading newspapers, listening to the BBC, going to the library and the pictures and, above all, seeing Udo and their English friends again. Their only regret was missing my mother.

Oma and Opa were bowled over by the tolerance and generosity being shown them in England. They were not only received into the country, but given ration cards and a cash settling-in allowance. When they told Aunty Gertie their good fortune she shook her head in despair, saying: 'Aren't we fools?' Oma and Opa evidently agreed, since they refused to remain dependent on the state. Though Opa was now seventy and Oma sixty-seven, they had found themselves a joint residential job in the kitchens of an old people's home in the East End of London and this was where they took me to spend a couple of nights. They had a little flat in the attics of the glum Victorian building but, true to form, Oma had made even those improbable quarters look cheerful and homely.

They had discovered that several of their closest pre-war friends weren't alive any more, but they received the warmest possible welcome from those who were. Only Mr George and his family refused to have anything to do with them; they could never forgive Oma and Opa for having been Nazis. Given Oma's disposition to make the best of every situation, she never said much about this rejection, but I could tell from the regularity with which Mr George's name cropped up in her conversation that she deeply regretted the loss of his friendship.

Aunty Hopey herself wasn't politically minded, but her family's tradition of radical socialism could equally have disposed her to cut off all ties with my family when their fervent support for Hitler came to light. How generous of Aunty Hopey to allow her love for my mother and my grandparents to overcome her disgust at their politics and to come to their rescue again as staunchly after the Second World War as she had during the first.

Even Mr George's family, the Rossells, don't appear to have held the politics of the older generations against the children. Several times while Udo was at school in Staines, Aunty Hopey had him in tow when she visited them, or they her. Mr George discovered Udo's love of history and started taking a real interest in him, giving him books. Then, soon after my bicycle accident, when Aunty Hopey came on her annual visit to me in St Ives, she appeared with a large jar of ointment that Mr George had made specially for me to one of his own recipes. He had heard that the accident left me with facial scars and sent me the message that if I rubbed the ointment in, night and morning, the scars would disappear. I did as instructed and, in due course, most of them did.

In addition to socialising with her old, as well as her more recent English friends, Oma was, as always, conducting a large correspondence. When Germany's post-war turmoil started to die down, she had managed to re-establish contact with quite a number of relatives and friends, including Onkel Arno, Onkel Max and Herr Freyer, their teacher friend from Köpenick. They also traced their friend Annie, the widow of one of Opa's fellow-internees in the First World War, now living alone and in isolation in Berlin's Russian sector. But they never found any other members of the Anglo-German circle who had been their close friends for nearly thirty years.

At the end of my short stay with them at the old people's home, Oma and Opa took me to Liverpool Street Station to meet up with Udo and a party of unaccompanied school children travelling to join their parents serving in the British Occupation of Germany.

If I had expected my German trip to be in any sense a return to my roots I was going to be disappointed. My mother was living in considerable luxury with about a dozen other English residents, including Bill, in a Control Commission mess in a wealthy Hamburg suburb. All the domestic staff, including the cook, were German and though only German dishes were produced, they didn't recall for me many gastronomic experiences of the war or post-war periods.

My mother was working as the personal interpreter to Judge O'Hanlon, a British circuit judge sent out to hear cases which, for any reason to do with the occupation, came under British jurisdiction. One morning we were allowed into the court to watch her at work. She was wearing a flattering, figure-hugging navy-blue uniform and looked extremely important, up on the dais, a few feet away from the judge. Without a second's hesitation she was translating every word spoken, in either language, by any party to the proceedings. Even for someone with her skills it was a challenge that she found exhausting but also exhilarating. Occasionally she had extra interpreting assignments for one-off events, as when a Labour MP for Plymouth, called Mrs Middleton, visited Hamburg to address a socialist women's congress. On that occasion she committed the worst misdemeanour known in the interpreting profession – she abandoned her text and expressed an opinion. 'They were such a rude and badly behaved audience', she told me afterwards. 'They blamed the British for not stopping Hitler earlier and heckled everything the speaker said. It was a very smoky room, she could hardly make herself heard and I just couldn't stand it. I turned on the audience and told them to show better manners.'

When my mother and Bill weren't working they took us on expeditions to the Baltic coast and around Hamburg, including to orchestral concerts of the Hamburg Symphony Orchestra under their guest conductor, the young Sergiu Celibidache. They took us to a skating rink where my mother demonstrated her ice-dancing skills for us, not forgotten since her Köpenick days. When we were on our own, Udo and I hung about at the English club, swimming and playing tennis, watching cartoon films and going on organised outings with other English children.

On 18 June 1948, just a week or two before our arrival, Germany had experienced its most significant event of the next forty years, a successful currency reform. Overnight, long empty and desolate shops were filled with goods that Germans hadn't seen for a decade – if ever. I wasn't complaining, but the Germany I experienced that summer bore no resemblance to the one I had known, which no longer existed in any shape or form, but with which, deep down, I still identified. I had returned as an expat, to an expat England making itself comfortable in the first days of *Wirtschaftswunder* Germany.

I returned to St Ives in time for a few trips to the beach with Mary and my favourite blackberrying expedition with Aunty, before school started again. I was really looking forward to my new school and was not disappointed; of my many schools – thirteen by now – the Penzance County School for Girls has always stood out as my overall favourite. It was much bigger than St Clare's with classes twice the size, but it was excellently organised and I found its calm, unthreatening work ethic much less stressful than the giggly permissiveness in force at St Clare's. All its special events like concerts, speech days and even Christmas parties were rigorously rehearsed and conducted with style. For some reason to do with the age at which I took the 11 Plus, I was immediately put into the second year and introduced to Latin, child's play for an expert in German grammar like me and destined to become my favourite subject.

I was thriving at school but, in the year that followed, my home life suffered a serious setback. I knew that Dr Kleine's operation had only been a short-term measure and that both my feet would need more drastic corrections, including bone-grafts, when I was older. Now the time had come and I had to spend the whole of the following summer term in the Royal Cornwall Infirmary in Truro. With staggering disregard for my feelings on the matter, while I was incarcerated in hospital, Mary's family moved away from

Upalong St Ives to Carbis Bay, several miles away and, more to the point, on a different bus route. After I returned from hospital I rarely saw my beloved friend any more and missed her terribly. What made my situation still more desperate was that Tommy and Barry, our erstwhile Monopoly partners, had entered the most critical phase of their adolescent withdrawal, refusing to have anything to do with girls. I felt genuinely isolated. Aunty Hyne was always cheerful company but I couldn't discuss with her, as with Mary, all the things I was either learning or, more likely, not learning at school, but was desperate to find out about, like politics, religion and sex. Mary, nearly two years older than me and overpoweringly clever, had answers to my every quandary and had become my all-purpose guru. As none of us had cars or telephones, communications between us never recovered from this blow and, other than at school, we rarely saw one another any more.

The unremitting cycle of routine at Chy-an-Mor kept me busy enough but instead of, as before, spending my spare time going to the pictures and playing games with my friends, I developed the habit of going for long solitary walks on the cliffs and moorland above St Ives. The walks became ever longer and more frequent; I was becoming addicted to getting away on my own to brood and introspect about everything under the sun, from life and the universe to more specialised interests like Papa and Nazism. Just when there was a danger that my secret life might soon take over altogether, help arrived from a surprising quarter – Mrs Boon, one of Aunty Hyne's circle of gossips.

Like the others, she was a short, round chatterbox but, while their thoughts rarely ventured beyond the domestic domain, Mrs Boon was prisoner to a grand passion, Cornish nationalism. She told us that she was fluent in ancient Cornish, a claim impossible to test as the language had not been spoken in earnest for several centuries. She certainly knew the meanings of the local place names and told us that Chy-an-Mor meant 'House-by-the-Heather'. Mrs Boon also played a musical instrument, not unlike a zither, that she said had been a popular feature of early Cornish culture. From the day she moved into her cottage up the lane opposite our bungalow she became a daily visitor and, once in full flow on her favourite subject, nobody else got a word in. I was normally too preoccupied with my own obsessions to listen to her until the day she got on to the subject of druids. I pricked up my ears. She was telling us that those huge, mysterious-looking granite boulders which I passed daily on my walks and, after a particularly exhausting spell of introspection, sometimes sat down on for a rest, had once been altars. Thousands of years ago, before there was Christianity, they had been used for human sacrifices. I was spellbound. And was I aware, she went on, that twice daily on my school bus I was passing close by Chysauster, the oldest known site of human habitation in the British Isles? A whole new perspective on the world – and my position in it – swung into focus.

There is no doubt that the grandeur of the Cornish coastline and the haunting beauty of its desolate, rock-strewn hinterland were part of the attraction that drew me on my solitary walks, but there was more to it. Like countless other observers of the Cornish coastal scene, it inspired in me an inexplicable feeling of timelessness and mystical presence. Listening to Mrs Boon its meaning suddenly became crystal clear. The mysterious presence I sensed was that of the ancient Celts who had lived along that coast thousands of years ago. The next time I went for a walk I could practically see them, bearded, wearing white robes and laurel wreaths, playing their zithers and performing their rituals amongst the granite pillars. Somehow, Mrs Boon's lively evocation of the prehistoric scene at the top of my road put the events of my own lifetime that so troubled me into a more bearable context. My personal worries suddenly seemed quite insignificant and even Hitler was cut down to size. At last I could appreciate the profundity of Reg's favourite saying when he came up against a problem to which there was no easy answer, 'Ah well, it'll all be the same in a hundred years.'

24

RETURN TO MY ROOTS

S ometime during my third autumn in St Ives my parents'
divorce came through and I received a letter from Papa.
Though my mother had warned me that she would be giving him
my address, seeing the letter before me still gave my system a jolt.
I recognised his writing at once, bold and characterful and in the
same dark blue ink he always used. When I was last with him four
and a half years before I still couldn't read grown-ups' writing.
Now I could but I still found his letter difficult to read – and it was
not just the script.

Papa's letter was affectionate but guarded. He wrote that he
was well, living in Lautenthal at Tante Kätchen's. Her father had
retired leaving him, Papa, in charge of the electricity works. He
asked about my school and my feet but mentioned nothing from
the past or our life together. I confined my answer to similar
practical topics but even that proved a test. I hadn't spoken or read
German for two and a half years and, except when doing
arithmetic and reciting the times tables to myself, parrot-fashion,
in the language in which I had learned them, had long ceased to
think in German. I was shocked to discover how difficult it was
to write my letter, yet, compared with the other obstacle to
communication between us, the language issue seemed quite
minor.

How could I ever make sense to Papa of my life at Chy-an-Mor? And what was I going to do with the acquisition of a father like him in the life I was leading there? How should I answer Aunty Hyne's questions about my interesting-looking letter with the fancy stamps? The truth would expose my mother's lie that my father had gone missing on the Russian front; anything else meant introducing yet another lie. I had long believed that if only I could get into contact with Papa again, my troubles would be over; now I was and I could see that a whole new set was about to strike.

Soon after Papa's letter came one from Mutti with the news that she and Bill had got married. She enclosed a picture of them, arm-in-arm, coming out of a church. Mutti was dressed in a New Look costume and cartwheel hat – the height of fashion at the time. They were surrounded by their friends, many of whom I recognised from my Hamburg holiday, laughing and smiling and bombarding them with confetti. Udo and I both liked Bill. He had an easy-going, sunny temperament that couldn't have been a greater contrast to Papa's, yet we recognised that underneath he was as solid and reliable as could be. In a subtle, quiet way he had insinuated himself into our family almost before we had noticed. Now he was a fully fledged member and if there was a danger it was that the rest of us would take him too much for granted. The fact that I could find no fault with my new stepfather, however, did nothing to release me from the old fantasy of my German family being reunited one day.

That year – 1949 – Udo and I were invited back to Hamburg for Christmas. This time it was arranged that we would spend the final weekend of the vacation with Papa in Lautenthal. We would be staying in the same house I had visited when I went to the Harz Mountains to recover from whooping cough at the age of four. We would be with Papa, Tante Kätchen – Mutti's long-time best friend – and her sons Dieter and Klaus, playmates of mine from as long ago as I could remember. For Udo, who had long ago distanced himself, emotionally, from Papa and cut loose from his German past, it was a duty visit; for me it was the moment I had longed for – the closest I was ever going to get to returning to my roots.

Tante Kätchen hadn't changed a bit, in personality or appearance. She was as bubbly and looked as charming as ever in yet another of the strikingly individual dirndl outfits that defined her style. The same could not be said of either Papa or me. Papa, with less hair and more lines on his face, fatter and in civilian clothes, looked very different from my memory of him; I, meanwhile, had metamorphosed from a dainty little girl of not yet nine, into a fairly lumpish thirteen-year-old. Then came the shocking realisation that I could hardly speak German any more. It wasn't that I had forgotten anything I previously knew, but that the thousands of new concepts I had acquired in the last three years were all in English. I needed them to express myself. Whenever I opened my mouth to say something perfectly ordinary to Papa I ended up tongue-tied, desperately searching for words that wouldn't come for the very good reason that I had never learned them in German. I quickly noticed that, provided I stuck to language not much more elevated than baby-talk, there wasn't a problem.

Undaunted by all the obstacles, Papa and I slipped easily into our old relationship. It is possible that my linguistic regression to a younger age made it easier for us to pick up where we had left off. It certainly ensured that our relationships would never progress very far beyond that of 'Papa and his little girl'.

The weekend had some magic moments. As on my first visit to Lautenthal the little town of half-timbered houses, encircled by pine-covered hills, looked enchanting under its blanket of snow. God! How good it was to breathe frosty air and to feel my face tingling with cold! How I had missed the bracing tonic of a proper snowfall in those mild, Atlantic Cornish winters! We tramped through the snow up to the Waldkater Hotel where we had stayed nine years ago and where I had been introduced to the delights of downhill tobogganing and miniature skis. As we climbed the steep path hand in hand, Papa told me about his two years in a British POW camp at Fallingbostel and about what a harsh and humiliating experience it had been. The whole time he had been ill and hungry. On his release, he came directly to Lautenthal, our agreed point of contact; that was the first he heard of our departure to England. He had suffered some kind of physical and mental breakdown, but Tante Kätchen nursed him back to health and even got him a job in her father's electricity works. It turned out that Papa and Herr Beume had, by chance, studied not only for the same engineering diploma but, at different times, at the same college. Herr Beume was delighted to have someone he could trust take over his responsibilities and Papa was enjoying the challenge.

He also told me what had happened to our other relatives. His younger brother, my Onkel Jochen, had settled with my grandmother Olga's relatives in Waldeck. Not so Papa's sister, my Tante Kiki. Like so many women terrified by graphic stories of the Red Army's behaviour as it overran Germany, she had taken her own life and given poison to her children. My little cousin Klaus, about five at the time, had thrown up his dose and was the only one of the three who survived. He was now living with his father somewhere in South Germany.

Later in the day Tante Kätchen took me aside and gave me her version of the family's recent history. She said that she had only met Papa once in the war before he and Mutti had, in effect, become separated, but that this single encounter had been enough to make her *verknallt* (besotted). After that, whenever she came to stay with us in Recklinghausen, she saw and heard how desperate Mutti was to get away from him and go to England. Thus, when he first contacted her from his POW camp asking for our address, she decided not to reveal to either of my parents the whereabouts of the other. She argued that to do so would not only have been dangerous for my mother and the rest of us, it would have destroyed any chance of repatriation to England, the future she had set her heart on. Tante Kätchen therefore determined not to reveal to Papa my mother's plan to desert him until we were safely in England.

She still appeared confident that she had done the right thing and confided in me her hope that she and Papa would one day make a permanent life together. Wasn't this exactly what I had foreseen so clearly when, at the age of five, I first heard about the concept of divorce?

I was having to radically revise the picture I had cherished for years, of a broken, despairing Papa with nothing left to live for. He was certainly a very different man from the one I remembered, but broken he was not. He was a fully going concern, doing a responsible job, living in a charming place with a beautiful woman who adored him. He had picked himself up, dusted himself down and become a perfectly successful civilian in the new West Germany.

What interested me much more about him than any of this, however, was what had happened to his Nazism. For all our previous life together, his fanatical commitment had been the most striking feature of his personality, yet there was no sign of it now. I found it hard to credit that, as everyone else in Germany appeared to have done, he had renounced his former beliefs outright the minute they became inconvenient – that he had, in effect, been *untreu*. Perhaps he was keeping his old ideals locked away in his heart, afraid to reveal them to anyone else, especially his 'English' children? Other possibilities were that he had either been genuinely 're-educated' or that, like me, he had tried to sort out for himself what had been daft and what had made sense about it all. However he had come to terms with it, the whole Nazi episode in his life must have left a huge scar somewhere in his soul, yet there was no clue as to its nature. Important though it was for me to find out how he was coping with his past, I couldn't bring myself to mention the subject. Either way, it had to be extremely painful and I could sense that it was as taboo here with Papa as everywhere else in Germany. As a result of my cowardice I missed my one and only chance to be released from the obligation that Papa had instilled in me as long ago as I could remember, the obligation to live the life of a loyal and committed Nazi.

On our last afternoon Tante Kätchen went down to her cellar and emerged with an antique film projector and some ancient rolls of film. They were silent films made in England, going by the clothes, not long after the turn of the century. First came a Lord Peter Wimsey whodunnit, then some comedy shorts set on Brighton Beach, consisting entirely of characters dressed in absurd bathing costumes chasing one another in and out of tents and bathing machines and falling into the water. We all rolled about laughing until we cried or were in such pain that we had to stop looking at the screen for a while. Then Tante Kätchen played the reels backwards and we became hysterical. By the end we were aching all over and could hardly stand up any more.

After a final festive meal in our honour we got ready to return to Hamburg. Papa walked us down to the station. On the way his manner suddenly changed. He had been so calm and jolly the whole weekend, now he started speaking urgently and with emotion. He was telling me that he would never understand why Mutti had left him. Their thirteen years together had been perfect. If she wanted to get out of Germany and he couldn't go to England then we could all have emigrated and met up together again in a new country, Australia or Canada. He said he still loved Mutti and always would. By now he was close to tears – so was I.

After all the tramping in snow, struggling with German, eating, travelling, laughing and crying, I returned to Hamburg exhausted. My mother came up to my room to wish me goodnight. That was all I needed to set me off on another of my by now famous bouts of emotion. Once again my mother did her best to find out what the matter was and to calm me down, getting terribly upset herself in the process. Once again I couldn't tell her as I didn't know myself. All I could be sure of was that each time I was on the point of getting a grip on myself I instantly collapsed into a further bout of hysterical sobbing.

Then something reminded me of the last time I disgraced myself like this. It was in Recklinghausen, the night before we left for England, exactly three years ago. I could remember how I felt then, torn in two between excitement at starting a new life in England and grief at leaving my old one; I could recall my fear of a future in which I would all the time have to conceal who I really was and pretend to be somebody else, living like two people rolled into one, a permanent double life. So much had happened in those three years. I had acquired a new name, a new nationality, a new language, a new stepfather, even a new pair of feet! Yet over this weekend with Papa I had been exactly the same Katrin Thiele as before. How accurately I had foreseen my predicament.

Then I tried to imagine what I would have been like now if we hadn't gone to England, if I hadn't been forced to learn English and those other thoroughly un-German activities, like thinking for myself and using my imagination, if I had never got to know the Aunties Hopey and Hyne, Reg, Miss Haydon, Mary, Tommy and Barrie, Cornwall, Mrs Boon, the ancient Celts, in fact, everything and everybody I knew now. It was an impossible – and futile – exercise. I *had* got to know them. My life was in England now, that was it. For the time being, anyway, I had no choice in the matter and had better just get on with it. At last I managed to stop crying and turned my thoughts to packing.

Next morning a Control Commission car drew up outside the mess. A uniformed driver came to the door to collect Udo and me and our luggage and to take us to the station to join the rest of our party. I had been here before. It was 6 December 1946 all over again.

25

POLITICS, BRITISH STYLE

At the end of the following term, for the first time in my life, I had a bad school report. I was quite put out as I hadn't consciously been slacking. One extra-curricular activity that had, however, claimed a lot of my attention was the February 1950 General Election. Mr Vibert, the Leach Pottery manager-cum-magician, and his wife were following the campaign minutely. They went to every election meeting staged and, thinking that I might also find them interesting, invited me to join them. The meetings were held in the town's biggest cinema and were always packed to standing room only. Formal speeches were followed by question and answer sessions and the whole thing was generously spiced with heckling and repartee. I loved them.

The incumbent MP was a Conservative but, Cornwall being in the Celtic Fringe, the Liberals were putting up a strong challenge. Labour never attracted very much support in those parts and especially now, with Attlee's post-war Labour Government running out of steam, it didn't stand a chance. It had the most glamorous candidate, though, in the person of the twenty-five-year-old Peter Shore, destined to become a Cabinet minister and elder statesman of his party. He was the youngest candidate in the country and told us that, if elected, he would enter the House of

Commons at the very age that Winston Churchill had started his political career.

I always found myself agreeing with whoever had been speaking last, but at the end of the campaign was in no doubt that if I had the vote I would support the Tory. For reasons I couldn't explain, his whole approach, with its emphasis on law and order, respect for authority and discipline, somehow felt right.

Curiously, I never made any connection between the politics I was seeing in action in St Ives and those I had lived under in Germany. They didn't strike me as remotely the same order of thing. The purpose of politics here was for the people to choose the policies they wanted their government to introduce for the good of the country. The Nazi politics of my experience were neither about people choosing, nor about policies, nor about anything the government was going to do for the good of the country. Quite the reverse. They consisted of the government *telling* the people what was for the good of the country and what every one of *them* had to do to achieve it. The two were so different that it was years before I could concede that what I had known in Germany was politics, too.

That Easter when Udo came to St Ives for his annual visit we received a letter with exciting news. My mother and Bill wrote that they had saved up enough money to come back to England for good. They were going to buy a business somewhere in the West Country, it was just a question of finding the right thing in the right place. We were told to sit tight until the end of the summer term at least, but to prepare to move to join them after that. Soon afterwards, for my fourteenth birthday, I received a lovely letter from Opa. He didn't often write but was obviously prompted on this occasion by the memory of his own fourteenth birthday. In the previous century in Germany, that was the age one started one's apprenticeship, so one's fourteenth birthday must have been special, like reaching one's majority. 'Believe me, life goes by so quickly, it does not seem so very long ago when I was fourteen.' Opa wrote. 'I felt like a prince, so many presents I had and everybody making a fuss of me.' Opa, too, mentioned the forthcoming move in which he and Oma were to be included and sounded excited about us all being together again soon.

The news gave me such a surge of energy that, instead of continuing in my scholastic decline, I ended the school year in a blaze of academic glory. No doubt the fact that it was the time of the year when my famous examination skills could come into play helped me leave the school where I had been so happy on a high note. In her leaving report my form-teacher wrote how sorry the school was to lose me, I was such a 'public-spirited' pupil.

When my summons to rejoin my family at last arrived, I was elated but Aunty Hyne cried. She reproached me for not being in the least sorry to leave her. I wished I was better at pretending but there was no way I could conceal my joy. I tried to comfort her by saying that I would write, that I would come back to see her often and that we would invite her to visit us in our new home but she wouldn't be consoled. Thank goodness it was the Bed and Breakfast season and business was flourishing, but I knew she would be terribly lonely in the winter with nobody to 'do for'.

Though I couldn't feign regret at leaving I was in no doubt about the debt I owed her. She had set me up to survive, cope and even succeed in a life to which I had no right by birth, circumstances or conviction, but into which I had been catapulted and which was my only chance. It was the life of that which I could never truly be, an ordinary English schoolgirl.

26

Journey Between Two Selves

It was a beautiful day in July 1950. I was the only occupant of my compartment on the Plymouth-to-Exeter stopping train, the last stage of a journey I had started that morning in St Ives. On the floor beside me stood a Heinz Baked Beans carton secured with string and punched with holes, through which the whiskers and tabby nose of my cat Flip could be fleetingly glimpsed. On the rack above me was a battered suitcase containing everything else I owned.

The little steam train was chuffing through some of the prettiest countryside in England, with the outlines of Dartmoor visible in the distance. The local stops all had charming names like Cornwood, Bittaford and Ivybridge. I would have enjoyed my journey whatever the destination but, watching the lush Devonshire scenery roll past that day, my state was close to ecstasy.

My instructions were to get out at a place called Totnes that I had never heard of. There, as I understood it, my entire family, now somewhat reconstructed, was going to be reunited in a home of its own, the first since leaving Mahlsdorf seven years before. In the interim we had, between us, lived in nearly thirty different places and Udo and I had attended twenty-four schools. Since coming to England, my mother, Oma and Opa had worked in a dozen jobs. I scarcely dared believe the contents of the letter that summoned me to this rendezvous. If it was to be believed, my mother and my new stepfather were in the process of buying a house for us all to live in. For the first time in my life I was even going to have my own room.

My mother was meeting me at the station. Over the last three years I'd only seen her once or twice a year in the school holidays, most recently at Christmas. With my head I could understand why we had to be separated for so long but with my heart, every minute I had missed her. I knew, too, that the separation had been as bad for her. She once told me that for the whole three years she spent away from us, working for the Control Commission in Germany, she had a lump in her throat. It didn't go away till we were together again.

It would be wrong to conclude from my joyous state in the train that day that my three years in Cornwall as Mrs Hyne's fifth Little Woman had been actively unhappy; the reverse would be nearer the truth. In every way but one they were idyllic, a serene, secure and enriching interlude of my growing-up, providing the benign environment I needed to practise my new English identity and become integrated. They were my most constructive formative years.

Their imperfection lay not so much in the separation from my family – that I learned to cope with. It was having to live as an imposter. I had the permanent feeling that this wasn't really me, my real life. I felt like an exile or an actor trapped on stage in a never-ending play. Yet, if anyone had asked me where or what my real life was, I wouldn't have had an answer. It wasn't in any known place or context, not Germany or England, not with my mother or my father, but all of these mixed up together in a turbulent confusion that I couldn't express but that was ever-present in my consciousness.

With hindsight, I know that nothing disastrous would have happened if I had accidentally blown my cover, yet at the time it was my worst dread. As a result, my outer life of a well-behaved and lively foster-child felt like a masquerade. My real life was the secret one inside me; it was the source of much perplexity and pain but, whatever the demands of the world outside, also the source of all the strength I needed.

Now I could leave my secret life behind; I was on my way home – who cared if it was going to be in a place I had never even heard of? All that mattered was that I could at last stop acting and be myself again – or so I thought.

27

OURS IS A NICE HOUSE, OURS IS

The train drew into Totnes station and my mother was there to meet me, as happy and excited as I was. Leaving me to grapple with the awkward Heinz carton, she picked up my battered suitcase and led me briskly in the direction of the steep little town. We climbed up a narrow, walled passage, through an archway in some medieval ramparts joined to a moated earthwork atop of which perched a small but perfectly formed Norman castle and proceeded through a narrow, winding High Street into a little square. Overlooking it from a corner position was an oddly proportioned end-of-terrace house. It was on three floors and, though it stretched back as far as the eye could see, it was only a few feet wide; furthermore, it appeared to be on the point of falling down. This was Waterloo House, my new home.

Totnes turned out to be extremely ancient, just then preparing to celebrate the thousandth anniversary of its borough charter with a pageant in the castle grounds. Its street plan was Anglo-Saxon, like a herring-bone, with a main thoroughfare running through the middle of the town and rows of individually owned strips, or 'burgher's patches', spreading out on either side. This arrangement meant that houses built on any of the original plots and fronting on to the High Street were likely to be abnormally slim and to have an equally narrow strip of garden stretching behind them. Waterloo House was one such and this history explained its curious layout.

It was built – we never found out when – on the side of a hill and in stone at least two feet thick. Signs of its most recent use, as a laundry, remained in the form of assorted boiler rooms and drying lofts built on to different levels of the rear. These were connected by steps that merged into a path leading in a long, thin garden. While the outhouses were fully equipped with stone sinks, copper boilers and drying racks, the domestic plumbing of our grandly named house was confined to one cold tap and an outside lavatory. There was no electricity but each of the downstairs rooms boasted a couple of gas lamps suspended from the wall on copper brackets. They cast an unobtrusive silvery light that was very attractive. Further unique features were that the staircase had collapsed from an infestation of death watch beetle and the ceilings of all four bedrooms hung down at the angle of a hammock with someone – a fairly heavy someone – lying in it; bits of ancient wattle and daub building materials protruded from the flaking ceiling plaster.

It was the most beautiful house I had ever seen and the room that was going to be mine, with its cast-iron fireplace and a window-seat that offered a full-frontal view of the toy castle, was the most beautiful in the house which, at £800, was undeniably a snip.

Builders were already at work and in the course of the summer made it liveable enough for the rest of the family to descend and stake their claims.

First came Udo, in exuberant spirits. He was seventeen and had just passed his School Certificate, the required qualification for any form of higher education. He was all set to study for his A Levels – being introduced for the first time that year – at the Torquay Technical College.

Last to arrive were Oma and Opa. They had worked in several more residential jobs since the one in the old people's home I visited, most recently for a family whose house backed on to the

Virginia Water golf course. Opa had really aged and looked tired and broken. Oma was the reverse. The prospect of this latest change of fortune had given her a new lease of life and she was brimming with energy and high spirits. As my mother and Bill were going to be working for a local business in which they had bought a share – their reason for choosing Totnes – Oma was designated to be the housekeeper for the rest of us, a challenge she seized with relish.

When they selected the West Country for our new base, they were unaware that economically it was the most depressed region of the country, with the highest rate of unemployment. At first their business venture didn't work out and the whole seven years we lived in Totnes were dominated by financial worries. Yet despite our abject poverty – and with the exception of one problem that I will come to later – our home life was remarkably cheerful and content. The credit for this was, of course, due to Bill who, quietly and with a light touch, assumed the role of head of the family in a way that made everyone feel valued and secure.

Our odd-ball extended family, two teenagers, two geriatrics and two newly-weds, quickly settled down together in the grandly named architectural curiosity that was now our home. Oma liked to sing an adaptation of one of her old music hall songs about it, 'Ours is a nice house, ours is'. The original contained the line, 'The front's at the front and the back's at the back', but Oma's version went:

> Ours is a nice house, ours is,
> It's got no rats or mouses,
> The front's at the side and the back's at the side,
> Ours is a nice house, ours is.

It was big enough for everyone to have their own space, with the focal point of family life a cosy kitchen with a dresser and a Rayburn stove flanked by comfortable chairs. One of them was officially Opa's. He spent most of his time there, reading travel books, newspapers and doing the football pools. He still went off for little walks, however, and had even started another tobacco plantation.

There was always a high-spirited atmosphere in the house and – with the single exception I am still coming to – no discord or quarrels. Oma, our domestic anchor-woman, set the tone with her songs, wit and ingenuity. She made light of the affliction that had dogged her for nearly forty years, chronic insomnia from the time her nerves were shattered in the First World War. We often came down in the mornings to find that while the rest of us were sleeping she had baked a cake, cleaned the silver or done the laundry.

Though the rest of us couldn't help becoming integrated, to some extent, in the local community through going to work or school, Oma and Opa remained completely isolated. I don't think they ever went into anybody else's house, yet they didn't mind or, I think, notice. They liked going to the cinema and taking a bus to nearby resorts like Torquay or Dartmouth to walk along the seafront and admire the flower gardens. Apart from that they were content to bask in the enjoyment of living with all of us again in our own home and, above all, in England.

Oma still conducted a lively correspondence with their old friends and relations and some of them started coming to spend their holidays with us, including Miss Green, the doughty Salvationist who had helped us in Recklinghausen, the Aunties Hopey and Kath and even Aunty Gertie, now widowed, as well as Oma's other sister, Nellie, who had come back to England. When Aunty Gertie came to spend Christmas with us, at least five years after our last encounter, we must have passed muster as sufficiently anglicised, for when she died soon afterwards she left us each a little legacy.

Opa lived for two more years and then died peacefully, at home, aged seventy-four. After that Oma sometimes made trips to London to stay with her surviving sister and the faithful First World War friends. Another link with that era of her life was, however, quite local.

It was my school speech day. Although, in most ways my

Totnes school was more laid back than the one in Penzance, in preparation for this event Miss Pendlebury, our music teacher, every year drilled all 300 or so of us for a high-class performance of a single, ambitious choral work. We had to learn these songs so thoroughly that, to this day, I can still sing some of them. For the year in question she had chosen a most unusual piece, an exuberant hymn in praise of children's singing. It went thus:

> Come music-makers, lift up your song,
> To set the echoes ringing,
> A song of truth
> In the heart of youth
> A song for the joy of singing . . .

Oma attended the occasion and afterwards said how much she liked the song. Furthermore, she told me that, according to the programme notes, the composer was someone called Martin Shaw. Could this be the Martin Shaw who had been the organist of St Mary's Church, Primrose Hill and their tenant on Haverstock Hill when my mother was a baby? We looked into the matter and discovered that he was the very one.

After two years at the Torquay Tech studying for his A Levels, Udo went off to medical school at Manchester University, leaving the rest of us, especially me, bereft. After that he often brought home foreign students who had nowhere to go in the vacations, exotic characters whose appearance on the streets of stodgy Totnes invariably caused a frisson of excitement. Our Biafran visitor told us he was glad he had come to Devon and to discover that, contrary to the other evidence at his disposal, England was not built up from one end to the other in a seamless extension of Manchester. Oma was delighted with these engaging house-guests and they were, I think, charmed by her refreshingly direct approach to their racial and cultural differences. One young man called Agit Buthoo Singh, a Sikh from Tanzania, aroused her professional interest with his explanation for wearing a turban. As a devotee of Guru Nanak, he had never in his life had his hair cut and there it lurked, beneath his imposing head wear, in its natural state. This was something that, in more than forty years of hairdressing, Oma had never seen and she became seriously interested in the hair-management techniques used by someone in his situation, which he was happy to demonstrate. He also taught her how to launder and starch a five-foot muslin turban.

Of the six of us, I, through attending the local school, was best placed for putting down proper local roots. Compared with St Ives, where distance had made it impossible ever to see class-mates at weekends or in the evenings, here, with my school just a few minutes' walk away, making friends was easy. Then a neighbour invited me to join the Rangers – Girl Guides, but older – a contact that not only introduced me to the delights of local history, hiking, camping and sleeping out on Dartmoor, but gave me a definite place in Totnes society.

One weekend the Totnes Rangers joined up with another South Devon group for a special area camp. Girls from different companies were mixed up together and I had to share a tent with a tough-looking, red-haired girl from Plymouth. I can't remember what set her off but, as we were unrolling our sleeping bags and making up our beds, she launched into an emotional account of the night her whole family was killed in a wartime air-raid on Plymouth. She worked herself up into quite a frenzy and told me in gory detail what she intended to do to the first German who ever crossed her path. Murder was too kind a word for the scene she described. There was no way this girl could have had an inkling about my German origins, but I was terrified. Hunched up in my sleeping bag, I lay awake all night sweating and trying to work out what to do if in the middle of the night she suddenly leapt up to attack me with her Girl Guide knife.

I must have made a good recovery from this traumatic incident since it didn't deter me from other expeditions with the Rangers, or from enjoying most things about my life in this historic little town that, more than anywhere else I had lived since leaving Mahlsdorf, had truly become home.

28

VERRÜCKT

A curious feature of our life at this time was that for 364 days of the year no visitor to Waterloo House, not even a fly on the wall, could have guessed that any of us had ever set foot in Germany. (On the 365th they would have seen us celebrating Christmas German-style, with not a Christmas stocking, a cracker or a funny hat in sight. It wasn't a conscious plan, but just happened, automatically.) There were no German books, pictures or memorabilia to be seen; no German cooking was done. Only in an emergency, when there was no English equivalent, was a German word used or memory recalled. Considering that the six of us had, between us, spent 133 years – more than half of our joint total of 248 – living in Germany, this was quite an achievement.

It started as a policy of concealing our German origins to avoid possible hostility, a policy that, after my encounter with the Plymouth Ranger, I fully supported. But then it went further, to a concealment of our past from ourselves, blocking out reality as though the whole German period of our lives hadn't happened. On the rare occasions that reference to it couldn't be avoided, the facts were distorted to suit the perspective of the normal English family we pretended to be.

The discord in the family I referred to earlier arose from a fundamental disagreement about how to handle our past. I knew I must keep it alive, so that I might make sense of it one day, a position that required me to talk about and have as much contact with Germany as possible. The others, including Bill – whom Mutti had spared no detail of our involvements – were committed to exorcising the whole episode, not only from the curriculum vitae they shared with others, but from their minds. For them any reminder was not only an assault on their new identities, but a threat to their security. They hadn't made a conscious decision, more an intuitive, but – except for one – unanimous, pact. The battle lines were drawn and, even with a five-to-one line-up, conflict was inevitable.

The focal point of discord was invariably something to do with Papa. Though he never came anywhere near Totnes, he certainly made his presence felt. As I was the one keeping the link with him going I became the harbinger of discord, the trouble-maker. The others couldn't understand why was I going out of my way to be so difficult and I acquired the reputation of being 'barmy' – well, it was just another way of saying *verrückt*.

I was so happy to be back with my family, I didn't immediately notice what was happening. True, when Papa and Tante Kätchen sent me some curtain material for my new room – fixing it up was my overriding passion at the time – it puzzled me that the others couldn't bring themselves to admire it. The very arrival of the parcel seemed to strike them as an affront, calling forth some extremely derogatory remarks about the sender from Oma who, if my memory served me right, had once been his good friend.

The first serious upset came at the time of our first Christmas together in Totnes, once again precipitated by a parcel from Papa. I put it under the Christmas tree, ready to open with the other presents. Oma told me it was out of place; I had better take it up to my room and open it there. I obeyed but then, at the height of the festivities, left the cosy family circle to go upstairs and open it. I returned wearing some outlandish new clothes and trinkets and gnawing on a piece of aromatic *Lebkuchen*, a German

Christmas delicacy. The others couldn't take it. Accusing eyes were cast at me, my mother was in tears and it was conveyed to me that I was spoiling everyone's Christmas. As I saw it, they were spoiling mine. Why should I continue to cut Papa out of my Christmas, as I had had to for all these years, now when there was no longer any need?

Later that night my mother called me into her bedroom. She was still red-eyed but, for the first time ever, she talked seriously to me about the problems I was creating. She told me that when she had planned our repatriation she had fully intended to sever all our German connections. She assumed that I would forget Papa and would want to become a hundred per cent English, instead of which I was being like this and making life difficult for everyone else. She admitted that she had come to realise that children do perhaps need contact with both their parents, whatever the circumstances, but she implied that she had learned this lesson too late to do anything about it in my case. I think she was asking for my understanding of everyone's feelings and begging me to go easy on them.

The aspect of living with my own family that I had longed for more than any other had been the opportunity to shed my secret life. It didn't matter if the others were less interested in the German thing than I was, so long as I was with people who would understand what I was talking about and who would let me be myself. Now things were turning out differently. Instead of helping me grapple with my German hang-ups, the others were struggling with far more serious ones of their own. I had been so young at the time that I could still confidently expect to sort out my confusion one day, rationally. They, older and more directly involved, couldn't hope to do that. Like millions of other Germans they were having to eliminate a large chunk of their experience, – that which had usually been the most dramatic part of their lives – and to build up meaningful new lives, and selves, from scratch. And here was I, messing up even that desperate way out of my family's dilemma.

Oma and Opa had had to do something like this to themselves once before, when they were deported from England. They had internalised their hurt and anger and it had become a demonisation of England. Now the process was being reversed. Oma, the most outspoken and expressive member of the family, became quite passionate in her condemnation of everything to do with Germany, the country with which she had identified for more than twenty-five years.

This time my mother and brother, too, were freezing the wartime period out of the reservoir of memory on which a person draws and which becomes part of their personality. They found any reminders of that time, not only the ones forced on them by me, exceedingly painful. Thus when Dorli Winter, our Mahlsdorf neighbour, turned up at Udo's student flat in Manchester – she was in England as an au pair and Tante Kätchen had given her his address – gentle, kindly, perfectly mannered Udo couldn't cope. He got into a panic lest she reveal his true identity to his flatmates and shut the door on her. When Tante Kätchen tried to ring Mutti up once she, too, couldn't cope and wouldn't come to the phone.

As for me, I had nothing to forget or regret. I had enjoyed what many experts consider the perfect upbringing, with the double security of a loving family and a wider community where moral and cultural values were unambiguous and openly expressed. My experience of being German had been positive. It grieved me to see what the others were doing to themselves, but I could do nothing to prevent it. As for 'coming out' with my secret life, as I was determined to do, that was going to have to wait. I would make another attempt when I eventually left home and when it couldn't upset the family, but I could already foresee that it would create a horrible barrier between us, leaving me once more with a double life.

Some months after that, my mother knocked on my door and said she had something to show me. It was my 'pedigree'. She explained how it brought together into one schedule every legal document I would ever need to prove my identity. It had her and

Papa's marriage certificate, my birth certificate and her natural-isation certificate with me and Udo written into it and our name change explained. Udo was getting one as well. I was deeply touched. It was a powerful admission by her that my German roots would always be part of me and that, for all the pretence to the contrary, deep down she was aware that there was no way I could ever shake them off.

At the end of 1951 Papa and Tante Kätchen got married and, together with her boys, started a new life in Canada. Over the next few years Papa made several attempts to have me join them for a holiday, but my mother wouldn't agree to the suggestion. After the last occasion, she feared it would confuse and distress me all over again and put me off my stride at school. As a consolation, when I was eighteen, she sent me on a visit to Germany. Though it was yet another mirror-image repeat of her own visit to England as an eighteen-year-old flapper, it was not consciously intended. Nobody mentioned it at the time and I have only just noticed the similarity myself.

I was going to stay with Frau Krüger-Lorenzen, my mother's partner on their wartime radio programme. Jane and Janet had found one another again after the war when my mother accidentally bumped into Kurt Krüger-Lorenzen in a Hamburg street and they had resumed their friendship. (Herr Krülo had resumed his work in broadcasting and later became a well-known television personality with the *Südwest Rundfunk*.) The Krülos now lived in Bad Homburg, only half-an-hour's tram ride from Frankfurt, where Oma's tireless correspondence had tracked down Opa's brother, my great-uncle Max, after the war. Now she wrote to tell him I was coming and when I arrived at the Krülos a letter from him was already waiting. In an antique-looking, florid script – quite unlike Opa's perfect copperplate – and in an equally extravagant literary style he was inviting me to Frankfurt to spend a day with him, or rather, with *them*. Who else could possibly be involved in the 'we' of the invitation? I was intrigued. She – for it was a she – turned out to be a charming woman called Tilla

Kahlisch and it emerged that she and Onkel Max had been an 'item' since 1936, the year I was born. So much for his confirmed-bachelor reputation! They had got to know one another working at the Berlin Post Office and in 1945, some time after Oma and Opa's tramp, had also made the dash West together. They managed to resume their post office careers in the Bundesrepublik and now Onkel Max, looking just as I remembered him, lived comfortably retired, while Fräulein Kahlisch still worked. The three of us met up together for several more enjoyable rendezvous, taking in open-air concerts supported by large portions of *Kaffee und Kuchen* in the Palmengarten, and even a night at the opera.

When I related all this to the family back home, they were speechless. How could Onkel Max have concealed this relationship for all those years, under the cover of living with their ancient aunt, Tante Martha? Why had he never married Fräulein Kahlisch? And why, even now, were they not living together but, as I had to report, in adjacent flats? Not even someone as forthright as Oma felt she could ask these delicate questions in a letter. Only now has a possible explanation suggested itself to me. Could it be that Fräulein Kahlisch was Jewish and Onkel Max, caution personified, continued to see marrying her as too much of a risk?

Like my mother returning from England in 1928, I, returning from Germany twenty-six years later, had a difficult decision to make about my future. A letter from Papa was waiting for me, suggesting that I transfer to Canada for my college education. That way I could live with him and Tante Kätchen and, after our long years of separation, we could get to know one another again.

Papa's plan made sense in so many ways; part of me badly wanted to go. But I had set my heart on a course in England that fitted my interests exactly, everything I wanted to study. It was the Philosophy, Politics and Economics degree at Oxford. I hadn't seen anything else like it and my school was already coaching me for the entrance exam. At last, after a lot of agonising and feeling selfish and guilty, I rejected the Canadian proposal, at least for the time being.

Then I sat the Oxford entrance exam and, in due course, was invited for interviews at St Anne's College. The Philosophy Fellow at that time was Iris Murdoch and my first interview was with her. 'Why do you want to study philosophy?' she asked me. Easy, I thought, it's so obvious; I only needed a second to come up with my answer. 'I want to be wise,' I told her. To my consternation Miss Murdoch collapsed into peals of laughter. What was so funny? I couldn't see the joke at all and was quite put out, watching her fall about, laughing at my expense. It was only several days later, when I received a letter offering me a place on her course, that I could bring myself to forgive her.

29

Coming Out

The following October, 1955, I presented myself at St Anne's to begin my student life. The family worked hard to give me a good send-off; my mother made me clothes, Oma did my hair and Bill introduced me to the mysteries of having a bank account and writing cheques. Leaving home was going to be a wrench but also a liberation, the longed-for moment when I could stop pretending and be myself at last.

I had only once broken the family's rule of silence about our German history, to my best friend at school. I knew I could trust her not to spread the story, but also that I mustn't draw conclusions from her 'What a hoot!' response about how other people would react when I started going fully public, as I now intended to do.

My moment came much sooner than I expected, at an informal teaparty in somebody's room in my hostel, a few girls sitting on the floor, toasting crumpets on the gas fire. Unusually, the conversation turned to people's experiences of the war; the most exotic one being described, by far, was that of a girl who had been evacuated to Canada. At a suitable gap in the conversation I piped up, 'I spent the war in Germany.' There was a short hush, then one girl turned to me and said in a voice throbbing with concern, 'Oh, you poor thing! It must have been awful!' Another, equally sympathetic, added, 'I didn't realise you were Jewish.' Had I heard right? Hostility, ridicule, embarrassment, even acceptance, I was prepared for, but sympathy? Thinking I was Jewish? What was going on?

I pressed on. 'No, it wasn't awful and I'm not Jewish. My father was in the *Wehrmacht* and I had quite a good time really.' All eyes were now fixed on me and I was bombarded with comments and questions like, 'You mean, you weren't put in a camp?' 'Did your father take part in the July Plot?' and 'Did you know the von Trotts?' They were as bewildered by the story I was trying to tell them as I was by their extraordinary questions.

One thing not in doubt was that by drawing attention to myself with my tale I was ruining my new friends' teaparty. They couldn't cope with my revelations. I couldn't fathom why I was making them so uncomfortable, though, or why, when I had only 'come out' like that to make myself feel better, I was now feeling worse, more different and isolated than ever. For some reason, instead of breaking them down, letting my past hang out was creating a whole lot of new barriers.

It required several more incidents along the lines I have described to make me abandon my policy of unreservedly coming out with my German identity. It was not only failing to achieve the intended result, but proving to be seriously bad manners. Perhaps Oma's approach was right after all. Gradually, I came to understand that the English had clear, black and white stereotypes for wartime Germans. On the one hand were Nazis, vicious murderers with blood on their hands, not fully human and certainly not suitable for having to tea; on the other were victims and resistance fighters who had all suffered unspeakable hardships and whom one should go out of one's way to help. Harmless-looking creatures like me and my Totnes family didn't fit the Nazi stereotype and, I now saw, had always been automatically slotted into the victim category (a generous reaction I still meet in the 1990s when people first hear of my German connection).

That explained the many kindnesses we had been shown when we first came to England. Sadly, British post-war culture hadn't equipped the population for dealing with the overwhelming majority of Germans, including us, who had supported their country's war effort, but had not been involved in, or allowed themselves to know about, Nazi mass murder, who defied classification as either totally 'good' or totally 'bad' Germans. Attempting to explain what I had experienced and how much more complicated everything had been only disturbed the mental constructs people had adopted to help them to cope with their former enemy who, defeated or no, was never going to go away.

Thankfully, enough of the English way of doing things had by now rubbed off on me to enable me to work out a compromise position. From now on, I decided, there would be no more lying or pretence, but neither any full-scale unloading of my psyche, trumpeting truth for truth's sake from the rooftops, for my own gratification – and everyone else's discomfort. In future I would reveal as much – or as little – about myself as befitted each occasion.

Apart from that, I knew that I had better get used to the idea that my double identity would never go away. I would have to learn to live with it, like everything else about myself, stop fussing and concentrate on doing something with my life. I could even envisage a day when it might cease to be a problem for me any more and could become an asset, a bonus, an extra string to my bow ...

30

Papa and His Little Girl

In July 1956, my first long vacation from Oxford, I sailed to Canada for a holiday with my father. Nearly seven years had passed since that wintery weekend in Lautenthal when we were last together and more than eleven since the war's end and the break-up of our family.

Since then Papa had acquired a new wife and two stepsons and I a new stepfather. We both had new homes, Papa's in a new country with a different language. Each of us was involved in work or studies incomprehensible to the other. What did we have in common that could give our six or eight weeks together any meaning? Certainly, nothing from the here and now.

Papa met me off the boat-train in Toronto and we fell into each other's arms. Within minutes of being together again we had picked up where we left off; we were back to being 'Papa and his little girl' and, throughout the summer, everything conspired to keep us there. Though Papa now spoke fluent (Canadian) English, our relationship only made sense to me if we were speaking in German, a language in which I was still firmly stuck at the level of a ten-year-old. Our first conversation on being alone together was much like our last in Lautenthal, when Papa had spoken so emotionally about his loss of the wife and children he adored. In the second, when we talked about the war, Papa told me how he had loved being a soldier and how that military period when our family was still together had been the high point of his life.

Outwardly, Papa and Tante Kätchen were obviously making a success of their new lives as part of Canada's hard-working, ambitious, German immigrant community, yet Papa's confidences to me about his feelings for the past only reinforced my perennial pity for him and fuelled my determination to reassure him that, whatever he had lost, he still had a devoted daughter. The only way I knew of doing that was to remain his good little girl. I therefore spent the summer, perfectly agreeably, in a state of suspended animation, voluntary regression to a former self, living yet another double life.

Neither of us ever forgot an occasion that summer when, sitting on the grass in a park overlooking Lake Ontario, we managed something approaching an adult conversation. We were delighted to discover a subject, not from the past, that was genuinely important to us both and on which we could agree – the value to a society of having first-class public services. It was perhaps the only common ground between the Welfare State of 1950s Britain and the National Socialism of 1930s Germany. No doubt we always remembered the occasion because it was unique.

What was not mentioned between us in any shape or form was the overall Nazi philosophy, particularly the ideals of noble personal behaviour, that had so impressed me as a child. Though they never received any reinforcement – least of all from Papa – I had never abandoned the revised version I worked out for myself on my solitary clifftop walks in St Ives. By now its origins were lost and, in its revisionist form, it had become an ethical code no longer so very out of the ordinary, even by English standards of worthiness. Thus, *Pflicht*, *Treue*, *Willen* and serving the *Volk* had mellowed into every day virtues like 'dutifulness', 'integrity', 'determination' and 'making the world a better place'. What remained exceptional in my case was the fervour with which I clung to my ideals, as if driven by some unseen, higher authority that must be obeyed.

Papa didn't like it at all and couldn't understand my behaviour. He had adjusted superbly to North American values and culture and was for ever chiding me for my lack of personal ambition and dreamy idealism. Yet, though I no longer associated my personal agenda with my infant commitment to Nazi ideology, I have no doubt about its influence on the kind of person I became – a 'causes' person, a workaholic, but incapable of working for an employer or an organisation, only for an idea I could support, the more extreme or unpopular the better. Though Hitler would have detested every cause I cherish, I hold him directly responsible for this outcome.

The fossilised relationship I established with Papa on that first holiday together was to set the pattern of our relationship for the rest of his life, until he died in 1979. I suspect that it suited me rather better than him, for he often complained that I would never discuss politics with him, as he would have liked. I had quickly discerned his nostalgia for the Third Reich and, as for the Holocaust, he claimed reports of it were grossly exaggerated. Any honest adult discussion between us could only have led to one outcome, quarrelling, and that I couldn't cope with.

It was to be many years before I would feel ready to discuss the past with him adult to adult, and when that time came, he was already long dead. The events that – alas, too late – made this possible did not come about until 1992, when I had started to work on my family's history.

I had come to that chaotic period at the very end of the war when we were living at Süppling. I doubt if there were many – any – Germans around in that spring of 1945 whose lives were proceeding normally and intelligibly, unaffected by the fact that their society was collapsing about their ears. For me, in the years that followed, all the bizarre events of that time had merged together into a single confusion of memories. It was only when I started my project of trying to make sense of it all and writing it up that the special significance of one episode struck me – the never explained, intense military and police searches for Papa at the very end of the war. I cursed myself for my cowardice in never asking him to explain what on earth had been going on. Nevertheless, I decided that even now, nearly fifty years after the event, it was still worth having a stab at getting some answers.

I asked a cousin who lives near Magdeburg, not far away from Weissewarte, to make a trip to the village and to attempt to tune into the local memory of the final days of the war, a time that everyone alive at the time would surely remember. I hoped that the mention of the *WE Lager* and of Oberleutnant Thiele might ring a few bells and I was not disappointed. My cousin's reply set me off on a research trail that took more than a year to reach a conclusion – the most anguished year of my life.

The first person my cousin accosted in Weissewarte turned out to be the husband of one of our forester/farmer/landlord's two blonde daughters, Marga. She was now sixty-seven and living in the village. Süppling, my cousin learned, no longer existed. The house and farm had been systematically dismantled by raiders and looters. First came East European slave labourers and camp inmates, enormous numbers of whom were making their way homewards, forced to live off the land for their survival. A place as isolated as Süppling would have been powerless against plunder on such a scale, so the family abandoned it and returned to their house in the village. In the years that followed, anything that remained, especially potential building materials that were in desperately short supply throughout the life of the German Democratic Republic, was removed by ordinary local looters. The pond, too, was gone. The water level of the river that fed it had been lowered to provide water for industry and it had completely drained away. If one walked through the forest today, my cousin was told, there was nothing to indicate where the little settlement had once been. The farmer's daughter produced photographs of the old Süppling and commented that the years her family had spent there had been the happiest of her life.

Immediately the name of Oberleutnant Thiele was mentioned, however, she let forth a powerful tirade of abuse, which my cousin did his best to relay in his letter.

There had clearly been some nasty clashes between our two fathers, sparked off by their conflicting politics. It seems that Papa had pulled rank on Marga's father and threatened him in a way that ensured her family's hatred of his memory for ever more. Trying to separate the factual claims from the vituperation left me with two horrifying accusations.

The first concerned Papa's military behaviour in the last days of the war. It seems that he had been one of those Nazis who went on obeying orders to the bitter end, blindly fighting, risking lives and inviting the destruction of any building still left standing in the *Vaterland*, when common sense dictated surrender and desertion. Instead of sending the boys in his camp home, he had obeyed instructions to form his staff and any of the boys who were prepared to volunteer for active service into a combat group. About half of the sixteen- and seventeen-year-old trainees volunteered and were sworn in as members of the armed forces, whereupon Papa led them into a futile battle. They were quickly overcome by superior forces and, before many shots were fired, their operation fell apart; many were killed and Papa wounded.

Reading this made me sick. However stupid and wicked his actions had been, they didn't explain why in the days that followed so many people were going to such lengths to search for Papa. From a military point of view they were correct, following orders by the book. They threw no light on Mutti and Udo's interrogations by the American military police, the German police persecution of Oma, Opa and Udo after we left the area, or Opa's arrest and internment in Stendal prison. I read on.

The family's second accusation linked Papa with an atrocity committed twenty-four hours before the Americans reached the town of Gardelegen, some forty kilometres north-west of Weisse-warte. Marga told my cousin that the last time she saw Papa at Süppling was at dawn one morning, when she observed our whole family, children and all, driving off in the direction of Gardelegen, for Papa to participate in this atrocity. The details of her story were blatantly incorrect; someone at Süppling must have observed my parents' early-morning dash to deliver Papa into captivity and put their own interpretation on the incident. Nevertheless, there must have been a reason for associating Papa's name with the event at Gardelegen, where a large number of concentration-camp survivors, mostly Polish Jews, had been locked into a barn and incinerated.

I went to the Goethe Institute Library in London to hunt for books about the Holocaust – the kind I had never managed to make myself look at before. The subject had been too painful for me and I had ruled it out of bounds for my mental survival. The first book I opened, Martin Gilbert's *Atlas of the Holocaust*, had several maps which identified Gardelegen as the site of a Holocaust massacre in the final days of the war: 1,016 victims had perished. As I read on, a black cloud descended on me, freezing out every other thought and feeling. For several months the thought 'Gardelegen' was always with me. I couldn't tell anyone about my dread, not even my husband; I felt implicated, guilty, untouchable, a pariah.

I could no longer avoid confronting, in close-up, the detailed reality of what the Holocaust had meant for the individuals involved, victims as well as perpetrators. This was something that, like most other Germans, I had managed to do very successfully for nearly fifty years. I started reading Holocaust history books and survivors' literature; I had never managed to get past the first pages before. Now I read, in quick succession, Bettelheim, Primo Levi, Eli Wiesel, Janina David, Helen Fowler, George Clare and Louis Begley. I spent a day in the Museum of Mauthausen Concentration Camp, near Linz, the kind of place I would previously have done anything to shun. The book that most helped me through those grim months was *Hitler's Children*, Gerald Posner's collection of interviews with the – by now middle-aged – children of leading Nazi war criminals. There was a certain comfort in knowing that other members of my generation had gone through the same agonising mixture of emotions as I was grappling with now.

I became an habitué of London's Wiener Library collection about the Holocaust, digging for references to the Gardelegen incident. I had to find out beyond any doubt exactly what had happened, who was responsible and if Papa had really been implicated.

I discovered that the victims had been from one of the 'death marches', columns of former concentration-camp inmates that, in the last weeks of the war, were made to march, ill and starving, for hundreds of miles from one camp to another, to prevent them falling into the hands of the advancing Allies. I felt ashamed that I hadn't heard of these marches until now, though they were numerous and very many thousands of Jews and others died on them.

The Nazis in charge of Jewish policy couldn't tolerate the thought of any Jews still alive having the 'last laugh' on them, being liberated by the victorious enemy, yet the rationale behind the marches was as confused as the instructions to camp commandants and SS guards about their conduct. The result was that a column dispatched to the east, away from the Western advance could well have met another marching in the opposite direction, to get away from the Russians. By the end, the SS guards were seriously at a loss to know what to do with their sick and starving charges. The Gardelegen prisoners originated from Auschwitz, but had already been moved once to the Dora Mittelbau camp, in central Germany. Now they were being herded still further west, to Bergen-Belsen. They were about half way to their destination, near Gardelegen, when the SS guards heard that the British had already liberated Belsen. They didn't know what to do and went for help to the first Nazi contact they could locate, the SS headquarters in Gardelegen. The atrocity in the barn was the result.

Around thirty of the 1,050 marchers survived by hiding in the nearby forest; others who succeeded in digging their way out of the burning barn were immediately shot. One of several survivor accounts I found mentioned that the SS guards who drove the marchers into the barn were supported by some young boys in Hitler Youth uniforms. If Papa had really been involved, could he have been so utterly depraved as to make the boys from his camp participate? These were the thoughts that haunted me, day in day out, for months.

The Wiener's own material on the Gardelegen incident was incomplete, but from its index of Holocaust archives round the world I discovered where I might find more. The principal source appeared to be the Yad Vashem archive in Jerusalem and I wrote there for further information. Nearly a year after starting my search I received photocopies of the entire contents of their file on the Gardelegen incident.

There were further personal accounts by survivors and by the American soldiers who first arrived on the scene, when the barn was still smouldering. The item of greatest interest for me was a bulletin issued by the Simon Wiesenthal Documentation Centre in Vienna, in January 1991. It read as follows:

NS-CRIMES IN GARDELEGEN, (EAST) GERMANY

1,016 inmates were killed in this incident at Gardelegen. On April 13, 1945 (24 hours before the Americans liberated this area), an SS troop under the district commander of Gardelegen, Gerhard Thiele, steered inmates into a barn and set it on fire.

The report gives the details of the atrocity that I have already described, with the following additional information:

The Americans started investigating the crime right away. Some of the SS men whom survivors identified as the guards who had shot at them, after escaping the barn, were executed by the Americans on the spot. But the commanders, Thiele and another SS man who was only known to be of Austrian origin, could not be captured.

The bulletin ended with a report of a recent lead to the whereabouts of the wanted man, Gerhard Thiele, currently being investigated by the Wiesenthal Centre.

This bulletin explained much, but not everything. The man responsible for the massacre had the same surname as Papa, and a Christian name, Gerhard, that could have become confused with Papa's, Eberhard. Either Papa had come under suspicion because of a mix-up with names, or he really was the guilty man, and the Wiesenthal Centre had got some of its details wrong.

I wrote to the mayor of Gardelegen for more information and learned that the little town has a large memorial archive to commemorate the massacre, with its own archivist. He now confirmed to me that Gerhard Thiele was indeed the local SS commander and that the boys in Hitler Youth uniforms were locals – no doubt called up into the *Volksturm*, a kind of home guard made up of the young, old and unfit, that Hitler ordered to be formed in every community for the defence of the last hours of the *Vaterland*. The archivist wrote that he had never heard of my father or the Weissewarte camp. Yet more information came from my indefatigable cousin, who also visited Gardelegen. Gerhard Thiele had been a well-known local figure, a school teacher in the town before the war. My cousin even sent a photograph of him, looking striking in his SS uniform, but not in the least like Papa.

I am now satisfied that the urgent searches for my father in April and May 1945 were due to a case of mistaken identity. The hunt was on for Gerhard Thiele and it seems that the existence of another prominent Nazi called Eberhard Thiele, only forty kilometres or so away, was too much of a coincidence to be ignored. That was why my father came under suspicion in two quite separate operations, first from the American army and then from the German police.

I suspect that as soon as they had Papa in captivity the Americans checked him out and eliminated him from their Gardelegen inquiries. Some time after that he was transferred from American POW to British POW captivity, but I have not been able to discover when, or why, that happened. Stendal prison, where he bumped into Opa, could well have been a staging post in his progress to the appropriate punishment for somebody like him, not a big military or SS fish, but a long-standing Nazi Party official.

The interest in Papa of the civilian German police is most likely to have had something to do with the family at Süppling. Perhaps when they heard the news that a Nazi called Thiele was on the run after the Gardelegen atrocity they remembered seeing Papa surreptitiously leaving their house one morning; having experienced for themselves what a fanatical Nazi he was, they jumped to the conclusion that there was a connection between the two events. The farmer and his family were well connected to the local socialists who, having spent the war underground, were immediately given responsible positions by the new military government, including jobs in the civilian police. That connection could explain why Oma, Opa and Udo were watched and followed, evicted from their flat, deprived of their luggage and why Opa was arrested. It could also explain the terrible atmosphere at Süppling when they went back to collect their luggage and nobody would speak to them.

In those chaotic times it is not surprising that communications between the American military and the German police were a muddle and their search for Papa poorly co-ordinated. Yet though both had him in their custody at various times, neither appear to have charged him with a specific crime. Nor did his behaviour in years to come suggest that he felt guilty or feared he was a wanted man. Thus the mistaken-identity theory is my best guess for why so many people were after him that spring. He did end up spending two years in prison, most of the time not, I later discovered, as a prisoner of war, but as a civilian internee. As far as I can make out, this was a routine punishment for his twelve years' work as a Nazi Party employee and activist. For half of this time he was simultaneously serving in the armed forces but I remain doubtful that he was an ordinary soldier, more a political 'cheerleader' for the troops. That would explain his many little trips back from the front, and also his sudden switch from the *Wehrmacht* to the *Luftwaffe*, when he was head-hunted to take command of a *WE* camp.

It was an indescribable relief for me to know that my father was not the mass murderer I had for many months dreaded. However, during that time I became a different person and I would not now like to go back to the one I was before – too cowardly, frightened and ineffectually guilt-ridden to confront the reality of the Holocaust or to show Holocaust victims the respect of being well informed about their persecution and their sufferings. I am glad that I am no longer too squeamish to read the terrible, but uplifting survivors' literature, or to watch the most harrowing scenes and interviews with survivors in films such as Claude Lanzmann's astonishing nine-hour masterpiece, *Shoah*. Somehow, by the time I had found answers to the mysteries surrounding my father's wartime activities, I had moved on from my obsession with my own family and become more interested in deeper questions, such as the forces that made ordinary Germans willing to participate in murdering Jews, the origins, life histories and experience of Holocaust victims like those at Gardelegen and the strategies that the survivors – and the perpetrators – used to cope in the years that followed.

My search for answers can never be complete, not when reports of new research into the Nazi period continue to pour off the presses and, after fifty years of silence, the German population has started to debate, in public, the role of ordinary soldiers and civilians in Second World War atrocities.

My biggest regret is that I never faced these issues while Papa was still alive. Had I been able to make my personal journey before he died, I am in no doubt that we would have spent many hours together in honest discussion of this most difficult aspect of both our pasts. What is more, in the process we would have eliminated, once and for all, that ridiculous pair of fossils, Papa and his little girl.

EPILOGUE

On Saturday, 12 September 1993, my closest living relatives and I met up together in Totnes cemetery. There were seven of us: my mother and Bill, Udo and his wife, my husband Luke, my daughter Kitty and myself. We had come to set up a memorial stone to both our grandparents on Opa's grave. There was no reason for choosing that particular date, other than it being the first that was convenient for everyone, once we had made up our minds to lay the stone. That had taken forty-one years.

When Opa first died, doubts about the wording of an inscription proved an insuperable problem. There seemed little point in putting up a gravestone unless it properly identified Opa, German origins and all, but that Oma couldn't allow and the idea was dropped. Even after her death in 1966 the grave remained anonymous.

By 1990, when I started putting together my family's history, my mother and Bill had lived in South Devon for forty years. None of their friends and neighbours had any idea that my mother had ever set foot in Germany. The more than quarter-century she had spent there might never have happened. On the other side of the Atlantic Udo, too, had established a life for himself in which his first thirteen years didn't feature. When I told them about my plans to rake up the past and set as much of it as could be recalled on paper I couldn't be sure they would be pleased.

To my delight, both readily entered into the spirit of the enterprise and it became a family project. I already had in my possession Oma's memoirs; now the other two wrote or dictated contributions, allowed me to interview them and produced additional materials I had no idea existed, such as a batch of letters and postcards sent to Aunty Hopey from Köpenick in the 1920s. In 1961, when Aunty Hopey died while on a visit to us in Devon, they had somehow found their way into Udo's hands.

Despite all their assistance, I couldn't bank on it that my mother and brother would approve the result and that it wouldn't turn out distressing for them. Lest my reconstruction of her life upset her, I only allowed my mother to read my first draft when I was present to catch her reaction. I should have known better. As pragmatic at eighty-two as at thirty-two, all she did was point out my mistakes, tell me additional details that reading the story had helped her remember and ask me if I would like her to translate the text into German. Soon after that she wrote me a sweet little letter, saying that she felt herself privileged to have her early life set out before her like that at an age where she was sufficiently distanced from the events described to be able to look at them dispassionately. She wrote that she considered my book 'a gift' and thanked me for writing it.

My brother, too, approved the outcome and gave it to his children to read. He had bottled up so much of his past that they had only the vaguest notion of what his childhood had involved. Now they started discussing it in the family and, sometime later, on a visit to check the accuracy of my final version, I had the pleasure of hearing him tell the story of his escape from the Russians to someone outside the family. Though not a man given to displays of emotion, he couldn't help shedding a tear when he read my account of his adventures with Oma and Opa.

In April 1992, Udo and I met up together for a few days in Berlin. We went to Mahlsdorf and discovered that several of our childhood friends were still living there. For both of us the highlight of the trip was to learn that Udo's Jewish friend, Günter, had survived the war and still lived in Vienna.

Of us all, writing the book benefited me the most. It released me from the compulsion to be for ever chasing impossible dreams. It brought me to earth and my causes and campaigns started to see results.

Working together on the project helped all three of us to live more comfortably with our past and led, inexorably, to a reconsideration of the gravestone question. By the time we met up in Totnes there was no longer any doubt about the wording. We had the stone made in Welsh slate and inscribed in copper plate, to remind us of Opa's immaculate hand writing. It read:

> In Memory of
> Richard Druhm
> born Luckenwalde 1878
> died Totnes 1952
> and his wife Ethel
> born 1880 died 1966

That said it all, really. A passer-by reading those sparse facts wouldn't need to know much twentieth-century history to work out the rest for himself; that a man born at that time and in that place, who married an English wife and died in Totnes in 1952 – and especially the wife – must have had troubled and disrupted lives. Given those basic facts, nothing, not even the pursuit of a profession as peaceful as hairdressing, could save them from that fate.

Chronology

1878	Richard Druhm (Opa) born in Luckenwalde, Germany
1880	Ethel Norris (Oma) born in London

1895	**Opa comes to live in England**
1905	Opa and Oma marry and set up shop in Hampstead
1907	Eberhard Thiele (Papa) born in Popilewo, Poland
1910	Elfreda Druhm (Mutti, my mother) born in London
1914	War breaks out. Opa interned in London
	Oma works for George Rossell, gets to know Elsie Hope (Hopey)
1916	Papa orphaned

1918	**War ends. Opa deported to Germany**
1919	**Oma and my mother follow to Germany**
1931	My parents meet and marry
1933	Hitler assumes power
	Udo Thiele (my brother) born in Berlin
1936	I am born in Berlin
1939	War breaks out, Papa is called up
1943	Thiele family leaves Berlin
1945	War ends, Papa interned at Fallingbostel Camp

1946 **My mother, Udo and I are 'repatriated' to England**
1947 Papa released from Fallingbostel Camp
I become Mrs Hyne's 'company'
Oma and Opa return to England c/o Red Cross
My mother appointed by the Foreign Office to work with
the Control Commission for Germany
1949 My mother marries Bill Jater
1950 Family reassembles in Totnes, Devon
1951 Papa remarries, emigrates to Canada
1952 Opa dies in Totnes
1955 I go to University
1966 Oma dies in Devon
1979 Papa dies in the USA
1992 I start researching the family history
1993 Family puts up memorial stone to Oma and Opa

Books Referred to in the Text

Louis Begley *Wartime Lies* (London, Macmillan, 1991)

Bruno Bettelheim *The Informed Heart* (London, Penguin, 1991)

Charles Booth *Life and Labour of the People in London* (London, Macmillan, 1902)

George Clare *Last Waltz in Vienna – The Destruction of a Family 1842–1942* (London, Macmillan, 1981)

Paul Cohen-Portheim *Time Stood Still – My Internment in England 1914–1918* (New York, Dutton, 1932)

Janina David *A Square of Sky* (London, Eland, 1992)

Desmond FitzGerald *A History of the Irish Guards in the Second World War*

Martin Gilbert *Atlas of the Holocaust* (London, Michael Joseph, 1992)

Primo Levi *If This is a Man* (London, Orion, 1960)

Helen Lewis *A Time to Speak* (Belfast, Blackstaff Press, 1992)

Panayi Panikos *Germans in Britain during the First World War* (London, 1991)

Sylvia Pankhurst *The Home Front* (London, Hutchinson, 1932)

Gerald Posner *Hitler's Children – Inside the Families of the Third Reich* (London, Heinemann, 1991)

W T Reay *The Specials; How They Served London. The Story of the Metropolitan Special Constabulary* (London, Heinemann, 1920)

Adrienne Thomas *Die Katrin Wird Soldat* (Berlin, Ullstein, 1930)

Elie Wiesel *Night* (London, Penguin, 1960)

INDEX

Lightning Source UK Ltd.
Milton Keynes UK
UKOW04f0617151213

223010UK00001B/4/P